ROUTLEDGE LIBRARY EDITIONS: WOMEN AND WORK

I0124655

Volume 1

WOMEN'S PLACE IN INDUSTRY AND HOME

WOMEN'S PLACE IN INDUSTRY AND HOME

SYLVIA ANTHONY

Routledge
Taylor & Francis Group

LONDON AND NEW YORK

First published in 1932 by George Routledge & Sons, Ltd.

This edition first published in 2022
by Routledge
4 Park Square, Milton Park, Abingdon, Oxon OX14 4RN

and by Routledge
605 Third Avenue, New York, NY 10158

Routledge is an imprint of the Taylor & Francis Group, an informa business

© 1932 Sylvia Anthony

All rights reserved. No part of this book may be reprinted or reproduced or utilised in any form or by any electronic, mechanical, or other means, now known or hereafter invented, including photocopying and recording, or in any information storage or retrieval system, without permission in writing from the publishers.

Trademark notice: Product or corporate names may be trademarks or registered trademarks, and are used only for identification and explanation without intent to infringe.

British Library Cataloguing in Publication Data
A catalogue record for this book is available from the British Library

ISBN: 978-1-032-27038-8 (Set)
ISBN: 978-1-032-27295-5 (Volume 1) (hbk)
ISBN: 978-1-032-27310-5 (Volume 1) (pbk)
ISBN: 978-1-003-29221-0 (Volume 1) (ebk)

DOI: 10.4324/9781003292210

Publisher's Note
The publisher has gone to great lengths to ensure the quality of this reprint but points out that some imperfections in the original copies may be apparent.

Disclaimer
The publisher has made every effort to trace copyright holders and would welcome correspondence from those they have been unable to trace.

WOMEN'S PLACE IN INDUSTRY AND HOME

By

SYLVIA ANTHONY

M.A.

LONDON

GEORGE ROUTLEDGE & SONS, LTD.

BROADWAY HOUSE: 68–74 CARTER LANE, E.C.

1932

Printed in Great Britain by Butler & Tanner Ltd., Frome and London

DEDICATED

TO

THE MEMORY

OF

MARIA SHARPE PEARSON

CONTENTS

CHAP.   PAGE

PREFACE xi

I INTRODUCTORY 1

II THE DISTRIBUTION OF WORK 9

The proportion of occupied women to occupied men, and to the total female population—decline since 1881 —decline in paid domestic service—increase in unpaid domestic workers—estimate of number of latter—numbers of men and women in various industries—proportions of the sexes in different industrial grades—sex-differentiation according to arduousness of work—and according to occupation in or out of doors—geographical distribution of occupation by sex—summary of conclusions.

III THE REMUNERATION OF WOMEN WORKERS . . 21

Comparative remuneration of men and women—women's on an average lower—more women occupied on less-skilled work—are women concentrated in poorly-paid occupations?—women in Trade Board trades—wage-rates in Trade Board and other trades compared—wage-rates in women's non-industrial work: (a) Domestic service ; (b) Prostitution ; (c) Teaching ; (d) Nursing and Midwifery ; (e) Clerks and Shop-assistants—Juvenile wage-rates—Differential wage-rates according to sex—summary of conclusions.

IV THE CAUSES OF LOW PAYMENT OF WOMEN . . 38

Differences of physique a cause—but not sufficient explanation alone—differences of function—natural—conventional, connected with marriage : average age of occupied women—expectation of marriage—lack of capital resources—conventional obligations of marriage —maintenance of wife by husband—and of children— effect on comparative wages of men and women—restrictions on women's employment in well-paid work—effect on workers' organization—summary of conclusions.

V THE ECONOMIC CONVENTIONS OF MARRIAGE AND THEIR ORIGINS 55

Ancient custom of reciprocity of maintenance and service between husband and wife the basis of economic relationship of the sexes—social reasonableness of its establish-

CHAP.   PAGE

ment originally—early association of home with gainful occupation—domestic work of juveniles—changes due to industrial development—dissociation of home and gainful occupation—prohibitions of gentility—emancipation of women—distinction made by modern conditions between economic position of married and single woman.

VI   TESTS AND PLEDGES OF WAR TIME .   .   .   71

Agreements about terms of women's admission to men's work—success of women's work—previous low valuation partly due to low wages—industrial work found not harmful to maternity—appointment of War Cabinet Committee on Women in Industry—Majority Report—Minority Report—non-representation of women at industrial conferences and on other bodies—the vote.

VII   TRADE UNIONISM AND WOMEN'S WORK .   .   91

Industrial Revolution of eighteenth century the genesis of Trade Unionism—its effect on source of family income—competition instead of co-operation within the family—men's wages undercut by women—monopoly of heavy work by men not customary—attempted by male organization in wool, silk, coal industries—monopoly of all factory work by men suggested—opposed by women workers—monopoly proposed on grounds of women's welfare, in coal, pottery, metal, clothing industries—and on various other grounds—improvement of working conditions based on welfare of women—Equal Pay—early attempts to secure it—silk trade, cotton trade, metal trades—Trade Union Congress resolution—organization of women—difficulties—practical obstacles to proposals for equal pay—Trade Board practice—connection of Equal Pay and married women's work—limitation of sex-conflict in industry—by conventional absorption of women in domestic work after marriage and low wage-demands of others—Trade Union restrictions as partial cause of this—summary.

VIII   INDUSTRIAL LEGISLATION AND WOMEN'S WORK .   127

Industrial legislation differentiating between men and women—its paternal character—genuinely or hypocritically benevolent—international scope—conventions and recommendations of I.L.O.—differential legislation in Great Britain—differentiation in law but not in practice—effect of such legislation on women's employment—*pros* and *cons* of differentiation—conclusions.

IX   THE WORK NOT PAID WITH WAGES .   .   .   146

The work of home-making defined—its characteristics—the quantity of work—the details—the national cost of home-making labour—peculiar economic treatment of it—results of this treatment: restriction of demand for industrial goods and services—effect on wages—and on industry in general. Working-hours and effi-

CHAP.   PAGE
ciency of home-maker—results of inefficiency—(a) on
industry; (b) on children's health and intelligence.
Health of home-maker neglected nationally—and individually. Need for new social-industrial policy respecting home-making.

X   THE HOME-MAKER   167

Dissatisfaction with economic position—social significance of dissatisfaction—effect of economic position
on health—health of married women gainfully occupied
—of domestic women—maternal mortality rate—causes
of maternal mortality—connection with economic
position of women in general and of home-maker in
particular.

XI   THE DIRECTION OF CHANGE   183

New views of marriage—the Woman's Movement—
the philosophy of political freedom—Programme for
Change.

XII   EQUAL PAY FOR EQUAL WORK   194

The meaning of the phrase—opposition disguised under
similar titles—the effect of differential rates on industry
—aggravation of evil effect during periods of depression—effect on national expenditure through Unemployment Insurance Fund.

XIII   THE DIRECTION OF CHANGE (continued) .   .   .   212

Provision for families—disadvantages of present system—schemes for change—cash payments—provide a
basis for equal pay—extension of communal services
to family—less effective—Future of the Home—as a
family unit—as a small-scale unit—popular distaste
for co-operative home-service. New Economic Basis
for Marriage—failure of present legal basis—Christian
teaching—Swedish law—voluntary agreements—mutual
obligations. Future of Women's Work—still largely
domestic—domestic work less like slavery—freedom of
movement between domestic and industrial—based on
special organization therefor—advantages of this freedom—for domestic woman—for gainfully occupied
woman—for children under their care—for industry.
Women's work more diversified—and of higher average
grade. Conclusion.

INDEX   237

LIST OF TABLES

PAGE

I MEN AND WOMEN GAINFULLY OCCUPIED ; numbers of each, percentage of each to total male and female population aged 10 plus, and percentage of occupied women to occupied men, 1881–1921 (Great Britain). 11

II MEN AND WOMEN OCCUPIED IN VARIOUS INDUSTRIES, 1921 (England and Wales) 14

III MEN AND WOMEN OCCUPIED IN HIGHER AND LOWER GRADES OF PROFESSIONS (1921), numbers and percentages 17

IV MEN AND WOMEN ENGAGED IN INDOOR AND OUTDOOR OCCUPATIONS (1921), numbers and percentages to total of each sex employed, respectively. . . 19

V EMPLOYMENT OF MEN AND WOMEN IN TRADE BOARD TRADES 23

VI Statistical Basis for Chart showing correspondence between DEGREE OF TOTAL UNEMPLOYMENT AND PROPORTION OF WOMEN INDUSTRIALLY EMPLOYED . 204

PREFACE

This book is an attempt to outline the present economic position of women, to trace the origin of those features which most sharply differentiate Economic Woman from Economic Man, and to focus in a coherent view of the future the Will to Change which the present position inspires. Its subject is Woman and Leviathan ("that great Leviathan called a Common-wealth"): indeed it is a study of that huge beast by one securely enclosed within its entrails. Jonah investigates the workings of the whale; and if at times he attempts an attack upon Leviathan's internal economy, that seems but a natural reaction.

My gratitude is due to many people for information, encouragement, criticism, and for practical assistance not always directly connected with this book, but essential to its production. For all these things I owe thanks to Mrs. E. M. Hubback and to my husband. Miss Ivy Pinchbeck, Miss Dorothy Elliott (Secretary of the Women's Branch of the National Union of General and Municipal Workers), Mrs. E. Abbott (Chairman of the Open Door Council), Miss Douie (Librarian of the London Society for Women's Service), and Miss Anna Martin, of the Rotherhithe Guild of Women Citizens, are among those who have pointed the way to material for my studies and been themselves inspiringly informative. No one of them would necessarily have come to the same conclusions as are here expressed. Mrs. Valentine Downes and Miss Mary Roberts of Nant Peris have given me practical help in diverse form, while Paul Michael Hollis and Arolla Jane, though they have not exactly helped, have hindered much less than they might have done.

WOMEN'S PLACE IN INDUSTRY AND HOME

CHAPTER I

INTRODUCTORY

The tumult and shouting for women's political equality have died down ; captains and kings have departed. The aftermath of the sex-conflict somewhat resembles that of the European War : an economic chaos which promises woe to both sides, and a darkness of social philosophy which can be felt by all possessed of the appropriate sense.

There is indeed at the present day a curious lack of any accepted code to regulate the economic relationship between men and women in society. The effects of this void are visible in numerous instances of individual friction, and in disagreement on points of fundamental principle arising whenever the relationship demands discussion, and remaining still open and unsettled when the discussion ceases. A recent instance may be found in the Report of the Royal Commission on the Civil Service, when the Commissioners divided equally, for and against Equal Pay for the sexes, and could present no agreed or even majority recommendation on the matter.

The social conflict, the uncertainty of view, the lack of coherent philosophy, are a feature of other industrial communities as well as our own. An observer of personal problems in America writes of the conflict there " between the theory of equality (of the sexes) and the fact of competition " :—

" Everyone in America will agree that the sexes are equal. Most people will argue that equality has already been achieved. But the truth seems to be that the two sexes, on the whole, are very much frightened of each other. I read recently that there are a million women living on alimony in the United States. This sounds like an exaggeration; but at least it will draw attention to a quite remarkable state of affairs. Every day there are breach-of-promise cases for absolutely astonishing sums. If such facts exist, it is obviously untrue that women have secured economic equality with men, or have equal economic opportunities. If women felt that they had achieved equality they could not tolerate such a position of dependence. It is just as obvious that men have by no means achieved superiority."[1]

In England, though breach-of-promise actions have somewhat gone out of fashion, we have similar signs of a "quite remarkable state of affairs". The anomalies of the Unemployment Insurance Acts, for instance, are as nothing to the anomalies of social structure which their operation reveals. There is food for thought in the case of the woman who recently complained to the authorities because her husband, from whom she was separated, had not claimed the wife's allowance for her from the Unemployment Insurance Fund. She, presumably, was also unemployed. Theologically we have abandoned Miltonic orthodoxy—" He for God only, she for God in him "—but when husband and wife approach the altar of Mammon, the Exchequer, she still requires his intercession. Our economic philosophy savours curiously of the antique, and seems to consist of little but a savour. Where is one to look for the body of principle from which such savours are diffused?

For the organization of every human society must be based on some principle of the economic relationship proper to be maintained between men and women. Even complete disregard of sex, in industrial and political economy, would provide such a principle—and indeed a very remarkable one, which, so far as I know, has never been put into practice. It was not practised in this country under the strictest—or freest—régime of *laissez-faire*. It may be approached at the present day in Russia; but

---

[1] Mr. Alan Porter in the *Spectator*, January 31, 1931.

it is far from complete there, since it appears that though women receive equal pay under the Soviets, they enjoy also special industrial privileges in connection with their function of maternity.

The motive principles actually in force in any community at any time can only be discovered by a study of the actions that flow from them, and their success can only be judged by observation of the degree of equilibrium and national well-being that is maintained. Explicit statements of principle or ideal offer little aid in the search for the theory underlying current practice—such statements as " *Laissez-faire* " ; " With all my worldly goods I thee endow " ; " The rate for the job " ; " Equal Pay for Equal Work " ; " What the industry can afford to pay " ; " To each according to his need." These are straws showing, not the way the wind blows, but the point from which some believe they would like to feel it freshen. To find the implicit principles actually at work, one must attempt to discover what is the difference between the work available to men and women, and the forces determining this difference ; the work they each perform, and the economic reward they receive ; and what evidence there is of tendencies to change in these respects. These are the quarry of this book.

The immediate consequence of the natural physical differences between men and women is, that women as a whole spend more time and energy than men in reproduction—that is, in the natural processes necessary for the recruitment of the race. A broad line of economic differentiation between men and women therefore appears to be reasonable and necessary, namely, that in the general distribution of the profits of industrial work, women as a whole should receive a larger or more assured share than men, compared with the industrial work performed by each sex. Women must be partially dependent on the past or present labour of men, if the two sexes are to be maintained at the same economic level, and the race is to be normally recruited.

The recognition of this principle is doubtless the foundation for the custom, established in the Common Law of England and the legal systems of most other civilized countries, that the husband shall maintain his wife according to his means. For something over twelve hundred years, it seems probable that this phrase has described the central fact in the economic relationship of men and women to one another in this country, although its legal recognition seems to be some thousand years younger.

For a long time after this principle was established, money was scarcely in use at all among the common people ; industry was a domestic affair ; girls married at the age when nowadays they enter a secondary school, and their families were limited by little but mortality. Marriage did not seclude them from industry, though childbearing occasionally did so for a while. This interval of childbirth was the time when women needed assurance of other support, and the community specially needed that they should receive it. A woman, therefore, as child or wife (and she was usually one or the other) was to be assured of maintenance by husband or father ; conversely, the profit of her industrial labour accrued to the man ; but her maintenance was not dependent on her labour. For it was when she was incapable of work that her maintenance was most necessary.

This principle did not, in the centuries when it was first established in this country, involve the parasitic dependence of the wife on the husband, since her scope for " gainful " occupation was then scarcely more restricted than his. Rather it provided the woman with a second line of defence, and laid upon the man a permanent responsibility to provide support, in the military rather than the economic sense of that word. Their maintenance of one another was mutual, except at such times as she was incapacitated, when his special responsibility was called into play. Her economic freedom was less than his, but the ordinary man had not much of that either, before money came into common use.

The economic organization of society in which this

principle originally established itself has radically altered since, and complicated reactions have resulted from the survival of this ancient custom in the midst of change. The use of money ; later marriage and lesser fertility of women ; the supersession of the individual wage for the co-operative family return on work co-operatively done ; the departure of work from home to factory, and of men and women in its train—all these now normal features of our modern society have taken their part in undermining the sufficiency of the ancient plan. We now find families where the husband is in short-time employment or unemployed, and the wife is the chief contributor to the family income. We find large numbers of women earning independent incomes ; and often then a difficulty arises as to the principle to be observed in determining their just remuneration compared with that of men. For many men have these customary and legal obligations to domestic women, whereas the women who compete with them have not. Hence arises dissatisfaction, conflict and a sense of injustice among many different groups. Many women demand Equal Pay in the name of justice, and because they hold that the reward should be determined only with regard to the work done. Many men support the same principle. When women are paid less for the job, they are likely to drive men out of employment. " The principle that a man and a woman doing the same work should receive the same pay has always been accepted by the Labour Movement."[1]

At the same time it is frequently forgotten that for the majority of adult women, who work in their own homes, the economic problem is not one of Equal Pay but of Any Pay. By *Pay* is here meant money given as a recognition of and reward for work, carrying with it the usual right to freedom in expenditure, such freedom being limited but not normally extinguished by prior claims based on legal or conventional obligations.

Equal Pay between men and women in industry offers no solution of *this* problem ; it would probably accen-

[1] *Labour Party Report on Equal Pay for Equal Work* (1930).

tuate it. As a psychological factor in the economic relationship of men and women the question is increasing in
importance ; it is nearer the threshold of consciousness
in younger than in older women. Resentment or avoid-
ance of the economic dependence associated with conventional marriage is no longer restricted to the spinster or
the middle-class woman. It has an important bearing
on the falling and dysgenic birth-rate.

Yet as soon as one begins to consider the problem as
a whole, one becomes painfully aware of a void in current
political philosophy : the general lack of any attempt to
evaluate domestic work, or to co-ordinate it, economically, with other industrial activities and developments.
Do we wish the domestic work of the individual home
to be reduced to a negligible minimum by the extension
of infant crèches, nursery schools, co-operative housing
schemes that include in their design communal kitchens,
heating, and other services ; labour-saving devices and
better architectural planning for the individual home ;
and increasing centralization in the factory of processes
as yet domestic ? And then would we encourage married
women to occupy themselves in paid industry rather
than their homes, so as to secure *their* equal pay ?
Or do we want, while thus reducing domestic labour, to
confine the domestic woman to non-industrial activities,
and so gradually increase the ranks of the leisured and
semi-leisured ladies free to spend their time at bridge or
literary clubs, or on committees for improving the circumstances of those whom they suppose less fortunate
than themselves ? Or would we prefer to turn the clock
back, or fix it where it tells the present hour : encourage
the use of the maximum of domestic labour to produce
a given result ; discourage the industrialization of any
work which housewives have been wont to do themselves
in the past, or economies effected by co-operation between
individual homes ; or the application of machines to domestic work that has previously been done by hand ; or the
planning of houses with a view to reducing the labour of
keeping them clean—and then keep all married women

in their homes working on these lines, by dint of refusing to allow them to do anything else ?

The first policy seems to be roughly that of Soviet Russia ; the second appears to represent the American ideal ; the third, the prevalent English policy.

The attitude of those who oppose the employment of married women in paid work outside their homes appears to possess some inherent reasonableness, based upon the existent conventional economic relationship between men and women. But the dignity of the home, which is presumably supposed to be promoted by this policy, is really endangered by it, and also the industrial progress of the nation, as will be indicated later.

What has been described as the Soviet system, however, is probably not suitable for this country, either as an immediate practical policy or even as an ideal. It appears to need to be based on a low standard of material living (such as an acute and widespread housing shortage would cause), and/or on a " will to community " in the provision and enjoyment of domestic services which many centuries of preaching of Christ's doctrine on the matter have not yet succeeded in instilling among our countrymen. The prevalence of one or both these conditions may see the Russian through thick and thin, but the Englishman has a preference for individual home-services which only the enjoyment of a super-income seems usually capable of eradicating. This preference may be founded on a perfectly sound view of the function of the home in relation to modern industry, industrial fatigue, and the Englishman's individual psychology (none of which, of course, applied to Christ's disciples) ; it is probably fortunate that no practical statesman would dream of attempting to change it.

But the Soviet system is not the only one which, if it were in force among us, would cause dislocation of industry and much individual sense of distress. The present system does the same. If there were no other condition of modern life difficult to reconcile with our sex-economic-conventions, the existence of unemployment of men side by side with industrial employment of women would be sufficient to disturb the ancient order.

The economic relationship which is sanctioned by conventions may be thus summarized :—

(1) It is right that men should maintain their wives and their young children. It is also fitting that they should maintain or partially maintain other adult women of their family if they wish to do so.

(2) Men shall be deemed to have a prior right to the possession of money or property. It follows that they should receive (a) more remuneration for the performance of similar work ; (b) a preference or monopoly of the better-paid work ; (c) prior right in matters of inheritance.

(3) The personal service required in a man's home shall be performed by the woman or women he maintains, unless he can afford to engage others to do it.

(4) In so far as is consistent with the above, it is fitting that women whom men do not wish to maintain should maintain themselves, either wholly or partially.

The most brilliant and comprehensive attack made on these conventional principles in recent years, in the field of economics, was launched by Mrs. Sidney Webb in the Minority Report (signed by herself alone) of the War Cabinet Committee on Women in Industry (1919).

These conventional principles are proving inadequate in the organization of modern life. Mrs. Webb's suggestions are not, in the view of the present writer, entirely adequate as a substitute, but the consideration of them must be deferred to a later stage, when facts and frictions have been more fully described.

CHAPTER II

THE DISTRIBUTION OF WORK

The proportion of occupied women to occupied men, and to the total female population—decline since 1881—decline in paid domestic service—increase in unpaid domestic workers—estimate of number of latter—numbers of men and women in various industries —proportions of the sexes in different industrial grades—sex-differentiation according to arduousness of work—and according to occupation in or out of doors—geographical distribution of occupation by sex—summary of conclusions.

The conditions of employment are at present abnormal. The number of the unemployed ranges between two and three millions. This state of affairs is favourable to the employment of women as compared with the employment of men. Retail trade has increased at the expense of primary production and manufacture; the heavy industries are more hardly hit than the average; light automatic machinery is being more and more used. All these conditions (and others to be considered in later chapters) favour, comparatively, the employment of women, and are among the reasons why women have latterly absorbed a higher proportion of paid jobs than in 1920.

Whatever the future holds in store for British industry, however, there is no doubt that efforts will be made to return to the old norm of employment. Even if the abnormal conditions of industry become in some respects the new norm, yet in the numbers of those employed at some wage or profit, in some kind of gainful work, no one doubts that a great struggle will be made to absorb in industry the same proportion of the population as was considered normal to be gainfully occupied at the period when the Unemployment Insurance Fund was established. It is almost inevitable that these efforts should include

9

an attempt to return to the previous norm in the comparative employment of men and women.

The question then arises, what was that norm ? It was not stationary. The idea has been for a long time popularly accepted that from the end of the nineteenth century there were an increasing number of openings for women, in an increasing number of callings, and that Woman's Place was no longer, in any exclusive sense, the Home. If it was normal for the gainful employment of women to be on the increase compared with that of men, and compared with that of the total female population, it may seem that the present depression has only speeded up an acceleration which was already begun.

Actually, however, statements about the increasing gainful employment of women were largely current fiction. They had a limited application only, to certain sections of the population—more particularly to the professional or middle classes. But when it was suggested that more and more women, in proportion to the numbers of their sex, or in proportion to men, were entering into possession of Economic Independence, it simply was not true. The proportion of women compared with men now employed *is* seen to be abnormal, when one studies the trend of employment previous to 1921.

For the forty years previous to 1921, the proportion of women gainfully employed had been gradually decreasing. (The decennial Census did not fall to be taken during the war years, which was an exceptional period in this respect.) The figures were clearly set out in the Report of the Balfour Committee on Industry and Trade (*see* facing page).

The Table shows that between 1881 and 1921 there was a gradual decline in the proportion of women gainfully occupied, amounting in all to about 3 per cent. in comparison with all adult women, and to about the same in comparison with occupied men. In the words of the Balfour Report, there was previous to 1921 " as regards females . . . an appreciable decline in the proportion (not in the total number) of women and girls returned as fol-

TABLE I [1]

SHOWING THE NUMBERS OF MEN AND WOMEN IN GREAT BRITAIN
GAINFULLY OCCUPIED, THE PERCENTAGE OF EACH TO THE
TOTAL MALE AND FEMALE POPULATION AGED 10 PLUS, AND THE
PERCENTAGE OF FEMALES TO MALES OCCUPIED, 1881–1921

Census Year	M		F		M : F
	No. employed	Per cent. of males aet. 10 +	No. employed	Per cent. of females aet. 10 +	Per cent. of employed women : men
1881	8,851,486	83·3	3,887,128	33·9	43·9
1891	10,010,324	83·2	4,489,408	34·4	44·8
1901	11,548,164	83·7	4,763,375	31·8	41·2
1911	12,929,619	83·7	5,423,944	32·3	41·9
1921	13,655,895	82·8	5,701,424	30·8	41·7

lowing definite occupations ". This proportion had " fallen
to a greater extent than can be accounted for by the decrease in the employment of girls under 14 ".[2] (The decrease in the employment of girls under 14 was caused
by the raising of the school-leaving age, which affected
both sexes.)

A marked decline, however, had occurred in the numbers of women " going into service ". Between 1911 and
1921 the number of women occupied in the Census class
Personal Service [3] fell by about 350,000, and the decline
was especially noticeable in Private Domestic Service,
being sufficient to account for a great part of the total
change during that period in the proportion of women
gainfully occupied.

So far as domestic work was concerned, the decline
in *paid* workers was partly counterbalanced, as it would

[1] *Report of Balfour Committee on the State of Industry and Trade :
Survey of Industrial Relations*, H.M.S.O., 1926, p. 59 (except the last
column, computed by the author from the figures given).

[2] *Ibid.*, p. 60. See also *The Numbers Occupied in the Industries of
England and Wales, 1911–1921*, by A. L. Bowley, 1926, p. 3.

[3] The Census classification *Personal Service* includes, besides Private
Domestic Service, employers and employees in Lodging Houses,
Restaurants, Inns, etc., also Charwomen and Laundry Workers. The
numbers employed in commercial houses *increased* 1911–1921.

appear, by two other simultaneous changes : the proportion of married women increased, and the proportion of married women working for gain decreased. In 1901, of every thousand women in England and Wales, 395 were single, 497 married, and 108 widowed. In 1921, the corresponding figures were 368 : 520 : 112.[1] In 1911 the percentage of married women " occupied " was 15·3 ; in 1921 it was 14·7.[2]

The paid servants were leaving the homes, but the married women were more and more staying in them— and more and more women were married. *There was on balance little change in the extent to which woman's workplace was the home.* As for women's economic independence : in so far as that may be supposed to consist in earning the money for one's keep, it had evidently *decreased* in extent, since 1881.[3]

Despite the decline in Personal Service, about one-third of all " occupied " women were employed in it in 1921 —a large proportion, which is not likely to have materially altered. But the number of women so occupied would (in the words of the General Census Report, 1921) " be immensely increased if account could be taken of the females occupied with the domestic duties of the home, although classified as unoccupied because not working for payment or profit ".[4] To obtain a complete view of the occupational field for both sexes, we should take account of this immense area hitherto uncharted by the Census (as it might be represented in an ancient map, " Here be Hous-wyves "). An estimate needs to be made as to how many of the undistinguished ruck of women so classi-

---

[1] *The Social Structure of England and Wales,* by Carr-Saunders and Jones, 1927, p. 10.

[2] *Balfour Committee, op. cit.,* p. 427.

[3] But in so far as economic independence may be said to consist in *legal* right to hold or inherit wealth, earned or unearned, the independence of women was established, by the passing of the Married Women's Property Act of 1882. The decline in women's independence, referred to above, is only to be understood to have occurred in respect of the comparative proportion of *earned* incomes, and technically can only be dated from the year when the right to enjoy any personal possession became possible for women.

[4] *General Report on Census of England and Wales,* 1921, p. 126.

fied really are unoccupied (that is leisured, aged, invalid, etc.) and how many are employed in regular unpaid work. These workers are each their own mistress, so there is no check on the time they spend working. But that is no reason against the attempt to reckon them, for the same fact applies to many other independent workers—to many stockbrokers, small shopkeepers and costermongers. A certain proportion of housewives employ paid help, and some of these may be regarded as doing only part-time work. This is also true of workers in other industries and professions. Many a man, for instance, may be listed as a barrister, or an architect, who often has little to do, or who arranges to have the less-skilled or routine labour performed by employees, and does not spend seven hours a day at work.

The great majority of " unoccupied " women are doing a regular, comparatively hard, and comparatively long day's work all the year round, with no more holiday-time than their men-folk, and no more weekly Days of Rest. If they are omitted from the Plan of National Industry, whenever that plan is drawn, the result is falsified.[1] Only by their inclusion can we gather some idea of the way national industry is distributed as between men and women. With their inclusion the main divisions are as follows (*see* p. 14).

It is evident that the adult male population is distributed among all the main divisions of industry. A considerable number of men are engaged in Personal Service. But this type of work swallows up so many persons in all, that in addition to a considerable number of men it provides the employment of the great majority of occupied women. Consequently the proportion of women employed in all other types of work is comparatively low.

___

[1] The deceptiveness of the classification of all married women not working separately for gain as " unoccupied " is incidentally illustrated in the Report of the Ministry of Agriculture on the Practical Education of Women for Rural Life (1928). It is there estimated (p. 13) that there are roughly 10,000 women with an "independent" interest in agriculture (i.e. working for individual gain), and 1,000,000 with a " co-operative " interest (i.e. working for family gain). The latter do not appear in the Census figures of industries and occupations.

TABLE II [1]

SHOWING THE NUMBERS OF MEN AND WOMEN OCCUPIED IN CERTAIN
AND IN ALL INDUSTRIES OF ENGLAND AND WALES, 1921

Industry	M	F	Total
Fishing	39	2	40
Agriculture	1,038	85	1,124
Mines and Quarries . . .	1,275	11	1,286
Metal Mnfrs.	1,904	221	2,126
Textile Mnfrs.	489	654	1,142
Clothing Mnfrs.	312	503	815
Food, Drink and Tobacco Mnfrs.	342	200	541
Paper, Printing Mnfrs., etc.	221	119	340
Other Mnfrs.	1,449	249	1,699
All Mnfrs. . . .	4,717	1,946	6,663
Gas, Water, Electric Supply .	158	109	163
Transport and Communication	1,164	39	1,204
Commerce, Finance, etc. .	1,533	742	2,275
Nat. and Loc. Gov. (inc. Defence, exc. Educn.) . . .	918	194	1,112
Professions and Education .	334	416	750
Entertainments and Sport .	78	38	116
Personal Service	518	1,507	2,025
Miscellaneous	342	80	388
Total gainfully occupied . .	12,113	5,065	17,178
Personal Service unpaid . .	—	8,430 [2]	—
TOTAL (Workers) .	12,113 [3]	13,495	

For footnotes, see facing page.

Anything over the rate of 1 woman to 3 men is above the average, and occupations in which there are more than this proportion may be considered at least as much " a woman's job " as a man's, under present conditions.

Within each main division of industry there are a great number of branches and sub-divisions, in all of which the proportion of men and women employed may differ from one another very much. Thus under Metal Manufacture one finds Engineering, which (excluding Marine or Electrical Engineering) employs about half a million men and 33,000 women—a proportion of 15 men to 1 woman—and Tin Box Manufacture, in which about 4,000 men and 8,000 women are employed.

Certain main branches of industry, nevertheless, stand out as pre-eminently " women's work ". In the Clothing Trades as a whole, there have for a long time been about twice as many women as men employed ; in Textiles the proportion of women for the last forty years has been about 3 to 2 men. In the Food, Drink and Tobacco industry taken as a whole, that proportion is reversed ; it is still a high one for the women. In the Printing and Paper Industries, and those grouped with them, the proportion of women has for a long period been more than

---

[1] See *The Numbers Occupied in England and Wales*. It will be noticed that when classification is according to industry, it is not possible to separate those occupied in clerical work.

[2] This figure is obtained as follows :—

Females aet. 12 plus, non-gainfully occupied .		10,543 000
Ditto attending educational institutions, full-time	912,000	
,, aet. 70 plus	698,000	
,, in asylums, hospitals, etc. . .	303,000	
,, Leisured, or occupied in non-gainful work, non-domestic (estimate) . . .	200,000	
	2,113,000	
		2,113,000
Ditto, occupied in unpaid domestic work .		8,430,000

[3] The difference of over a million between the final totals for men and women workers may be attributed to the fact (*a*) that a larger number of occupied men than of occupied women are absent from the country when the Census is taken, e.g. fishermen, men in the Defence Forces, Mercantile Marine, etc. ; (*b*) that there are more women than men in the total population.

1 : 2. The same is the case for certain branches of Metal Manufacture, the Pottery Industry, and a number of other manufacturing industries or branches of industry, such as Rubber, and the Upholstering branch of the Furnishing Trades.

In the Distributive Trades the proportion of women occupied is more than 1 : 2, and the same is true of those branches of employment which are grouped under the head of Commerce, Banking, Finance, etc.

At this point we find ourselves instinctively making a further distinction. On a recent country holiday I was informed by the landlady of my humble lodgings that a former visitor had brought " his young lady, who is on the Stock Exchange ". Foreknowledge of the differences between the employment of the sexes in this favoured circle, and under the head of Commerce, Banking and Finance in general, prevented the information being misleading. A famous comedian used to sing a song which (according to the probably faulty tradition of my family) began

> " My brother is awfully clever,
> He's head of a very large firm ",

and concluded

> " Oh, well then, he sweeps out the floor."

But no one would accuse the lodger's young lady of similar tactics, for her statement could not deceive. A young lady " on the Stock Exchange ", in the usual sense of the phrase, would be indeed a rare bird.

In almost every branch of industry we find a distinction between the work of men and women, roughly following the line of distinction between the more and less skilled grades of work. This may be illustrated by the state of affairs in the Professions—another branch of work in which, as a whole, the proportionate number of women is much above the average, being 3·5 to 3 men.

Women are strongly represented in the professions of teaching and medicine, being much in excess of the men. But whereas in the higher grades of the teaching profession there are nearly 2 women to 1 man, in the lower

TABLE III [1]

SHOWING THE NUMBERS AND PERCENTAGES OF WOMEN COMPARED
WITH MEN IN CERTAIN AND IN ALL PROFESSIONS (1921)

Occupation		Highly-skilled		Less-skilled	
		M	F	M	F
Teaching [2]	No. . .	58,095	110,670	10,760	76,682
	Per cent. .	100	180	100	713
Medicine [3]	No. . .	34,055	1,573	16,862	118,086
	Per cent. .	100	4·7	100	695
All Professions	No. . .	252,176	134,788	54,654	225,194
	Per cent. .	100	54	100	412

grades there are more than 7 women to 1 man ; and in
the medical profession whereas there were in 1921 about
20 men to 1 woman in the higher grades, the position
in the lower grades was much the same as in the teaching profession—about 7 women to 1 man.

Throughout national industry the same conditions may
be observed. In industry proper, the owners, agents,
managers, foremen and superintendents are usually men.
It is so common for women to preponderate in the less-
skilled branches of work, and men in the more skilled,
that problems of women's labour are frequently treated
as similar or identical with problems of unskilled labour.
In commerce and clerical work it is a matter of common
observation that a disproportionate number of the females
employed are in positions of lesser skill or trust. The
secretary or shorthand-typist, who is typically female,
usually takes dictation from a man. Where there is a

[1] The figures (not the percentages) in this Table are from Table XL,
p. 68, *The Social Structure of England and Wales*.

[2] The term " Highly-skilled " includes certificated, college-trained
and certain others ; the term " Less-skilled " includes uncertificated,
not college-trained, and supplementary teachers.

[3] The term " Highly-skilled " includes Physicians, Surgeons, etc.,
and Dentists ; " Less-skilled " includes Sick Nurses and subordinate
Medical Service, Mental Attendants and Midwives.

counter-saleswoman, there is often a frock-coated shop-walker in charge.

It may be suggested that there is yet a third line of cleavage between men's and women's work. Their distribution in the different types of industry is in different proportions : their distribution in the higher and lower grades of work within these branches is different : it may be said that there is also a difference between the arduousness of the work undertaken by men and women as a whole, and that whereas men undertake the major part of the world's heavy or disagreeable labour, women are occupied with the lighter forms of it.

Disagreeability is, of course, a subjective quality impossible to estimate statistically : it depends not only on the character of the work, but also on the conditions of it, and the physical and mental character of the worker. Heavy, or even dirty, work, is not in itself necessarily disagreeable, though one may suppose it always to be so when it overtaxes the health of the individual employed on it.

One may, however, state generally, that industrial work requiring a high degree of physical strength, or involving much risk of danger, is in the majority of cases performed by men, and many women are occupied in light, automatic or sedentary work. On the other hand there are many homes from which an unburdened man departs in the morning to spend his eight-hour day at an automatic machine, or on an office-stool, leaving behind a woman to occupy herself with the more varied, possibly pleasanter, but often heavier, activities of the house : the wash-tub, floor-scrubbing ; perhaps the carrying of coals, water and babies up tenement stairs which seem as high as Jacob's ladder—an unwelcome kinship between heaven and home.

Distribution of work between the sexes according to " weight " or agreeableness is therefore not a subject apt for scientific estimation. There is, however, another line of cleavage between the work of men and women which may be measured with some exactitude, and is of great interest in connection with the question of suitability of work for men and women on grounds of individual and racial health. What proportion of men, and of women, are occupied in and out of doors ? The figures given below refer to the year 1921, but it may be supposed that little change has occurred in this respect, of a permanent nature. There is much unemployment of men at present in out-door work, which might temporarily lower the figure under this head (or lessen its reality) ; but the increased indus-trial employment of women has not occurred in outdoor occupations. There seems every reason to suppose that the picture presented by Table IV represents, with approxi-mately permanent correctness, an established feature of our economic organization :—

TABLE IV [1]

INDOOR AND OUTDOOR (PAID) OCCUPATIONS : THE NUMBERS AND
PERCENTAGES OF MEN AND WOMEN SO EMPLOYED IN 1921
('000s)

Type of occupation	Males		Females	
	Number	Percentage	Number	Percentage
Indoor . .	5,642	46·6	4,805	95·0
Outdoor . . .	3,379	30·9	148	2·9
Mixed	2,732	22·6	112	2·2
TOTAL . .	12,113	100·0	5,065	100·0

Ninety-five per cent. of the women who do paid work are occupied indoors, and probably quite as large a pro-portion of those domestic workers whose work is *not* done for profit. The corresponding percentage for male workers is less than half the women's percentage. It is evident that the increase of indoor work, which is such a marked feature of modern industrial economy, affects women more than men—though this distinction between the sexes may have existed to some extent for a very long time, before

[1] *The Social Structure of England and Wales*, p. 53.

indoor work became the preponderating condition in industry.

A further interesting distinction may be observed between the distribution of men's and women's work, in respect of geographical area. This is a distinction which is fluctuating too rapidly to admit of exact illustration. New industries are arising in the South of England which employ a large proportion of women. Hitherto, for over a century, the South has been richer in establishments of comparatively leisured and wealthy families (including many retired Army and business men) which employ a high proportion of female domestic servants; in Lancashire, Staffordshire, Yorkshire and the Black Country there is considerable concentration of manufacturing industries which employ women; so that in these districts the proportion of women employed, compared with the men, is relatively high. In South Wales, and other mining areas, on the other hand, the proportion of women occupied in paid work is low, both because they are excluded from sharing in the chief local industry, and because the neighbourhood is not sufficiently salubrious to be chosen by employers of domestic servants.

There are many other significant distinctions in the distribution of work between men and women : and these distinctions may be considered from an historical, geographical, physiological, eugenic, or many another point of view. To sum up the distinctions which have been touched on in this chapter ; we find that

1. Women's occupations are less diversified than men's.
2. More than half the women who are occupied, do not receive direct remuneration for their work.
3. The proportion of women to men in the less-skilled occupational grades is considerably higher than the proportion in paid work as a whole.
4. Paid work involving a high degree of strength or risk is usually performed by men.
5. Women are more occupied in indoor work than men.
6. The geographical distribution of women (paid) workers is not identical with that of men workers.

CHAPTER III

The Remuneration of Women Workers

Comparative remuneration of men and women—women's on an average lower—more women occupied on less-skilled work—are women concentrated in poorly-paid occupations?—women in Trade Board trades—wage-rates in Trade Board and other trades compared—wage-rates in women's non-industrial work: (a) Domestic service; (b) Prostitution; (c) Teaching; (d) Nursing and Midwifery; (e) Clerks and Shop-assistants—Juvenile wage-rates—Differential wage-rates according to sex—summary of conclusions.

If we could construct a table showing, for every branch of national industry, not only the numbers of men and women employed, but also the rate of remuneration received, we should find that the total at the foot of the female column was very much less than that at the foot of the male column, because so many women do not receive remuneration for their work. Supposing, however, that we were to disregard all the unpaid workers, and then take an average for the remuneration of men and women gainfully occupied: it is generally agreed that the average remuneration of the men would still exceed that of the women.

It is not possible to construct such a table of remuneration because there has been no complete inquiry into rates of earnings since 1906. What then are the reasons for supposing that the average remuneration of women is normally less than that of men? Briefly these reasons are (1) the concentration of women in the less-skilled grades of industry and professions; (2) the concentration of women in poorly-paid occupations; (3) the lower average age of women workers and the low pay of juveniles; (4) different rates of pay for men and women doing similar work.

We have already observed that there are more women in the less-skilled grades of each occupation, proportionately, than there are men. The ratio of remuneration of less-skilled to more-skilled work has risen considerably during the last twenty years, but it is still the rule that less-skilled work is paid at a lower rate than more-skilled in the same industry. So because women are concentrated among the less-skilled occupational grades, their average remuneration tends to be lower than that of men.

But in the determination of relative rates of remuneration there are other considerations as, or more, important than that of more or less individual skill. The lower grades of one occupation may receive as much reward or more than the upper grades of another ; nor can such differences be accounted for simply on the grounds of the comparative skill required by the practice of the occupation as a whole. Leaving for the moment out of the question the reasons why such differences exist, it is relevant to consider whether, in the occupations in which women are chiefly congregated, the workers generally are comparatively well or ill rewarded. If the latter, this would provide further evidence that the average remuneration of women is low.

Although it is scarcely possible to conduct an independent inquiry into the wages of women workers in every industry and profession, much evidence on these points can be collected (1) by studying the proportion of the sexes in occupations in which wages are notoriously low ; and (2) by studying the wage-rates in those occupations employing large numbers of women.

We have a guide to the former group, in the scope of the Trade Boards. Trade Boards may be established by the Ministry of Labour in trades in which (owing to lack of organization of the workers, or any other cause) wage-rates are found to be " exceptionally low as compared with that in other employment ". Since the passing of the first Trade Boards Act in 1909, Trade Boards have been set up for 39 trades. The number of workers employed in these trades is estimated at over $1\frac{1}{4}$ million

(February, 1931). The proportion of men to women in this total is not available, but it has been roughly estimated for each trade separately, with the result shown in the following Table :—

TABLE V [1]

SHOWING THE RELATIVE DEGREE OF EMPLOYMENT OF MEN AND WOMEN IN 39 TRADES AFFECTED BY TRADE BOARD LEGISLATION

Sex Ratio.	Number of Trades.	Total Nos. Employed.
Women exclusively . . .	2	7,000
Women mainly (i.e. over $\frac{4}{5}$) .	9	442,000
Women in a majority . .	16	529,000
Men and women equally .	7	64,000
Men in a majority . . .	3	71,000
Men mainly (i.e. over $\frac{4}{5}$) . .	2	160,000
TOTAL . . .	39	1,273,000

Although no exact conclusion can be drawn from these figures, it seems evident that more than two-thirds of the workers in Trade Board trades are women.

Of all the main branches of manufacturing industry, the Clothing Industry is most strongly represented among these trades : on a rough reckoning, about one-half the workers affected by Trade Board awards are occupied in some branch of the Clothing Industry. And this is, after Personal Service, the woman's industry *par excellence*.

The Textile Industry, which also employs an exceptionally high proportion and a large number of women, is not strongly represented among Trade Board trades. The main body of textile workers, including the women, is well organized in Trade Unions. The method of remuneration is in most cases by piecework, according to complicated lists, so that it is difficult to make comparisons of

[1] See *Annual Report of Ministry of Labour* (1928), Appendix XVII. The figures there given provide only a rough indication of the comparative size of the trades concerned, and no exact numerical deductions can be drawn from them. In February, 1931, it was estimated that the number of workers employed in Trade Board trades was 1,300,000. Information on this subject was kindly supplied by the Ministry of Labour.

wages with those prevailing simultaneously in other industries. The Balfour Committee estimated, from returns of different firms employing altogether nearly 90,000 workers, that the earnings of cotton operatives averaged in May, 1925, about 37s. 6d. a week, and of woollen textile workers about the same. This rate was somewhat low even compared with general labourers in some other industries (e.g. shipbuilding), and distinctly low as an average rate.[1]

The Textile Industry is however, in the main, an exception to the rule that manufacturing industries employing a large proportion of women have been substantially affected by the establishment of Trade Boards.[2] Those branches of the Food, Drink and Tobacco industry, of the Paper industry, and of Metal Manufacture, which employ a considerable proportion of women, are all represented among the Trade Board trades.

Some commercial occupations have also come under Trade Boards. Such are the Milk Distributive and the Grocery Distributive trades. The latter Board has not functioned. The question has arisen of setting up Boards for the Drapery and the Catering trades. The application for the former was recently dismissed; the establishment of the Catering Trade Board has been opposed in the Courts by a group of employers on technical grounds, following the decision that there was cause for its establishment.

In all these commercial occupations except the Milk Distributive trade, the proportion of women employed is above the average. Many of the employees concerned are Shop Assistants; others are on the staff of hotels and other catering establishments, and fall under the heading of Personal Service. In all these non-localized occupations, wages and conditions of work differ widely, and some highly-skilled workers may receive good wages, but the inquiries make it clear that large numbers of

[1] *Balfour Committee, op. cit.*, pp. 82 *et seq.*
[2] Certain branches of textile manufacture do, however, come under Trade Boards, notably the Jute industry, in which women are in a majority of the employees.

those employed are paid exceptionally low wages ; and a high proportion of these workers are women.

A group of workers who also come under the occupational head of Personal Service, and for whom a Trade Board has been established for a long time, are the Laundry workers. These are nearly all women.

Although the fact that a Trade Board has been set up for an industry is evidence that wage-rates were low therein at the time of establishment of the Board, it may be said that once the Board is in existence, the wage-rates are raised up to or even above the average ; and consequently, that the concentration of women in trades so regulated cannot be taken as evidence of a low average remuneration of women at the present time.

If the Boards made a practice of fixing wage-rates on some definite theoretical principle of need based on the requirements of a certain uniform Standard of Living, there would be every likelihood that the rates fixed would be high compared with those prevailing in a number of other trades, especially in times of industrial depression. As a matter of fact, it is generally observed that the Boards are not mainly concerned with fixing wages on any such principles, but proceed rather on the same lines as those on which wages are usually determined. The Board gives facilities for collective bargaining in industries where weak organization has previously prevented the workers from safeguarding their interests. The extra weight thus thrown by the State on the side of the workers is rarely much more than sufficient to give them the strength and opportunity to present their case before the Board, and it is inevitable that the independent members of the Board should feel it beyond their powers to press for the fixing of rates higher than those obtaining in other industries in which no special machinery for wage-determination has been set up on the ground of insufficiency.

In general, therefore, it may be said that industries in which Trade Boards have been established, are likely to be among those paying comparatively low rates of remuneration. But wages fixed by such methods have a greater tendency to rigidity than those of industry in general ; [1] in times of falling wages and industrial depression, workers on Trade Board rates are likely to benefit compared with those in other industries. It seems likely, therefore, that at the present time the average remuneration of women, compared with that of men, is abnormally high. But in so far as the fact is due to this cause, it is bound to be a temporary phenomenon ; the lag is not approved by impartial supporters of the Trade Board system ; in times of depression it brings the whole system into danger by the opposition of the employers, and in times of rising wages discredits the Boards among Trade Unionists.

The workers who have been affected by Trade Board legislation, and even many of those who have benefited by the lower wage awards, are not exclusively occupied in processes of little skill. Much of the work connected with the manufacture of Clothing, in particular, is considerably skilled. The prevalence of comparatively low wages (at normal times, if not also now) in many Trade Board trades is due to other economic causes, and not to the degree of skill required in the practice of them. Whatever those causes may be, it seems evident that in the Distributive Trades, in industrial branches of Personal Service, and in the Manufacturing Industries, the majority of those branches of trade for which Trade Boards have been established, or there has been question of the need for them because of the low rates of wages, are trades in which a very considerable proportion of women are employed. It follows that in anything approaching normal trade periods, the average remuneration of women in industry is low.

Something is learnt of the average pay of women by the realization that a large proportion are to be found in many of the lower-paid branches of industry. What of the wages ruling in those other occupational groups in which the largest number of women are employed ?

---

[1] Some Trade Boards have fixed wage-rates on sliding scales according to the cost of living, but these are a minority.

Among these, private domestic service is pre-eminent. Is the pay in this occupation so high that it raises the average standard of women's remuneration even perhaps above the average man's?

Rates of wages and conditions of work in domestic service are not standardized. Their average is not easily assessable, and the difficulty is increased by the fact that the majority of workers " live in ".

The charwoman is the domestic general labourer who does not live in. Her work may vary considerably : it may involve heavy labour almost exclusively, or general or special skilled work. Charwomen are practically un-organized, but certain hourly rates of payment are with some uniformity recognized as the standard within any one area. In London at the present date, and for some years past, 9d. to 1s. an hour has been a normal rate for general or special daily domestic work when no meals are provided. This is probably nearer the maximum than the minimum rate ; it would tend to be lower outside London, and individuals conscious of less than average qualifications may offer their labour at a much lower rate. I have before me an advertisement offering daily domestic work at 4d. an hour—April, 1931.

Trade Board *minimum* fixed wage-rates for adult women (based on piece-work rates) range from 6d. to 10d. an hour ; awards for skilled workers (women) range upwards from 1s. an hour in several trades. Charwomen's wage-rates can therefore only be considered high when com-pared with *minimum* wages for *unskilled* work. Taken by and large, and compared with other casual general labour, charring cannot be considered a highly remunera-tive occupation.

Servants who live in, however, are generally judged to be comparatively well paid. The demand is (or until recently has been) greater than the supply of workers, chiefly, it would seem, because the conditions of work are uncongenial. It is impossible to state with any attempt at exactitude what are the average or standard wage-rates of these million and more workers, who are practically inarticulate collectively in so far as their work is concerned.[1] One may say, however, that the hours of work (or of work and duty) tend to be long, compared with those of industrial employment (ten hours a day, sixty-four a week, would, I believe, be a moderate computation of the average amount of time of a domestic servant's duty) ; most branches of the work are skilled, some highly skilled, and some are of the highest responsibility.

Sixty pounds a year, with board and lodging, is a very fair rate of pay for a highly-skilled (female) private servant in London. An experienced cook or trained children's-nurse may be engaged on such terms, though many instances might be discovered of more, and of less, than this amount being paid, to workers whose qualifications may differ little.[2] A housemaid or general servant will rarely receive so much, though in their case also exceptions may be found, for upper servants of large households, "generals" in houses where a small staff is *preferred*, or women whose wages have been gradually raised over a long term of years in the same employment. Probably £45 a year represents favourably the average wage for adult women private domestic servants in London at the present time.

The value to the worker of board and lodging received varies not only according to what she actually receives, but also according to what she would spend if not living in. One pound a week seems a very fair average estimate of this value.

On this estimate the sum of £100 represents a fair

[1] Since this was written, interesting figures for domestic servants' wages in London have appeared in Volume II of the *New Survey of London Life and Labour.*

[2] The domestic care of children has become of late years a subject of specialized professional training, and women who have qualified by such training may command salaries rising from the above figure a good deal higher. On the other hand able and experienced women with such training may be found to ask £4 a month, or even less. The decline in the middle- and upper-class birth-rate, which reduces the demand for such service, counteracts the rise in wages which might be expected to follow the improvement in qualifications and status of those supplying it.

average remuneration for an adult domestic servant in London, received in cash and kind. Very few indeed are likely to receive more than the equivalent of £150, the few exceptions having either special professional qualifications or being in positions of management—and some undoubtedly receive less than the equivalent of £100, in cash and kind.

Compared with other *skilled* employment, a wage equivalent to £2 or even £3 a week cannot be considered a high rate of pay for 60 or 64 hours a week on work or on duty.[1]

There is another branch of Personal Service, occasionally referred to as an ancient and honourable profession. Prostitution would be difficult to include among the listed occupations in the Census, but it is one of the methods by which a considerable number of women earn, try to earn, or supplement, their living, and it is not illegal traffic. Some two to three thousand prostitutes are arrested for alleged annoyance every year in London. Over the whole country the figures vary between three and four thousand. Many of these cases are the arrest of the same woman over and over again, while many professional prostitutes, of course, never come into the hands of the police. A competent observer [2] suggests that the figure of 10,000 is "a very large estimate" for the number of prostitutes in London.[3]

As to the amounts, or the average amount, of money earned, it is even more nearly impossible to suggest an estimate than in the case of private domestic service.

[1] In the recently-published Labour Party pamphlet *What's Wrong with Domestic Service?* the value of servants' wages is summarized as follows : " Wages in domestic service are very varied. They vary from beginners at the rate of 4s. 6d. to 7s. 6d. in the provinces to skilled cooks at £2, together with board and lodging. The value of board and lodging may differ almost as much. If this is reckoned at £15s. to £1, the wages of the hardest-worked servants, the generals, are about the same as adult women under Trade Board industries, i.e. in formerly sweated trades " (p. 5).

[2] Miss Alison Neilans, Secretary to the Association for Moral and Social Hygiene.

[3] If this estimate is approximately correct, it would indicate that prostitution has considerably declined per head in London during the last century. In 1793 an estimate, quoted in Mayhew's *London Labour and the London Poor*, suggested a ratio of 1 per 20 of the population ; Miss Neilans' estimate suggests 1 : 750.

" I suppose, from what I have heard," states Miss Neilans, " that prices received range for the street-walking class from a couple of pounds down to fourpence, the latter figure referring, of course, to the very lowest class of homeless wanderer . . . there are many grades in prostitution, even of the habitual kind. At the top a woman might get almost everything she wanted. At the bottom she sells herself for a pot of beer."

Mrs. Cecil Chesterton (*In Darkest London*) has vividly described the penury to which prostitutes may be reduced by unemployment or low rates of pay. Arnold Bennett, in *The Pretty Lady*, describes the haunting fear of superannuation and destitution felt by a rather more skilled and prosperous prostitute, and her characteristic boast of the friend who wishes to monopolize and maintain her—place her " among her furniture ". Robert Graves describes how, during the war boom, girls in Béthune took up this occupation for a few busy weeks, and then retired on their earnings, " pale but proud ". But war conditions are abnormal. It seems unlikely that a large proportion of those who practise prostitution as an occupation in more normal times acquire any considerable fortune.

In professional work proper, it is comparatively easy to discover what is the standard of remuneration, and especially in the profession of teaching, in which so large a number of women are employed. The salaries of teachers in State-aided schools are based on the Burnham Scale. They were reduced by 10 per cent. in 1931. It is common for private schools of good standing to offer salaries on the same scale to assistant teachers. Before the 1931 reduction, certificated elementary school teachers received *on an average* £334 per annum (men) and £254 per annum (women). The average salary of uncertificated teachers was £143 ; uncertificated women teachers therefore averaged below this rate. Graduate teachers in secondary schools received *on an average* £436 (men) and £348 (women) ; non-graduates, £397 (men) and £330 (women).[1]

---

[1] *Report of National Expenditure (May Committee)*, 1931, pp. 48–50. It must be remembered that teachers also receive superannuation pensions in addition to these salaries.

An intelligent young woman of my acquaintance is an uncertificated teacher in the Infants' Department of a National-and-Church School in rural Oxfordshire. She is engaged to be married to an able young agricultural labourer. She receives £95 a year, he £2 a week. It is of interest to see the overlapping of wage-rate of agricultural and semi-skilled professional work.

For men of the professional classes, the salaries ruling in the skilled grades of the teaching profession are comparatively low. Certainly some professional men, barristers, architects, artists, writers, may receive not merely little but nothing in profit, during their lean early years ; but if they reach the higher ranks of their professions they may expect to earn five to ten times as much as a headmaster. Setting aside the question of vocational urge, teaching is therefore a profession suitable for those without capital resources, but not one which offers the plums of economic reward for intellectual ability.

The less-skilled grades of the medical profession, in which also a great many women are employed, are less standardized than teaching, in respect of remuneration. A trained nurse, by undertaking private nursing, may earn 3 to 7 guineas a week and her keep, but such work is casual ; it is too intense in its demands on time and energy to be kept up continuously, and the problem of residence and service in the interim periods is in many cases extremely difficult. Consequently, many private nurses find it necessary to work through organizations by which they are guaranteed a regular income, and board and lodging when off duty.

Private nurses on the staff of the London Hospital earn £60–£90 a year (and their keep) : in general the rates of pay at the London are comparatively high. The scales of salaries approved by the College of Nursing for qualified nurses range from £60 for Staff Nurses to £150–£500 for Matrons, for residential posts, and £250–£500 for non-residential posts such as those of District Nurse and Superintendent. It is clear from the Second Interim Report of the *Lancet* Commission on Nursing, recently published, that many hospitals pay lower rates than these approved minima.

The profession of midwifery has been attracting much attention of late because of its importance in connection with the attempt to stem the high maternal mortality rate. Those who have received bills for 20 guineas a week from Harley Street maternity homes may be of the opinion that midwifery is a lucrative profession. In general this is not so. It has been stated recently by the Committee set up by the Ministry of Health, that

> "In addition to disabilities . . . serious enough . . . to deter all but the most courageous . . . must be added the further disadvantage of insufficient remuneration normally gained for long hours of unremitting toil. . . . According to the testimony of the Incorporated Midwives Institute a large number of whole-time independent midwives earn from £90 to £120 per annum. . . . These are gross figures, and bear no relation to the amount which actually remains for the midwife's personal use after paying . . . for domestic assistance in her own home, and for . . . various items of equipment which she is bound to provide for her own use and the use of patients. . . . She must often find the utmost difficulty in eking out a somewhat precarious existence."[1]

Of the occupations employing a high proportion and a considerable number of women, those of Clerk and Shop Assistant especially remain to be considered.

Clerical work is a peculiarly hybrid occupation. It includes members whose interests are bound up with commerce, others whose special skills and services give them a claim to professional status, and some whose wages have been affected by Trade Board industrial awards.

In the wage-rate awards for the Milk Distributive trade, the rates for Clerks were fixed as follows :—

Rural Areas		Non-rural Areas		London	
M	F	M	F	M	F
60s.	38s.	67s. 6d.	42s.	70s.	48s.

These amounts probably represent somewhat favourably

[1] *Report on Training and Employment of Midwives* (*Ministry of Health*), 1929, p. 39.

the remuneration of clerks in commercial houses at the present time.

A number of women clerks learn at their own expense the special skills of shorthand and typewriting. Although these skills (and the former especially) require a considerable degree of intelligence, education and manual dexterity for their efficient practice, the occupation is commonly regarded as somewhat derogatory, among middle-class people, just as the skilled occupation of domestic worker is regarded in a lower social stratum. A shorthand-typist without other special qualifications may expect to earn 45s. to 60s. a week in London at the present time. Compared with the wages earned in skilled work in manufacturing industries, these weekly earnings are not particularly high.[1]

Wage-rates among Shop Assistants are difficult to estimate even by those who best know the conditions under which they work, because they are so often reckoned by commissions in addition to a minimum sum, according to receipts. A general average may be suggested by the practice of the National Amalgamated Union of Shop Assistants, which aims at securing £3 a week for adult women and £4 for men, while resigning itself in most cases to the acceptance of wages at £1 a week under these figures while the task of fully organizing the workers remains so difficult.[2] Hours worked are frequently very long, so that the hourly *rate* is not so high as these figures might suggest to industrial workers.

An inquiry made by the Ministry of Labour into wage-rates in the Drapery and Allied Trades, of which the report was published in 1926, gave the rates for women

[1] In the autumn of 1931 a London business woman advertised for a secretary-shorthand-typist willing also to help her with the care of her baby. From the eighty-nine applicants she selected a young woman with the required training, excellent references for previous experience, and a Scottish M.A. degree, and engaged her for resident work at a salary of £1 a week.

[2] For information about wages and conditions of work of Shop Assistants I am much indebted to Miss Ethel Turner, Secretary of the Women's Section of the National Amalgamated Union of Shop Assistants, Warehousemen and Clerks, but she has no responsibility for any statement made in the text.

of and over 21 as varying from 30s. to 45s., those for adult men as 50s. to 90s.[1]

As we turn from one to another of the occupations in which exceptionally large numbers of women are employed, we find everywhere a general tendency for wage-rates to rule low. It is not sufficient, however, to consider only adult wage-rates, since the large proportion of women who are under age during the greater part of their wage-earning life makes the wage-rates of juveniles especially relevant to the attempt to estimate women's average remuneration.

Every wage-rate and salary so far quoted, refers to the adult worker. Juveniles (girls under 18 years old being reckoned as such, or sometimes up to 21) usually receive lower pay than women engaged in the same occupation. The young domestic servant, the nurse-probationer, and the juvenile in trade and commerce, are all liable to receive lower rates. Young girls at the present time are coming to " service " in the South of England, from the distressed areas of South Wales and Durham particularly, for resident wages of 7s. a week and upwards. In November, 1930, a young girl of my acquaintance applied at a Labour Exchange in the Marylebone district of London, for any available work, non-resident. She was sent to an employer who required a domestic servant, and was there offered a non-resident post, with working-hours 60 a week inclusive of meal-times, and wages of 12s. 6d. a week with three meals a day. Unfortunately it was never discovered whether this would have been considered suitable conditions and remuneration by the officials of the Ministry of Labour.

A case recently came to my notice of a young girl, the daughter of an officer killed in the war, herself particularly charming and distinctly intelligent, who on leaving her secondary boarding-school after passing the School Certificate examination, was found a post at 12s. a week and her keep, as domestic worker in a Ladies' Residential Club.

---

[1] *Report of Ministry of Labour on an Investigation into the Rates of Wages and Degree of Industrial Organization in the Drapery and Allied Trades*, 1926.

This wage, little as it may seem, is comparatively high for a juvenile worker. The same money, *non-resident*, is commonly offered to juvenile shop assistants. In provincial towns the average is probably lower for beginners. The following was the experience of a girl who is now (1931) in service in London, aged 19. On leaving school she went to work in " an egg shop " in her home town of Gateshead. Her working hours (which varied from day to day, being very long at the end of the week) totalled about 53 a week, exclusive of meal-times. Her wages were 8s. 6d. a week. She was engaged to sell eggs, but most of her time was spent in washing off the stamp from imported eggs so that they could be sold as English. This shop went bankrupt. The manageress transferred her own and the girl's activities to another of her ventures—" a wallpaper shop ". Here the working hours totalled 54, and the girl's wages started at 9s. 6d. and rose to 12s. After she had been at this work for eighteen months, she fell ill of the type of poisoning which afflicts those who deal in wallpaper (she calls it lime-poisoning), and retired home to bed for three months, without pay or compensation.

The rate of wages was, at the egg shop, just under 2d. per hour ; at the wallpaper shop, at the maximum, under 3d. per hour. This is lower than many Trade Board awards for juveniles in industry.

In industrial occupations, variations in wages according to age may be stereotyped and extremely elaborate. This occurs in certain of the Trade Board trades. The comparatively simple award for girls in the Button-making trade (made in 1922) may be taken as an example : [1]—

Age.				Award, per hour.	Earnings on basis of 48-hour week.
					£ s. d.
Under 15	.	.	.	3d.	0 12 0
15–16	.	.	.	4d.	0 16 0
16–17	.	.	.	5d.	1 0 0
17–18	.	.	.	6d.	1 4 0
18 and over	.	.	.	7d.	1 8 0

[1] *The British Trade Boards System*, by D. Sells, p. 68.

In this instance the usual practice is followed of reckoning that women receive their adult, or maximum, wage-rate at 18 years and over. Where the wage-rates are regulated in detail, either by a Trade Board award or by independent agreements, the impression is given that the women are thus deprived of the benefit of further rises which they might have had up till the age of 21. But it must be realized that the point around which the bargaining centres first is the adult wage-rate. The women's representatives are therefore very anxious to secure the recognition of the necessity of the adult, or maximum wage, for women, being given them at 18, partly because so many women retire early from industry after receiving junior rates for a large proportion of their service, partly because of the grave social danger of the payment to women physically adult, and over the age of consent and marriage, of wages below the level of independent subsistence. This danger is by no means completely averted by the payment of wages at their present rates.

There remains to be considered last a cause of women's low average remuneration, as compared with men's, which is, if not the most important, certainly the most obvious ; that is, the fact that when they are doing similar work they frequently do not receive equal pay. Over the whole field of gainful work the instances of men and women doing similar jobs are not very many, or, at least, they do not cover a very large proportion of women gainfully employed. But the instances of their receiving the same pay as men for such work are very much less. The distinctions are clearly visible in a study of Trade Board awards, and of the Burnham awards to teachers. In the latter, the proportion of men's to women's salaries is fixed at 5 : 4. Trade Boards usually fix men's and women's rates at about 5 : 3. The same practice of differential payment prevails in the Civil Service in Great Britain (though not in the Irish Free State).

The Cotton Weaving branch of the Textile industry is the classic exception to this rule. There are also a number of women occupied in the upper grades of professional work, in entertaining, sport, the arts, and independent commercial business, who earn incomes equal to those obtained by men of equal standing in similar work, and often of considerable amount.

But the number of such women is small compared with the number of all women gainfully occupied, although the significance of their proven ability and economic position may be great.

Remembering them in our summary, it is also necessary to remember their converse : that is, the considerable number of *men* now employed at extremely low wages in male occupations, such as coal-mining and agriculture.

But despite these counterbalancing factors, a general survey does lead to reaffirmation of the common view, that the average remuneration of gainfully occupied women is lower than that of men. For we find that

(1) Women tend to be concentrated in the less-skilled grades of industry and the professions ;

(2) Women tend to be concentrated in those branches of manufacture and commerce in which wages are comparatively low ;

(3) The average rates of wages in other occupations in which women are largely employed, also tend to be low ;

(4) The average age of women workers is low, and a great many of them therefore receive the low pay of juveniles;

(5) Women frequently receive less pay than a man would receive for similar work.

It becomes overwhelmingly evident that the present economic organization of society tends to depress the position of the woman wage-earner, as compared with that of the man, in some way not solely attributable to physical or mental differences of constitution. The causes of this depression are the theme of the next chapter.

CHAPTER IV

THE CAUSES OF LOW PAYMENT OF WOMEN

Differences of physique a cause—but not sufficient explanation alone
—differences of function—natural—conventional, connected with
marriage : average age of occupied women—expectation of marriage—lack of capital resources—conventional obligations of marriage—maintenance of wife by husband—and of children—effect
on comparative wages of men and women—restrictions on women's
employment in well-paid work—effect on workers' organization—
summary of conclusions.

The differences of the two sexes in body and mind form
a subject of infinite attraction at every altitude of thought
—in the anatomical theatre, the "legitimate" theatre,
the talkie, the nursery, the daily paper and the individual
sub-consciousness. They are the proper and the improper
study of mankind. One might attempt to describe the
differences made between the sexes in the economic world
solely in these same familiar terms of anatomy and function. But the attempt would fail to convince, for Time,
the fourth co-ordinate, and the conflicts caused by different rates of progression in history, are elements also
to be taken into account. The sex-differentiation that
exists to-day cannot be adequately described by reference
only to the reaction between our existent economic organization, and the two differing human structures with their
natural functions.

Yet these differences do have certain immediate reactions on the relative industrial position of the sexes.
They render the work of women less valuable than that
of men in occupations involving heavy "manual" labour
—such occupations, that is to say, as form a large part
of the work of erection and repair of buildings and ships ;
coal-mining, quarrying, stoking, etc. There are reasons,
based on the physical differences between the sexes, for

the usual allocation of such branches of labour by preference to men, so long as they are performed in the way
at present customary. Physical differences also render
the work of women *more* valuable than that of men in
occupations involving especial manual dexterity, such as
certain processes connected with bookbinding, the manufacture of electric lamps, scientific-instrument making,
and light automatic work in general.[1]

Heavy industrial work, which is more economically
performed by men, has for many years been gradually
decreasing in comparison with that of a lighter or more
automatic character. This development inevitably accompanies the continual increase of mechanical invention, and
the increased application of non-human power. It does
not *necessarily* imply a decrease in the prosperity or importance of the so-called "heavy" industries, which is
so marked a feature of the present industrial depression.
The decline in the heavy industries has been accompanied
by a certain comparative increase in the employment
of women. But the decrease in heavy manual labour
throughout industry as a whole, due to new inventions
and the use of power, has had little if any effect on the
comparative employment of the sexes. This change had
been in progress for fifty years and more before the slump
of 1921 began, yet, as we have seen, the employment of
women in comparison with that of men had been gradually
declining during that time, and though the definitely industrial employment of women had not declined as much
as their total paid employment, it had certainly not
accelerated in the proportion of this increase of mechanization. The amount of industrial work which was not
suitable for women to do (in the sense that it was not

---

[1] There are processes in connection with the making of electric-lamp
globes in which it is found useless to employ men because they have
not the necessary delicacy of touch. On this point in general, see *Report
of War Cabinet Committee on Women in Industry*, pp. 88–9, 104–5 (*Maj.
Report*), and notes to pp. 278, 281, 282 (*Min. Report*), H.M.S.O., 1919 ;
also *Home Office Report on Substitution of Men by Women in non-Munition
Factories during the War* (1919). For an example of division of labour
along these lines in the Printing Trades, see *Women in the Printing
Trades*, by J. Ramsay MacDonald, pp. 3, 5.

considered an economic proposition to put them to it) was continually lessening, but the comparative employment of women in industry was increasing, if at all, to a much less degree.

This seems to show that the physical differences between the sexes are not a sufficient cause to explain the comparative degree of their employment in industry, since their employment did not vary in the same ratio as the work suitable to them varied.

But physical differences are of function as well as of structure. Such are the obligations which marriage imposes on women by nature, to bring forth and multiply, to suckle and care for the young. In Great Britain, however, and in many other countries, these obligations are now, on an average, decreasing. In the last sixty years the birth-rate has declined from 35·5 (1871) to 15·8 (1931) per thousand. If natural differences of function were the determining factor in regulating the gainful employment of women as compared with men, we should have expected their employment to be on the increase during that time. Which on the whole it was not. One would have expected particularly a rise in the employment of married women, whereas in this respect the decline has been marked.

But civil marriage entails legal and customary, as well as natural obligations, which differ for men and women. These conventions affect the employment and the payment of men and women in almost every department of economic activity. Along innumerable different paths one may trace the segregation and low payment of women workers to the laws and customs associated with marriage.

One speaks of " women workers ". " Girl-workers " would be a truer description. The great majority of women retire from paid work on marriage, and comparatively few return to it. Consequently the average age of gainfully occupied women is low.[1] Nearly 50 per cent.

---

[1] See *Women in Modern Industry*, by B. L. Hutchins ; pp. 81–3 ; also *The Social Structure of England and Wales*, pp. 45–6 ; *The Numbers Occupied in Industries of England and Wales*, pp. 14 and 18.

of them, in 1921, were under 25 ; nearly 70 per cent. under 35 years of age. Whereas with men at the same date, only 27 per cent. of those occupied were under 25, and less than 50 per cent. were under 35 years of age.[1]

The low average age of the woman worker inevitably results in a low average wage for women as a whole. It is probably a more important factor in lowering the average than inequality between the wages of men and women doing similar work, for in many cases of juveniles, boys and girls, doing similar work, the wages are equal, or more nearly equal than those of men and women in the same circumstances. Wage-rates fixed by Trade Boards for girls and boys on an age basis tend to be the same, or nearly so, up till the age of 18 years, when the female rates usually become stationary, and the male rates continue to increase to the age of 21 or above. In this the Boards follow the customary practice of industry. Instances may be found (resulting from collective bargaining) of women's wages being higher than those of men of the same age on the same job, when the women have already attained their maximum and the men have not. Thus it is recorded in 1921 that in the Silk-weaving industry in Staffordshire the weekly rate for women aged 18–18½ was 36s., while the men's at that age was less. But at the age of 22, the men were due to earn 60s. 6d. while the woman's rate was still 36s.[2]

The retirement of women on marriage may be partly attributed to what may be classed as the natural consequences of marriage. A certain number of those retiring would, if they had remained, have been incapacitated from effective industry over certain subsequent periods of time by childbirth, consequent invalidity (supposing them to have received medical and midwifery services at their present standard) and the need for giving personal care to their children. But in the main this retirement, immediate and continued as it commonly is in each case, is due to the *conventional* obligations and privi-

---

[1] *Abstract of Labour Statistics for* 1930, p. 3.
[2] *Women in Trade Unions*, by B. Drake, p. 135.

leges of marriage, which rule that women, be they fertile or sterile, shall devote themselves to domesticity after marriage, and depend for their livelihood on a share of their husband's income.

Retirement on marriage lowers the average remuneration of women in a second, indirect way. The expectation of short service discourages the training of girls in special skills, and thus leads women into, and keeps them in, the ranks of the less-skilled workers. The chances are that the technical instruction of girls will not bring in as high an economic return as the instruction of boys. This aspect of the problem affects those concerned with the organization of labour in almost every social class, and from every point of view. The middle-class parent, pondering the family budget and the future of his boys and girls, cannot fail to take into account the fact that the preparation of his son for skilled work is likely to be a lifelong economic benefit to the young man, and that his chances of setting up later not only a motor car but a perambulator, depend upon it ; whereas any similar expenditure he incurs for his daughter may cease to bring in any assessable return if she later marries, and follows the convention commonly associated with marriage, that is, if she then retires from gainful work.

Among wage-earners the problem is no less acute, though it presses more heavily on those who organize labour than on the individual parent. Unless boys are trained and qualified to earn a skilled worker's and family-man's wage by the time they are adult, they present a difficult problem to Trade Unionism and their employer. The product of their labour is not worth in the market what they need or claim in wages. A girl, on the other hand, if untrained, will probably be released from her cul-de-sac on the wings of matrimony. Consequently it seems reasonable by those responsible for the organization of labour to encourage girls, but not boys, to take up " blind-alley " occupations ; that is, occupations of low status or pay, in which no opportunity is given for acquiring sufficient skill or standing for a later advance in remuneration. Instances of the expression of this view are constantly to be found in contemporary reports. Thus with reference to the Printing trade :—

"Major M. C., speaking at a luncheon of the London Master Printers' Association . . . said that . . . they would have to consider the introduction of a class of labour at a lower rate than the skilled rate. The trade unions were realizing the difficulty of dealing with boy labour when the age of 21 was reached, and were prepared to regard with sympathy an extension of the amount of work women and girls could do. . . . In theory they ought not to employ in the trade more boys than they could find work for when they grew up, but it must be admitted they had been taking boys into a ' blind-alley ' occupation. If girls were employed instead, they could still afford to keep them when they became adults."[1]

It is stated in the Report of the 1931 Royal Commission on the Civil Service :—

"The writing assistant class of the shorthand typist and typist classes are confined to women. . . . In our view there are two main reasons which make it advisable that the present practice should be maintained. First, it is undesirable . . . that persons who have capacity for better work should be kept too long on routine work. A turnover of staff is therefore an advantage in this connection, and the retirement of women on marriage is an important factor, whether or no such retirement is compulsory. If the staff for these duties is recruited from girls alone, the problem of avoiding blind-alley occupation is less acute than it would be if the class was recruited from . . . both sexes."[2]

The expectation of marriage, and the conventions customarily associated with it, have had this same wage-lowering effect on women's work for centuries : it is not a peculiar feature of modern industrialism. In medieval times, girls were seldom regularly apprenticed. They often acquired a high degree of skill in their father's, and then in their husband's craft, and were very useful to the male members of the family as the only form of cheap, casual labour that Guild regulations permitted. Thus

[1] *The Times,* December 4, 1928.
[2] *Report of Royal Commission on Civil Service,* H.M.S.O., 1931, pp. 14-17.

the use of female labour was profitable to the men, but by its casualness it

> " had the result of keeping women in an inferior and subordinate position in the working world. . . . Though they worked hard and the total amount of their labour has contributed largely to our industrial development, it was only exceptionally that they attained to the standing of employers and industrial leaders. . . . The lack of apprenticeship led inevitably to their taking a second place. . . . " [1]

Women did not, in early days, give up sharing in productive work after they were married, but since it was customary for them to help their husband, they could not know, at the usual age for apprenticeship, what trade they would afterwards be engaged in. In this way the expectation of marriage, and the conventions associated with marriage, contributed to prevent their regular apprenticeship ; and led to the subordination already described. There has thus been a continuous effect, and probably through the force of precedent a cumulative effect, of expectation of conventional, civil marriage, on the economic standing, and so on the average remuneration, of the woman worker.

In occupations in which the salaries or profits may be high, the cost of qualifying, or the preliminary capital necessary, are often also high, and vice versa. Most of those who qualify and set up as barristers, architects, first-division Civil Servants, doctors, have benefited from the expenditure of considerable sums of money, devoted to this end. On the other hand, those who become hospital nurses, certificated elementary school teachers, midwives or cooks, may also have paid for their qualifications, but certainly less. There are more men than women in the former professions, and more women than men in the latter ; the difference in access to capital resources is without doubt one of the reasons for this distinction.

The laws and customs regulating the inheritance and disposal of property tend to place financial resources preponderatingly in the hands of men, and the income that is earned to support a whole family is usually received by male members of the family exclusively. In so far as expenditure on qualifications, and capital for setting up in a career, are made by parents or guardians, we have already noted that the expectation of the girl's retirement on marriage makes the parent less willing to spend such money for her than for the boy. And since the deciding parent, in questions of such expenditure, is usually the father, it may be that there is apt to be in some cases a further sex-bias in favour of expenditure on the boy. In so far as the expenditure is undertaken by those who are themselves to benefit, there is no doubt that men, in general, are in a favourable position, compared with women, to obtain the qualifications or fulfil the necessary conditions for engaging in the more highly remunerative occupations—for they are much more likely to have the means of paying for them. And so for this reason also, women tend to be segregated in the less remunerative professions.

This difference between the sexes in capital resources is not of one generation only : men frequently benefit by exclusive inheritances from the past. Most of the higher educational foundations in this country are dependent on endowments ; the student rarely bears the whole cost of his instruction. The inheritance of the increment of these immense capital resources is reserved, in the great majority of cases, to men. The fact that men, in the past, had money to dispose of, while women had not, has secured to men at the present time much easier access than women have to the technical instruction and other qualifications which enable them to earn the greatest amount of reward.[1]

In industry, the expectation of marriage herds women into unskilled or low-paid occupations ; in the professions and commerce their comparative lack of funds adds force to the same tendency. It is so common for industrial

[1] This is more gracefully expressed by Mrs. Virginia Woolf in *A Room of One's Own*.

women to be semi-skilled or unskilled, that the problems arising from competition between men's and women's employment are often classed as identical with, or simply a part of, the problems arising from the divergent interests of skilled and less-skilled labour. Essentially I believe this to be a false and delusive identification. The circumstances which place a disproportionate number of women in less-skilled occupations or occupational grades, are different from those affecting the less-skilled in general. The competition of women with men has special characteristics. This is evident from the fact that the employment of women, as such, has constantly been regarded with special apprehension by men's organizations, and special measures have been taken to obviate the difficulties, and the danger to the general standard of life, arising from it.

The danger in question has no origin in nature. It arises from the difference between the legal and customary obligations of marriage for men and for women. The husband's obligation, which is recognized in law, is to maintain his wife (and his children, if he has any, while they are young). The wife is expected, by custom, to occupy herself with domestic, or other unpaid, work. Wives form the great majority of the 8½ million unpaid domestic workers. Though they are not paid wages, nor receive financial profit, they do receive economic reward for their domestic work ; that is, their share of the welfare they produce for their family, and also the maintenance to which they are in any case entitled from their husband, or from the State through their husband if he be unemployed, or from the State direct, if he be dead.

The economic relationship between husband and wife is therefore in some respects similar to that between employer and employed, or between partners in business ; but in many respects it is different from either. Firstly, it is contingent on the woman's performance not of domestic tasks, but conjugal obligations ; and even her conjugal obligations may be annulled if the husband does not fulfil his own, without corresponding annulment of her right to be maintained by her husband. Secondly, the wife retains her right to maintenance from her husband, even if she undertakes other, paid or profitable, work in addition to, or instead of, domestic tasks at home. Thirdly her reward is not proportionate in amount to the work she does, according to any recognized way of reckoning wages or profits. If her output is more than the next worker's—her house cleaner, her family more numerous and better kept—or if she spends more hours working— no one expects her to receive more income than her neighbour-wife, in consequence. Some relationship may be found between her " reward " and her husband's worktime or work-energy, not her own.

Although there is a relationship, therefore, between the wife's domestic work and her right to maintenance, established by the custom of centuries, and in some degree similar to the wage-payment or profit-sharing relationship, there are dissimilarities also of an economic nature which are fundamental and important. This is a peculiar relationship within the Body Economic, and as such it affects the whole body in a peculiar way.[1]

What are these peculiar effects ? Firstly, it is generally assumed that all married women, since they have a legal right to maintenance, receive maintenance. Therefore, if they enter the labour market, their needs are supposed to be less than those of other workers ; therefore their labour may be obtained at a lower rate of wages. The actual circumstances of individual cases make no difference to this theory, or the effect of the theory on wages. It may be that half the married women in industry are there for special economic reasons (for in-

---

[1] It is interesting also to compare the economic considerations which affect the marriage contract with those which precede and affect other bargains and contracts, and to trace in English history the variation at different periods in the weight accorded by correct convention to such considerations when sentiment is placed in the opposite scale. The interest of Jane Austen's works is largely derived from observation of the working of this balance in the human heart, and the opening of *Mansfield Park* is a delightful example of the frank recognition of the economic motive, which the Victorian age preferred to disregard. See also the stories of Miss Smith and Miss Watson, in De Quincey's *Autobiography*.

stance, the need for extra expenditure on invalid dependents, beyond what one wage-earner for the family can provide ; or the fact that the husband against whom they have been granted a Separation and Maintenance Order has emigrated)—reasons which economically cancel out all advantage they get from their legal right to maintenance. Nevertheless, the view dies hard, and has received few knocks as yet, that married women do not need to receive so much pay as other workers.

The wife's right to maintenance thus acts as a subsidy to her employment, of which employers have in the past frequently taken advantage. The employer's advantage is a double disadvantage to the married working woman, if her right to maintenance from her husband is not translated into reality, for she loses, from the remuneration for her work, the amount which she is supposed to be, but is not, receiving at home. Her position then illustrates that paradox : "From him that hath not it shall be taken away even that which he hath."

Secondly, we find that the obligation to do unpaid domestic work in return for maintenance tends to be extended to all women, and side by side with that, the assumption that they are in some degree maintained tends also to be extended to all women ; and so it is assumed that women as a whole should receive lower wages than men. In other words

"The ordinary view of the subject is that a woman need not be paid as much as a man, because her requirements are less, and she is likely to be partially maintained by others." [1]

Where a standard rate is in force, the effect of some women being supposed to be wholly maintained will be the same, or will enhance, the effect of all being supposed to be partially maintained. The lowering effect on wages will be "spread out thin" among married and unmarried.

Thirdly, we have the converse of these things. Since married men are obliged to maintain their wives, it is

[1] *Women in Modern Industry*, p. 89.

agreed that they should receive wages sufficient to permit them to do so, without any reckoning of profit from the wife's labour. Just as the assumption that married women are maintained is extended to all women, so the assumption that married men are maintaining their wives is extended to all men, and it is assumed that they must all receive sufficient remuneration to keep a wife. But since it does not seem sense to suppose that each industrial worker requires the exclusive service of a full-time domestic help-mate, all other workers (i.e. women and young persons) are expected to be satisfied with a lower wage, reckoned basically on unit subsistence needs, instead of one reckoned on the two-plus subsistence needs which are generally admitted as the rightful claim of the adult male.

The "plus" is the obligation to maintain dependent children. Under the law this obligation is common to both parents, but in so far as the provision of money is concerned it customarily falls upon the man, because he is by custom the earner of money.

To differentiate between all men and all women workers on the grounds that men have to maintain children is somewhat unreasonable, because less than 50 per cent. of adult male workers at any one time have children dependent on them.[1]

But indeed the maintenance of young children is not, I would suggest, at the root of this problem of differential remuneration. It is about half-way up the tree. The obligation of both parents towards their children, and of each member of a family towards other members (apart from the conjugal relationship) is actually in law the same. The primary responsibility of the father or adult male, which is customarily accepted, is based on the fact that he is commonly the earner of money, or the earner of more money, than the mother or the woman wage-earner. The cause of this is, partly, the natural obligations of marriage, but to a much greater extent, the conventional obligations of marriage. The responsibility for mainten-

[1] *The Disinherited Family*, by E. F. Rathbone, p. 16.

ance of dependents other than spouses therefore merely accentuates, in a large number of cases, the problems already arising from the different marital obligations of men and women. Financially this responsibility falls firstly on the man, *because* he, as a general rule, is paid money for his work and the woman is not, or because he is paid more than she. It then gives men a reason for claiming that they *should* be paid more than women ; but that is the second part of the same story.

In the processes of bargaining by which wages are usually settled, the two most elementary considerations taken into account are (1) the worker's conventional need (that is, the needs appropriate to the standard of living which it is generally agreed he should be able to maintain), and (2) the market value of the product of his work. The former has especial force in determining the minimum, the latter in determining the maximum wage to be paid.

When the wages of women are considered, in comparison or in competition with those of men, we find the conventional need being placed much lower. But the market value of the product of their work is often very little if any lower ; it may even be higher. The consequence is that the woman is a more profitable employee than the man, in these circumstances, and a tendency arises for women to drive men out of employment, or for men to be forced to accept work at the wage which is considered to be sufficient for the woman, but too low for a man. The men, many of whom need a dual-plus minimum wage, because of the obligations imposed on them by marriage, may be forced to work on a unit subsistence wage, because that is supposed to be sufficient for their female competitors.

The competition offered by women is limited in extent, because convention and the social organization resulting from convention prevents most married women from entering the labour market. But the women who do or potentially may enter industry, offer a real danger to men's wage-rates.

This is not mere hypothesis. It has been proved again and again in one trade after another. Men have been dismissed from employment, and women engaged for the work at lower rates of pay. In consequence of such experiences, men's organizations have taken various measures to prevent direct competition between their own labour and that of women. One of the most prevalent methods is the prohibition or discouragement of women's work in certain branches of industry, with a view to the stabilization of "men's" (i.e. comparatively high, dual-plus) wage-rates, salaries or profits. Such prohibitions are in many instances demanded of employers by the men's Trade Unions. The regulations (or tacit conventions) so made are various and numerous. Many came to light during the war 1914–1918, when, under pressure from the Government, which required the men for the Army, they were temporarily set aside with the recorded consent of both employers and employed. The records of these Gentlemen's Agreements of suspension were kept by the Home Office, under whose ægis many of them were made.[1] In each industry separately, the pledge of re-enforcement after the war (that is, the renewed exclusion of women from certain branches of work) was an important part of the pact. But it is not possible by pledges to keep industry *in statu quo ante bellum*, or in any other static condition, as regards differentiation in employment between men and women, because new branches of work are continually arising, in respect of which the old conflicts have to be fought out anew each time.

The restriction of women's labour resulting from such Trade Union action accentuates the tendency already noted of the concentration of women's labour within a comparatively narrow field. In order to prevent the demand for female labour being "artificially" increased by its cheapness, the demand is "artificially" diminished by Trade Union action and industrial convention. In times of bad trade, the demand for cheap labour is especially strong, and the Trade Unions are usually weaker, so that for this among other reasons, the comparative extent of women's industrial employment tends to increase during

[1] *Report on Substitution of Women by Men after the War*, Home Office, 1919.

industrial depression. But normally, women's labour is so much restricted by the prohibition of their employment in a number of trades or processes, that there is a disproportionate supply of it to meet the effective demand, and the average price they can command for it is consequently reduced. So the restriction of women to a limited range of occupations, in itself tends to make those occupations to which they are restricted, comparatively ill paid.[1]

The conflict of interests which arises between men and women workers as a result of the different obligations imposed on the sexes by marriage, is unfortunate for both. It is especially unfortunate in times of bad trade for the men, and most unfortunate in the long run for the women. For in the organization of this conflict the women are placed at a disadvantage. The men's " side " is composed of both sexes. The women whom they maintain have the same interests as their menfolk in raising the rates of *men's* wages, and preventing the undercutting employment of women ; whereas the female sex not only contends alone, but is even divided against itself, in the industrial field, by the *expectation* of marriage, and of subsequent maintenance on the man's wage.

> " Observations . . . on industrial women . . . show that . . . they regard themselves mainly from the point of view of the family, and believe that to keep up the standard of men's wages is as important as to raise their own." [2]

The statement that the female sex " contends alone ", is not intended to imply that the Women's Trade Union Movement has always trodden a separate path from the main, or men's Movement. On the contrary, it has at times been most materially aided, especially since the

---

[1] Disproportionate supply consequent upon restricted demand was the chief reason until recently given by orthodox economists for the low wages of women. Professor P. Sargent Florence, however, throws doubt on the existence of a supply of female labour excessive to the demand for it. He suggests that the convention of marriage-retirement prevents the supply of efficient adult female labour being even equal to the demand, and would point to other causes for the explanation of the low wages of women. (*Statistical Contribution to the Theory of Women's Wages, Economic Journal,* March 1931).

Women in Modern Industry, p. 193.

'nineties, by the organized men ; but I believe it is true to say that the helpful impulse has usually arisen from the belief that stronger organization of the women was in the interests also of the men.

" Please send an organizer at once, for our Amalgamated Society has decided that if the women of this town cannot be organized, they must be exterminated."

Such was the telegraphic ultimatum received by the Women's Trade Union League in its early days, from a branch of a men's Trade Union.[1] It expressed a common and surely comprehensible attitude on the part of the men. Obviously the organization of the women workers was demanded because it was a necessity for the maintenance of the Standard of Life of the male workers, not primarily in the interests of the women themselves, who would surely have preferred disorganization to extermination.

When the interests of men and women workers come into conflict, as they constantly do, the position of the women is difficult, and it becomes peculiarly difficult for women's Trade Union organizations to take a strong line. For the individual women workers themselves often feel a divided allegiance between their own body and that of the men, and a sympathy with their domestic mothers and married sisters.

The comparative weakness of women's Trade Union organizations, however, does not only become evident when the interests of the sexes come into conflict. Every factor already noted as a cause of the lower remuneration of women is also a factor in causing comparative weakness of Trade Union organization. The lower average age, the expectation of retirement on marriage, the performance of domestic duties at the end and before the opening of the day's work—all these things are a source of weakness to women's Trade Union organizations as compared with men's. Above all, the low wages of women are a hindrance to organization, and the lack of organization seemed for a long time an insuperable bar to any attempt to raise wages. Miss Mary Macarthur and her fellow-workers

[1] *Women in Trade Unions*, p. 31.

hoped to break that vicious circle by the establishment of Trade Boards.

It seems generally agreed that Trade Boards have had some effect in stimulating Trade Union organization, as well as in raising wage-rates among women. But Trade Unionism is still much weaker among women than among men, and while the other special conditions of weakness persist, it seems likely to remain so. It is therefore almost inevitable that where the interests of the sexes come into conflict, as individual industrial workers, Trade Unionism as a whole will favour the male, because of his greater Trade Union strength. Trade Union organization cannot, or is not in the least likely to secure for women a chance of competing with men on equal terms in every branch of industry—even for women organized in Trade Unions. It could not if it would, for men and women are not economically equal by the law of the land, so it is not within the power of the Unions to start them fair.

It follows that self-helpful Trade Unionism in itself is neither, by deficiency in the past, the sole cause, nor can be, by efficiency in the future, the sole and sufficient remedy, for the comparatively low industrial remuneration of women. This, and the segregation which goes hand in hand with it, may be traced partly to physical structure and function, but chiefly to the laws and conventions governing civil marriage. These act directly by withdrawing $8\frac{1}{2}$ millions of women from paid work, and indirectly by

(1) reducing the average age of the woman worker;

(2) reducing her opportunity for training in skilled work;

(3) reducing the force of her claim to remuneration sufficient for full maintenance at the recognized standard of living appropriate to her occupation or necessary for subsistence;

(4) increasing the force of the male worker's claim to remuneration sufficient for the maintenance of himself and at least one other;

(5) making her work cheaper than the man's, and thus forcing men's organizations to act in antagonism to her employment;

(6) reducing her ability to organize.

CHAPTER V

THE ECONOMIC CONVENTIONS OF MARRIAGE AND THEIR ORIGINS

Ancient custom of reciprocity of maintenance and service between husband and wife the basis of economic relationship of the sexes —social reasonableness of its establishment originally—early association of home with gainful occupation—domestic work of juveniles —changes due to industrial development—dissociation of home and gainful occupation—prohibitions of gentility—emancipation of women—distinction made by modern conditions between economic position of married and single woman.

The principles which are conventionally supposed to provide a basis for the economic relationship of men and women in this and most other countries of the European culture, have their origins in our earliest history. Their general sanction is based on custom rather than law. Custom makes cowards of us all, and it is difficult not to believe that conventions of such long standing originate in some deep-seated and immutable law of human nature. Just as the European races nowadays consider dusting, floor-scrubbing and home-cooking to be women's jobs, so the Indians of the Orinoco were found to delegate to women all agricultural operations, and the New Caledonians all manual labour. The Beni-Ahsen tribe in Morocco were horrified at the idea of a man fetching and carrying water, which is a woman's business ; on the other hand in Abyssinia " it is infamy for a man to go to market to buy anything ", but men carry water or bake bread, and it is their business to wash clothes.[1]

The diversity and contradictory character of such

---

[1] See *The Golden Bough*, by Sir J. G. Frazer (Orinoco Indians, p. 28, abridged edition, 1925) ; *The Mystic Rose*, by Crawley and Besterman (1927), pp. 63 ff. ; *The History of Human Marriage*, and *The Position of Women in Early Civilization*, by E. Westermarck.

55

customs among various peoples, and the fact, constantly observed by anthropologists, that the customs persist for generations after their causes have disappeared or been substantially modified, serve to prove that they are no more inherent in or essential to human nature and society than, for instance, male monarchy, or the practice of living in trees.

The present custom of most civilized nations, according to which the majority of women render domestic service in their own homes in return for maintenance, may (or may not) be expedient for the preservation of modern society, but it is certainly as mutable a characteristic of sex and humanity, as any of the practices mentioned above. In England this custom has no legal sanction. A wife has a right to maintenance in return for the rendering of conjugal obligations, but this need not (and among the leisured minority does not) involve an obligation to perform domestic work. Women who are not wives, but perform domestic labour in their family home, have no more right to maintenance by their male relatives than those relatives have to maintenance by them. (This is not to say that there is no such mutual right, but only that there is no legal basis for sex-differentiation in inter-familial obligation to maintenance, apart from the con-jugal obligation.) But custom demands maintenance for them in return for domestic work ; and further, in all but the most highly industrialized districts, convention requires that each home shall, if possible, offer one example at least of this peculiar economic relationship. There still survive social circles where an unmarried woman will be censured by public opinion for leaving her family home, for any reason but marriage, if it contains no other un-paid woman worker ; or for preferring, under such circum-stances, to occupy herself with paid work, extra-domestic, rather than unpaid domesticity.

The custom of the husband's maintenance of the wife being reciprocated by domestic duties on her part, is an ancient one, and may be considered to have been originally both reasonable and just, and a sound foundation for the economic relationship of men and women in general.[1] In the eleventh century in England, for instance, it may be considered to have been all this. For, firstly, the majority of adult women were wives, whose conjugal obligations involved them in a constant recurrence of activities which tied them to their homes. The age of marriage for women probably varied to some extent between the different social classes, being lower in the upper ranks of society where material provision was assured, and higher among the poor. There is little doubt, however, that the average age of women at marriage was lower than it is to-day. It is also almost certain that the female death-rate was higher than it is to-day, and that the average length of a woman's life when she had passed the age of childbearing was less ; so that the proportion of women who were married and of childbearing age would, in medieval times, have been much higher, in proportion to the total number of women.

The birth-rate was considerably higher than it is now, and also the infant mortality-rate. Child-birth, nursing and sick-nursing were therefore more frequent events for the majority of the female population, and, unless unforeseen emergencies occurred, they were domestic events, tying the mother to her own home, for there was little professional or institutional care available for mothers in child-birth and children in sickness, until comparatively modern times.

[1] Histories of early English law make little reference to the position of the married woman except in connection with property. The summary of her legal position given by Pollock and Maitland, however, may be taken to describe that of the propertied *and* unpropertied class : ". . . the main idea which governs the law of husband and wife is not that of an ' unity of person ' but that of *guardianship . . . the profitable guardianship*, which the husband has over the wife and over her property " (*History of English Law before the time of Edward I*, Vol. I, p. 485).

The liability of the husband to maintain his wife has been legally recognized for two hundred years (see E. Jenks, *Husband and Wife under the Law*, p. 51). Marriage-settlements became customary during the restless period of the Civil Wars. " The converse of the husband's right to his wife's personalty was his liability to maintain her . . ." but " the doctrine was, in a sense, negative. Where the husband's title was legal, the Court could not interfere " (*Short History of English Law*, by E. Jenks (1928 ed.), p. 227).

Such care as did exist of this kind was to be found in the work of men and women in religious orders. It seems probable that of the unmarried adult women, a very large number took religious vows. Their economic relationship to the Church was then very similar to that between profane spouses; reciprocal rights and duties were acknowledged, the Church being responsible for the maintenance of the " bride of Christ ", while she in her turn relinquished in its favour whatever property she might possess, inherit or earn.

The custom of domestic-work-in-return-for-maintenance drew much of its force from the fact that it provided child-bearing women with a simple and obvious guarantee of economic security. On occasions when she could not support herself by her own labour, she had a universally acknowledged claim on the fruits of the labour or property of another. Before money became the usual medium of exchange, the economic organization of society depended on a complicated network of acknowledged or statutory rights, duties and obligations. It is recorded, in or about the year A.D. 1000 :—

> " To all serfs belong a mid-winter feast and an Easter feast, a plough-acre and a harvest handful, besides their needful dues." [1]

The cotter must work for his lord so many days in the week, and he receives his reward in kind ; and

> " it befits him to have 5 acres (for himself) ; more, if it be the custom of the estate, and if it be less, it is too little . . . he shall pay his hearth-penny on Holy Thursday, as all free-men should " [2]

and he has duties in connection with his lord's military service. Such rights were difficult to enforce (" if it be less, it is too little ! ") and were susceptible of unjust and arbitrary assessment. The recognized right of every wife to be supported by her husband, apart from any reciprocal

---

[1] *Rectitudines Singularum Personarum*, quoted *English Economic History, Select Documents*, Brown, Bland and Tawney, pp. 7 and 8.
[2] *Ibid.*, pp. 5, 6.

obligation on her part, was an economic safeguard for the preservation of the race, which it would have been difficult then and for long after to secure in any more adequate way. The custom has many other roots in the history and economy of the family and society, but its economic reasonableness in this respect, little as it may have been the conscious cause of its establishment, must certainly be reckoned as a cause of its persistence.

The custom was not unjust to women, because so long as payments were commonly made either by exchange of goods, or of rights and services, or by a combination of these methods, the married woman who was secured livelihood but did not earn money by her work, was not in a peculiar economic position compared with many other persons of either sex. With the increasing use of money, however, and the development of capitalism, the disadvantage of being rewarded in this way has increased in constant and parallel measure. In a society based on money, this ancient custom denies to the domestic woman the degree of freedom and independence which the wage-earner has obtained.

But perhaps the most important of the differences between the modern and ancient economy—the chief consideration which originally made it not unreasonable that women should work in their own homes, is the fact that until about the eighteenth century, both the word " home " and the word " work " would have had in this connection quite a different connotation. The normal home would have included not merely a house or apartment, but also land owned or worked by the family, and the family right to use of common land. And domestic work was not synonymous with non-profitable work, nor did women perform it exclusively. In agriculture (in which the major part of the population was wholly or partially employed until the eighteenth century) there was no marked distinction between the character of the work done by men and women, caused by the restriction of married women to work in their own homes, so defined. Among the poorer people, both sexes might be employed as " servants in husbandry " before marriage, earning a small wage and their keep in return for work which either sex might be required to perform in the house or in the fields. Marriage for these people was supposed to depend, and frequently did depend, on the acquisition of a cottage with land or common-rights attached, and after marriage the wife's labours in raising crops or managing stock or poultry on croft or common were often not very different in nature, nor sometimes in profit, from her husband's work either for himself or a larger farmer. It is evident from contemporary literature of the thirteenth and fourteenth centuries that the housewife's care of cattle and poultry was a general rule, even among the poor and humble. In or about the year 1210, a bishop instructs three anchoresses :—

" Ye, my dear sisters, shall have no beast but one cat. An anchoress that keeps cattle seems more like a housewife, as Martha was, than an anchoress." [1]

Yet the gospels bring us no tidings of Martha's cattle : the bishop had presumed them among her cares, because she was a typical housewife.

Chaucer describes a poor widow who

" Was whylom dwelling in a narwe cotage . . .

Sin thilke day that she was last a wyf
In pacience ladde a ful simple lyf,
For litel was hir catel and hir rente ;
By housbondry of such as God hir sente
She found hirself, and eek hir daughtren two ;
Three large sowes hadde she, and namo (no more),
Three kyn, and eek a sheep that highte Malle,
Ful sooty was hir bour, and eek hir halle,
In which she eet ful many a slender meel . . .

A yard she hadde, enclosed al aboute . . .
In which she hadde a cok, highte Chauntecleer. . . .
This gentil cok hadde in his governaunce
Sevene hennes. . . ." [2]

---

[1] *The Ancren Riwle* (ed. Morton for the Camden Society, 1853, p. 416. Text modernized, H.S.A.).
[2] *The Nonne Prestes Tale* (*The Canterbury Tales*), Chaucer, c. 1390.

It is evident that housekeeping among the rural poor was almost synonymous with agricultural work and stock-keeping.

Cottagers' wives also undertook paid work occasionally. At harvest-time they commonly worked in the fields, and there are records of payments made to married women in the sixteenth century, for shearing of sheep, and other specialized agricultural work.[1]

The country gentlewoman, and the prosperous farmer's wife, as well as the cottage woman, had opportunities of occupation recognized as profitable, without leaving home, and were not considered to lose status by exercising these opportunities (except in the narrow circles of the highest fashion and wealth) until about the beginning of the eighteenth century. A sixteenth-century *Boke of Husbandrye*, recounting " what workes a wyfe should do in generall ", after bidding her sweep the house, lay the table, milk the kine, suckle the calves, " sile up " the milk, take up the children and dress them, and provide for her household's daily meals, continues with instructions for baking and brewing, butter and cheese-making, the care of swine and poultry, and of the kitchen garden ; the sowing and care of flax and hemp, and spinning from it, and making of sheets, shirts, and so on. And also

" It is a wives occupacion to winow al maner of cornes, to make malte, wash and wring, to make hey, to shere corne, and in time of nede to helpe her husbande to fyll the mucke wayne or donge carte, dryve the plough, to lode hey, corne and such other. Also to go or ride to the market to sell butter. . . . And also to bye al maner of necessary things . . . and to make a true rekening and accompt to her husband what she hath receyved and what she hath payed. And yf the husband go to the market to bye or sell, as they ofte do, he then to show his wife in lyke maner. For if one of them should use to disceive the other, he disceyveth himselfe, and he is not lyke to thryve, and therfore they must be true ether to other." [2]

The spinning and weaving which Sir Anthony Fitzherbert included among the housewife's domestic duties,

[1] *Working Life of Women in the Seventeenth Century*, by A. Clark, p. 62.
[2] *The Boke of Husbandrye*, by Sir Anthony Fitzherbert, 1523.

could alternatively be undertaken for industrial exchange. The textile industry provided work that could be done at home by women—websters and spinsters, married and unmarried—all over England. Men and boys sometimes took a share in the work, but it was generally considered the women's province. Chaucer's *Wife of Bath* stated (generalizing evidently from introspection and observation both) :—

> " Deceite, wepyng, spinning, god hath give
> To wommen kindely (i.e. by nature), whyl they may live." [1]

And everyone knows one of the earliest political slogans :—

> " When Adam delved and Eve span,
> Who was then the gentleman ? "

A great deal of this spinning was undoubtedly done for exchange. In medieval times wool and woollen-cloth were England's staple exports. Women made money by their domestic work.

They were also able to occupy themselves in many other gainful occupations besides agriculture and spinning, without leaving home, because most crafts (including retail trade) were carried on in connection with the home. In this kind of work, however, they usually worked as assistants or junior partners rather than as principals. For the industrial development of the crafts occurred simultaneously with the increasing use of money, and this placed women at a disadvantage. English laws of property and inheritance are partly based on the necessities of military feudalism, and partly on patriarchal Roman Law, so that they introduce considerations quite extraneous to the proper regulation of industrial relationships in a peaceable capitalist society, and inimical to the industrial status of women.

Nevertheless, so long as craft-work and trade were

---

[1] *The Wife of Bath's Prologue (The Canterbury Tales)*. It is worth noting that this independent-minded lady was a manufacturer in the woollen industry. " Of cloth-making she hadde suche an haunt, She passed them of Ypres and of Gaunt "—a description not likely to be forgotten by those who saw the Cloth Hall of Ypres before, or even after, its destruction in the 1914 war.

carried on in the home, the wife and daughter filled a recognized position as assistants to the master. The apprentice was subordinate to the wife as well as to the husband, and it was considered his business to assist in the whole work of the household, domestic as well as industrial. Defoe stated in 1724 :—

> "It is but few years ago, and in the Memory of many now living, that all the Apprentices of the Shop-keepers . . . submitted to the most servile Employments of the Families in which they serv'd ; such as . . . their Successors in the same Station, scorn so much as the Name of now ; such as cleaning their Masters' Shoes, bringing Water into the Houses . . . also waiting at Table. . . ." [1]

Women were at a disadvantage (as nowadays) through not being trained for skilled work by regular apprentice-ship so often as boys. The chief reason for this was (as nowadays) the expectation of marriage, and the association of marriage with domestic duties. But then, one of the domestic duties of the wife was to assist her husband in his trade ; if it was a skilled craft, she sometimes acquired considerable skill in it too, or else rendered special help in the financial side of the business. She was generally recognized as the man's business partner, and in many guilds the widow succeeded to the full Guild rights of the deceased.[2] The spinster was the chief sufferer by this system. She was a comparatively rare phenomenon. A wife was an economic asset, almost a necessary condition of prosperity, to the average tradesman and craftsman.

The custom of women working at home did not therefore prevent them from joining in recognized productive work, nor *in itself* serve to differentiate their work from that of the majority of men, until about two hundred years ago. This greater similarity between the occupations of the sexes cut both ways. It has been observed, of industrial conditions in the seventeenth century (when the old order was already changing) :—

> " . . . if women were upon the whole more actively engaged in industrial work during the seventeenth century

---

[1] *The Behaviour of Servants*, by D. Defoe, 1724.
[2] *Working Life of Women in the Seventeenth Century*, pp. 160 ff.

than they were in the first decade of the twentieth century, men were much more occupied with domestic affairs than they are now. Men in all classes gave time and care to the education of their children, and the young unmarried men who generally occupied positions as apprentices and servants were partly employed over domestic work. Therefore, though now it is taken for granted that domestic work will be done by women, a considerable portion of it in former days fell to the share of men."[1]

In earlier centuries, in the houses of the great and wealthy, the young pages and waiting-gentlewomen did much service that is now regarded as menial, just as the apprentices did in "middle-class" homes until Defoe's day. The schoolboy who must be served in all domestic affairs by a "scivvy", or a female member of his own family, would in medieval times have needed to possess very high rank to substantiate such claims, and even so he would have been failing to follow the highest examples of courtesy. The Black Prince waited on his prisoner at table, as the Knight's son, in the *Canterbury Tales*, did on his father; such services were part of the education of young boys and girls of the upper classes, to learn and practise which they were often sent away from their own homes, to the homes of other nobles or gentle folk.[2] This is the custom which, persisting into Elizabethan times, leads us often to misread Shakespeare, and to suppose that Maria, for instance—the waiting-gentlewoman to Olivia—is a servant, because she is called to bring "a stoup of wine", or ordered on other menial business.

[1] *Working Life of Women in the Seventeenth Century*, p. 5.
[2] The custom of sending children away to others' homes for their education and/or employment was very ancient, and probably of Germanic origin. It is also to be found among the Icelanders at the time of the prose Sagas. The following description of it occurs in *An Italian Relation of England*, 1500 (quoted G. G. Coulton, *Social Life in Britain from the Conquest to the Reformation*, p. 96) :
"The want of affection in the English is strongly manifested towards their children; for after having kept them at home till they arrive at the age of 7 or 9 years at the utmost, they put them out, both males and females, to hard service in the houses of other people, binding them generally for another 7 or 9 years. And these are called apprentices, and during that time they perform all the most menial offices; and few are born who are exempted from this fate, for every one, however rich he may be, sends away his children into the houses of others, whilst he, in return, receives those of strangers into his own."

Maria was no more marrying out of her proper station, when she wedded Olivia's uncle, than our own King's ancestor, the father of King Alfred, when he married the daughter of a butler—" Oslac, the famous butler of King Ethelwulf, which Oslac was a Goth by nation ".[1]

This is harking far back indeed, but not further than the custom of reciprocal domestic service and maintenance which is our subject.   The further back we go, the more clearly we see that this custom dates from a period when its significance and justification were utterly different from any it can bear in modern times.   The reasons for basing on this ancient custom the principles to be observed to-day in the economic relationships between men and women, have diminished and weakened.   The proportion of married women to the total population is probably less, and the married undoubtedly produce less children.   The special security which the custom originally guaranteed to mothers, is no longer to be guaranteed in this way : in fact, under the present economic organization of society, in which the State makes itself directly responsible (as a second line of defence) for the health and livelihood of the " independent " adult (which is recognized as being otherwise intolerably precarious), but leaves the " dependent " woman to the man's responsibility, the position with regard to security is directly reversed, and the child-bearing woman has less economic security than almost any other member of the community.

It has already been noted that the custom is inequitable because, in a society based on money values, it denies the domestic woman the independence which only property in money can give.   But this differential treatment is socially as well as individually unfortunate, for it prevents any economic value being assigned, by the ordinary balance of economic forces, to the product of the domestic woman's labour.   To this aspect of the subject I shall return in Chapter IX.

As influential as any other development, in weakening the economic justification of the custom, is the fact that

[1] Asser's *Life of Alfred.*

F

almost all the industries, trades and business which used to be carried on at home, have gradually departed from it to factories, shops, and offices ; the population has become increasingly urban ; agricultural work, like industry, has become more centralized and specialized ; thus the productive activities which can be performed with financial profit at home have progressively decreased, until the time has come when the work done in the home is considered and officially described as the antithesis of gainful occupation. It has decreased in variety, in value, and in popular valuation.

This development did not start with the Industrial Revolution in the eighteenth century ; bakehouses, breweries, and other craft-centres, had been set up as early as the thirteenth, competing with the usual domestic economy ; and the advantages of specialization for profit were already being weighed against the advantages of domestic production for some centuries before the eighteenth. The woollen industry, owing to the importance of wool as an export, was organized to some extent on a capitalist basis at a comparatively early date. Under Richard I, in 1197, an Assize of Cloth, intended to foster the trade, seems to have had, or been intended to have, some effect in restricting the sale of cloth which had been woven as a household occupation and encouraging thereby the sale of English cloth industrially woven.[1] Sporadic attempts were made in the seventeenth century, and possibly earlier, to gather wage-earning workers together, and so centralize the capitalist production of yarn and cloth. " These experiments ", writes Mrs. Clark,[2] " were discontinued, partly because they were discountenanced by the Government, which considered the factory system rendered the wage-earners too dependent on the clothiers."

It was the industrial, agrarian and philosophical revolutions of the eighteenth century, however (or the forces which caused them), which tipped the scale between

---

[1] *Growth of British Industry and Commerce*, by E. Cunningham, p. 192.
[2] *Working Life of Women in the Seventeenth Century*, pp. 98–9. See also *History of Trade Unionism*, by S. and B. Webb, pp. 32 ff.

domestic and centralized "capitalist" industry. The cottage woman, deprived of land and common rights, without hope of profit any longer from loom or spindle ; and her "betters", cut off from home-localized craft, trade, or commercial management—were faced with the alternative of gainful work away from home, or domestic work shorn of its former variety and value. If the woman belonged to the wage-earning class, and if she had small children, the choice was difficult, and the result often cruel.

" ' I do not think a great deal is got by a mother of a family going out to work,' said one who had been engaged in field work for twenty-five years, ' perhaps she has to hire a girl to look after the children, and there is a great waste of victuals and spoiling of things ; and then working in the fields makes people eat so much more. I know it was so with me always. I often say there is not fourpence got in the year by my working out . . . but generally I am in better health when I am out at work.' " [1]

" ' While working in the pit I was worth to my husband 7s. a week, out of which we had to pay 2s. 6d. to a woman for looking after the younger bairns. I used to take them to her house at four o'clock in the morning, out of their own beds, to put them into hers. Then there was 1s. a week for washing ; besides, there is mending to pay for, and other things. The house was not guided. The other children broke things. . . . Then when I came home in the evening, everything was to do after the day's labour, and I was so tired I had no heart for it ; no fire lit, nothing cooked, no water fetched, the house dirty, and nothing comfortable for my husband.' " [2]

Upper- and middle-class women were differently affected. The new industrial conditions deprived them of profitable work in their own homes, but also provided new wealth, which could be expended in supporting them in leisure, partial or complete. Much of the new industrial wealth was expended in this way : the leisure which had previously been a distinction of a limited minority of the upper classes spread downwards to women of the middle class. A code

---

[1] *Women Workers and the Industrial Revolution*, by I. Pinchbeck, p. 106, quoting *Report on the Employment of Women and Children in Agriculture*, 1843.

[2] *Ibid.*, p. 269, quoting *Mining Commissioner's Report*, 1844.

of conventional gentility and decorum arose which forbade all women of these classes, whether married or single, to occupy themselves with paid work outside their homes, if their male relatives could and would support them; and, in consequence, practically deprived them, under the new conditions, of all profitable work whatever.[1] The married woman with children had a slight advantage in the dignity of recognized economic rights under the law, and in virtue of her services in supervising a household and the upbringing of children. The spinster's lot under the new order is forcibly described by Charlotte Brontë in *Shirley* :—

" Look at the numerous families of girls in this neighbourhood : the Armitages, the Birtwhistles, the Sykes. The brothers of these girls are every one in business or in professions ; they have something to do : their sisters have no earthly employment, but household work and sewing ; no earthly pleasure, but an unprofitable visiting ; and no hope, in all their life to come, of anything better. This stagnant state of things makes them decline in health : they are never well ; and their minds and views shrink to wondrous narrowness. The great wish—the sole aim of every one of them is to be married, but the majority will never marry : they will die as they now live. They scheme, they plot, they dress to ensnare husbands. The gentlemen turn them into ridicule : they don't want them ; they hold them very cheap : they say—I have heard them say it with sneering laughs many a time—the matrimonial market is overstocked. Fathers say so likewise, and are angry with their daughters when they observe their manœuvres : they order them to stay at home. What do they expect them to do at home ? If you ask, they would answer, sew and cook. They expect them to do this, and this only, contentedly, regularly, uncomplainingly all their lives long, as if they had no germs of faculties for anything else : a doctrine as reasonable to hold, as it would be that the fathers have no faculties but for

[1] Writing became one of the very few gainful occupations which could be practised without loss of gentility, because domestically. Before the seventeenth century one may search literary records for the names of women writers *almost* in vain. The lack of leisure and the lack of female industrial specialization, rather than lack of education, deterred women from authorship. The rise of women in literature is almost simultaneous with the growth of capitalism, which enforced leisure upon a much greater proportion of them. It pre-dates by centuries the movement for women's higher education.

eating what their daughters cook, or for wearing what they
sew. . . . Lucretia, spinning at midnight in the midst of
her maidens, and Solomon's virtuous woman, are often
quoted as patterns of what 'the sex' (as they say) ought
to be. . . . The virtuous woman . . . had her household
up in the very middle of the night; she 'got breakfast
over' (as Mrs. Sykes says) before one o'clock a.m.; but
she had something more to do than spin and give out portions :
she was a manufacturer—she made fine linen and sold it :
she was an agriculturist—she bought estates and planted
vineyards. . . . King of Israel! your model of a woman
is a worthy model! But are we, in these days, brought up
to be like her?'' [1]

Shirley was written before the movement for the emancipation of women had got under weigh. In the field
of politics—the franchise—that movement has been successful; in the field of economics, not yet completely—
but it has gone a long way towards solving the problem
of the middle-class maiden, of which Charlotte Brontë was
one of the first publicly to complain. An historian of
women's work has noted, however, how this modern
development of economic freedom for women has to a
great extent passed over the married woman :—

   "One unexpected effect" (of the influence of economic
changes on the position of women) "has been the reversal
of the parts which married and unmarried women play in
productive enterprise. In the earlier stages of economic
evolution that which we now call domestic work, viz. cooking, cleaning, mending, tending the children, etc., was performed by unmarried girls under the direction of the housewife, who was thus enabled to take an important position
in the family industry. Under modern conditions this
domestic work falls upon the mothers, who remain at home
while the unmarried girls go out to take their place in
industrial or professional life. The young girls in modern
life have secured a position of economic independence, while
the mothers remain in a state of dependence and subordination—an order of things which would have greatly astonished
our ancestors." [2]

When one perceives the gradual decline of one after
another of the advantages, both to the individual woman

[1] *Shirley*, by Charlotte Brontë, 1849.
[2] *Working Life of Women*, pp. 11–12.

and to society, which originally sprang from the custom we are discussing—the reciprocity of domestic work and economic support, between husband and wife—one is naturally led to ask why it survives, comparatively so unquestioned. Doubtless there are many reasons : one, that not all its advantages have departed ; another, inertia ; a third, that this custom has given rise to another custom, which Mrs. Webb has dubbed " the vested interest of the male "—that is, the general recognition of the prior right of men to paid work, and particularly to well-paid work. This, reacting circularly, puts women at such a disadvantage in the labour-market, that many of them are unable to earn their living, and have to depend on men for all or part of their livelihood. The whole business therefore assumes a deceptive aspect of inevitability, and observers congratulate themselves on the recognition of cause and effect within this circle, without seeking to investigate the primary cause of the vortex, or the danger of such a whirlpool to those who are navigating the crowded river of life.

CHAPTER VI

TESTS AND PLEDGES OF WAR TIME

Agreements about terms of women's admission to men's work—success of women's work—previous low valuation partly due to low wages—industrial work found not harmful to maternity—appointment of War Cabinet Committee on Women in Industry—Majority Report—Minority Report—non-representation of women at industrial conferences and on other bodies—the vote.

The chemist tests his inorganic substances by standardized experiment ; weighs, heats, dissolves or precipitates, and so finally announces an indisputable comparison, description or analysis. The sociologist and historian have no similar resources at their command. But occasionally Time itself provides a cataclysm, which acts as a fiery furnace, a balance, a precipitating solution, on problems which are the subjects of their observation.

The European War of 1914–1918 acted in this way on the employment of women. Hypotheses became capable of proof, and some that had been held on high authority were disproved. It had been supposed that the restricted employment and industrial segregation of women corresponded closely with the lesser economic value of their labour. It had been stated that only the relative cheapness of women's labour offered any inducement to the employer to employ them in the place of men.[1] It had been said that the exclusion of women from trades or processes could not be laid at the door of the Trade Unions, which were in all cases powerless to bring about such a result, however much they might wish it, if a

[1] " No employer would dream of substituting women for men, unless this resulted in his getting the work done below the men's Standard Rate " (*Industrial Democracy*, by S. and B. Webb, 1898 ed., p. 497).

body of employers willed otherwise.[1] Above all, there was a consensus of public opinion, which had grown up during the previous century, that certain kinds of work (in general, light, sedentary, indoor work, especially such as did not require a high degree of strength or skill, intellectual or physical) were suitable for women, and that other work was of a nature not to be satisfactorily performed by the female sex.

War-time conditions provided an unexpected opportunity for putting these hypotheses to the proof, by calling upon women to fill men's places. The conditions, of course, had not the exact equivalence that would be required in a comparison staged in a laboratory. For one thing, there were some jobs or occupations undertaken by women during the war (such as all-round skilled and jobbing engineering work) for which the usual term of apprenticeship is longer than was the whole duration of the war. For another thing, there was some reluctance on the part of skilled men to teach women.[2] And there were, besides, special difficulties for everybody, in the peculiar conditions of war-time—of transport, of housing, of food supply (which took more time and energy than at normal times to procure, and so reduced the industrial energy of many workers), and of domestic service, paid or unpaid, of which there was less available per industrial worker, so that the women taking the place of men in industry had to do domestic tasks as well, to an extent quite unprecedented among the men whom they replaced.

Nevertheless, there was, during 1914–1918, an equivalence in the employments, and conditions of employment,

---

[1] " Wherever any considerable number of employers have resolutely sought to bring women into any trade within their capacity, the Trade Unions have utterly failed to prevent them " (*Industrial Democracy*, p. 499).

[2] " In every industrial district, almost without exception, there was continuous opposition to the introduction of women. In some cases this opposition was overt even to the point of striking ; in other instances . . . it took the insidious form of refusal to instruct women, or attempts to restrict the scope of their work or to discredit their efforts." *Report of War Cabinet Committee*, (*Appendices, etc.*, p. 55). See also *Home Office Report on Substitution of Women for Men in non-Munition Factories during the War*, 1919, pp. 11, 12.

of industrially employed men and women such as there has never been before or since, during the more modern period of history. And the disadvantages from which the women suffered were to some extent counterbalanced by a spurt of mechanical inventiveness and general receptivity to innovation, which resulted in the instalment of a large number of new labour-saving devices or methods.

The declaration of war did not, however, automatically cancel every prohibition, explicit or tacit, which restricted the industrial employment of women. Even the patriotism of the male wage-earners—which was probably no less widespread, no less genuine, and took a no less martial form, than that which in 1914 inspired the rest of the nation—was not enough to impel them to relinquish all that their Trade Unions had won, without securing any *quid pro quo*. In one industry after another, by countless struggles, they had succeeded in raising their wages, and had to some extent stabilized their standard of living, by refusing to work side by side with women, and by insisting on receiving, for " men's work ", a wage which might be supposed sufficient to support more than one person. If now, because of the war, they were to lower the dykes built up with such immense toil, what guarantee could they have that the flood of female labour, let in while they were fighting for their country, would not still be overwhelming their homes when the war was over, when the King's shilling (plus allowances) no longer supported them and their wives and children ?

The Government wanted the men for the Army, and it wanted them to come in voluntarily. Consequently it was anxious to facilitate the settlement of this difficulty. And at the beginning of the war there were doubtless many employers of labour who did not expect or intend to profit by abnormal conditions, and wished to set free their men for active service, without any expectation of benefit to themselves or shareholders in lowered labour costs. The Government itself was, of course, an employer of labour, on a very large scale.

The result was that agreements were made, between the Government and the representatives of a large number of Trade Unions acting in concert, and also between other employers or employers' associations and their appropriate workers' Trade Union, defining, for the satisfaction of the men, what the position should be with regard to substituted labour. The conditions demanded by the men, to which they believed the other parties to these agreements had in each respect pledged themselves, were (i) that the rate customarily paid for a job should not be lowered on the importation of a different type of labour (whether that of women, unskilled men, or juveniles) ; (ii) that the suspension of restrictions on such other types of labour should "hold good only for the duration of the war, or till such time as sufficient male labour should be again available ".[1]

The agreement between the Government and the Trade Unions was contained in the "Treasury Agreement" of March 1915. It was implemented, during the war by the Munitions of War Act (1915) and the Munitions of War (Amendment) Act (1916), and also after the Armistice, by the Restoration of Pre-War Practices Act (1918).

The Government also took a certain degree of responsibility for similar agreements in private industry, many of which were drawn up under the auspices of the Home Office. The records of these agreements may be found in the Home Office Reports, and provide a large volume of evidence of the recognition by the employers and the Government or Civil Service officials, as well as the men's organizations, of the men's customary right, and the reality of their exercise of the power, to exclude women from direct competition with themselves in industry.

Thus the stage was set for the almost unrestricted

---

[1] *Home Office Report on Substitution of Women by Men after the War,* 1919, p. 16. Agreements concluded by employers and men's organizations on these lines were by no means identical, even when drawn up under Home Office auspices. It would appear that the conditions mentioned were in some form common to all agreements recorded at the Home Office.

entry of women into industries which had never known them before, or not known them for generations, without opposition from the men, and at men's rates of wages. And although these pledges were, in the later stages of the war, most doubtfully honoured, still these conditions offered an unprecedented opportunity for testing the quality and value of women's labour, and the effect of industrial work on the women themselves.

Under these circumstances, the success of the women was so marked as to cause general surprise, and official comment. It would be absurd to recall now, fourteen years after, the superlatives called forth from innumerable observers of women's industrial ability and endurance—Lo, here ! Lo, there ! Lo, everywhere ! More convincing now to turn to the impersonal and sober records of the Blue Books :—

> " The opinion of the Factory Department is recorded that the substitution (of women for men in industry during the war) has proved successful in a great majority of cases ; that women have shown capacity to take up many of the more skilled processes hitherto reserved for men and to carry them out completely and well, and have displayed unexpected readiness for work which at first sight seemed wholly unsuitable for them." [1]

Here we have, then, a recantation of the opinion, so generally accepted before the war, that there were large categories of industrial work " wholly unsuitable for women ", and we have also the definite statement that work " hitherto reserved for men " was not so reserved owing to the incapacity of women to perform it " completely and well ". On the latter important point the War Cabinet Committee also made the most unequivocal statements :—

> " Occupations with demarcation between men's and women's work or duties . . . cover the bulk of the occupations in industry proper. *Though often the lines of demarcation are artificial, it is rarely that they do not exist. . . .*

[1] *Home Office Report on Substitution of Women for Men in non-Munition Factories,* Prefatory Note.

There are . . . many cases where women's work in one district or in one factory, is men's in another district or another factory." [1]

A number of employers and managers of labour gave evidence before the same Committee that they now found that in some branches of labour women were more valuable to them than the men whom they had previously employed, even when the women were paid the same rates of wages. If their attitude towards women's labour had indeed been, before the war, that its relative cheapness was its only attraction, then it certainly had not been a rational attitude.

Such was the evidence given by the manager of a Metal Works, with regard to ammunition work, and the evidence given by the Rt. Hon. J. H. Thomas, M.P., Secretary of the National Union of Railwaymen, as being the general experience among managers of railways with regard to the work of carriage cleaning. Similar evidence was given by members of the Federation of Master Printers. In a number of cases where women were paid less than men, their output was so much more, that the employers gave it as a reason for not paying them equally, that their output might then fall as low as the men's ! [2]

The type of labour in which women were usually found to be more valuable workers than men was light work of a repetitive character, or requiring special dexterity and delicacy of touch. Evidence was given before the War Cabinet Committee by representatives of the Engineering Employers' Federation, that " a woman will always beat a man " on work of this character. [3] It was reported that in the Hosiery Trade, " on many machines, owing to their intricacy and delicacy, the women are superior to the men " [4]—a fact recognized before the war—and the same was stated to be true of Cotton Weaving, in which men and women had been for a century, and are still, paid the same piece-work rates. But many of these

---

[1] *Report of War Cabinet Committee on Women in Industry*, 1919, p. 192.
[2] *Ibid.* (*Minority Report*), notes to pp. 281, 282.
[3] *Ibid.*, p. 83. [4] *Ibid.* (*Minority Report*), p. 278 n.

jobs at which women excelled, had been classed as men's work, and women had been excluded from them, before the war. The Agreement provided that, so far as that exclusion was concerned, industry should return to the *status quo ante bellum*.

The work of women, however, did not only impress observers by its superiority in light repetitive labour. It was not that the women were superior at *some* work that so surprised both the man in the street and in Whitehall, but the fact that they were so obviously equal to almost any work, when given anything like an equal chance. That is not to say that their output on heavy manual labour was on an average as high as a man's. (In work largely concerned with the handling of heavy loads it was suggested by the Chemical Employers' Federation that one man's work might be replaced by 1·6 to 2·8 of a woman's.) Yet even in this type of work, when it was paid by piece-work rates, the women were found to earn almost as much as the men :—

"Loading coke and coal and filling coke sacks was paid at piece-rates, which were identical for men and women, and the difference in earnings was very slight." [1]

There were skilled processes which had been considered definitely and exclusively men's work, before the war, at which women rapidly became expert :—

"In some skilled trades, such as acetylene welding, where the process, reserved before the war to fully-skilled fitters, boilermakers or coppersmiths, was more or less specialized, the women did 'interchangeable jobs with the men' and 'it was pretty generally accepted that the woman's output is equal to the man's . . . in some cases the output is said to be better.'" [2]

It was not any exact equality of output, nor any exact measurement of degree of difference, but the sight, and

---

[1] It was seldom possible for the women to have an "equal chance" for reasons already noted. But where comparisons of output were made between men and women working side by side, they cannot be taken as referring to a normal average for men in general, as men industrially employed during the war were likely to be of lower than average physique.

[2] *Report of War Cabinet Committee on Women in Industry*, 1919, p. 84.

the journalistic reports, of women doing so many different kinds of work and getting the job done—guiding the
plough, driving motor lorries, acting as bus conductors
under conditions exceptionally wearing, cleaning windows,
shovelling coal, and also undertaking work of the highest
responsibility, whether of industrial supervision, or of an
administrative or academic nature—it was the fact that
women could " stand up to " these types of work at all,
in such a way that the wheels did still go round, unentangled
in skirts or hair—this was the war's gospel for the general
public, so far as the work of women was concerned.

The gospel was spread not only by industrial employers,
by journalists, by enthusiastic statesmen, but by medical
observers and investigators as well.

" Most women enjoyed the more interesting, active and
arduous occupations, and in many cases their health improved
rather than deteriorated.   Medical officers of factories and
welfare supervisors have pointed out the beneficial effects
of open-air conditions (yard work, trucking in filling factories,
etc.) on the general health, and the success with which
properly selected women have undertaken work involving
the lifting of weights, heavy machine work, and even forge
and foundry work, without untoward physical consequences.
The whole experience tends to show that light sedentary
work is not by any means always the most suitable for
women, that operations involving a change of posture are
preferable and that *given adequate nutrition* many women
would have better health and greater physical vigour if
they followed more active occupations." [1]

" Given adequate nutrition."   The medical reports pointed
to one of the reasons why the industrial capacity of women,
as revealed during the war, was so much in excess of what
had been expected.

" The conditions under which women were employed before
the war were not such as to enable them to develop full
health and vigour.   Low wages, an unsatisfactory and inadequate dietary, long hours and lack of exercise in the
open air, resulted in physical and industrial inefficiency and

[1] *Report of War Cabinet Committee on Women in Industry*, 1919 (Memo.
by Dame Janet Campbell), p. 237.

caused both men and women to place too low a value upon the woman's strength and capacity." [1]

" The results of employment of women under war conditions have emphasized the importance to health of the good food, clothing and domestic comfort which can be obtained when the wages represent a reasonably adequate recompense for labour. They have also proved that properly nourished women have a much greater reserve of energy than they have usually been credited with and that under suitable conditions they can properly and advantageously be employed upon more occupations than has been considered desirable in the past even when these involve considerable activity, physical strain, exposure to weather, etc. Light, sedentary occupations are not necessarily healthy occupations." [2]

The conclusion was thus evident that before the war women had generally been paid such low wages that they could not feed or support themselves properly ; and this had set up a vicious circle of low wages—low efficiency —low valuation of their work.

In laying such stress on the wages received (and all that wages imply in expenditure) as the most important factor in conditioning the health of the woman worker, rather than the nature of the work done (apart from cases where Factory legislation already existed), Dame Janet Campbell, the writer of the Memorandum in question, did not forget that actual and potential motherhood are important considerations in connection with women's health. She considered that the national provision for maternal care and welfare was inadequate, and outlined proposals for its improvement. But she also pointed out that the evidence of war-time conditions did not indicate harmful effects to mothers or children, in the aggregate, from the employment of the mothers, as such, in industry. If heavy *double* duties were undertaken—domestic and industrial as well—any woman might be expected to suffer in general physical health,

[1] *Report of War Cabinet Committee on Women in Industry*, 1919, p. 250.
[2] *Ibid.*, p. 251.

and expectant or nursing mothers especially. But that was not a condition of industry.

"Employment under suitable conditions is not in itself injurious to the pregnant woman, while the money thus earned may enable her to be properly fed, a matter of the highest importance." [1]

Similarly, in the case of the infant ; the evidence did not indicate that babies had suffered from the increased industrial employment of women, compared with what they suffered from normal pre-war conditions. If industrial employment prevented the mother from breast-feeding her baby, or having the elder infants properly looked after, it was certainly a misfortune ;

" on the other hand, poverty or an insanitary environment may have an even more injurious effect than the mother's absence. This is borne out by the low infant mortality rates in 1916 and 1917, years during which a continually increasing number of married women was being employed." [2]

The experience of war-time showed that it was unreasonable that women should be confined to work that was unskilled, lacking in responsibility, indoor, sedentary, and light. It showed that the pre-war demarcations between "men's jobs" and "work suitable for women" were (in the words of the Majority Report already quoted) artificial. They were not scientifically founded on differences between the nature of the sexes. They corresponded more closely with lines drawn between better-paid and less-well-paid jobs. In fact, so much had this been the case, that medical opinion reported the ability of women to have been reduced and undervalued, compared with that of men, owing to their receipt of wages inadequate for subsistence, before the war.

But for the Trade Unions, war-time experience served also to point another lesson ; that pledges from an em-

---

[1] *Report of War Cabinet Committee on Women in Industry*, 1919, p. 251.
[2] *Ibid.*, p. 245. The Infant Mortality Rate has continued to decrease. The Birth Rate, the decline of which was conjecturally associated with the increased industrial employment of women during the war, has since fallen lower than it fell 1914–1918.

ployer, however solemnly contracted, were not sufficient to safeguard men's wage-rates or employment if women were admitted to compete with men. The contracts and pledges, even those made in conference with Cabinet Ministers, announced afterwards on public platforms, and embodied in Acts of Parliament, that women taking men's places should receive equal pay for the job, seemed to the men to have been subsequently broken, by quibbles about meaning, or by downright disregard. They had been broken (in the opinion of thousands of both men and women employees) as regards wages. The men were determined that, as regards the further pledge as to their reinstatement in employment, to the exclusion of the women who had taken their places, the contract should be kept. The law should be kept to the letter : they had learnt that only by their own organized strength could they see that it was kept in future in the spirit too.[1]

The allegations of Government bad faith, made by men and women workers, were referred to a Committee (the War Cabinet Committee on Women in Industry) which had been set up in September 1918, to consider the whole question of the employment and wages of women. The original terms of reference were :—

" To investigate and report on the relation which should be maintained between the wages of women and men having regard to the interests of both as well as to the value of their work. The recommendations should have in view the necessity of output during the war, and the progress and well-being of industry in the future."

Before the Committee reported, the war had come to an end. The pledge of reinstatement of the men found further legislative expression in the Restoration of Pre-War Practices Act, which, as a fulfilment of the pledge, gave rise to further dissatisfaction among Trade Unionists. The close of the war, and the pledges given by the Government to restore the men without consideration of the needs

---

[1] See Webb, S. and B., *History of Trade Unionism* (1920 ed.), p. 642 ; Drake, B., *Women in Trade Unions*, pp. 106 *et seq.*, and *Women in the Engineering Trades*, p. 131.

or views of the women, stultified the work of the Committee from the start, so far as concerned its practical recommendations. The Committee did a service of inestimable value in collecting and recording evidence relating to many aspects of women's industrial work, its value as compared with that of men, its extent and remuneration before the war, the opinion held of it by employers and independent qualified observers, the effect of it on the health of the women workers and the probable effect on the race. But the findings and recommendations of the Majority Report were based not so much on the evidence recorded as on certain assumptions of social principle, reconcilable with the Government's pledges to the men, but quite irreconcilable with a spirit of free enquiry on the lines of the Committee's terms of reference. Two of these fundamental assumptions were, that men had a prior right to paid employment,[1] and that the performance of domestic tasks was a function inseparable from womanhood.[2] On these assumptions, "the relation which should be maintained between the wages of women and men" was predetermined : the position and wages of women in industry must necessarily be inferior. The only matter undecided was, how, when men were to be given the preference in paid work, the wages of women could be maintained above the starvation level which, by medical evidence, had characterized them under such circumstances before the war.

The Majority Report contained a number of recommendations to this end. One group of these was based on the assumption that there would be a great increase in productive industrial activity after the war, and a greater total number of persons employed than previously. In addition, it was suggested that a National Minimum Wage for women should be laid down by law, based on the subsistence-needs of a single woman and graduated downwards for girls under 18. The wages of men, it was

---

[1] *Report of War Cabinet Committee*, p. 105, par. 116 ; p. 164, par. 187, etc.
[2] *Ibid.*, p. 69, par. 81.

thought, would still be adequately regulated by collective bargaining, and the man's minimum wage, secured by such bargaining, should be sufficient to allow for the support of children. To prevent women's wages or employment undercutting those of men, it was recommended that whenever women were employed on work not exclusively " women's work ", the employer should negotiate with the *men* before fixing the rate to be paid : the Committee suggested that piece-rates should be equal, and the ratio of 2 : 3 should represent the proportion of women's to men's time-rate wages. A Pensions scheme was advocated for women who had to support children without the aid of a man. The medical criticisms of national provision for maternal welfare were endorsed, and passed on to the Departments concerned.

The effect of these recommendations at the time was practically nil. The increased industrial production which was counted on, occurred only for a brief spell, and was then succeeded by a long period of depression and unemployment. No legislative provision was made for a national minimum wage for women. The suggestion of the Committee that if women's time-rates were fixed at a lower rate than men's (by arbitration, for which the machinery indicated never materialized), the women would nevertheless *not* undercut the men's employment because their industrial output was lower—this did not convince the Trade Unionist at all ; nor, considering the contrary evidence offered in the Report itself, was it likely to convince anyone else. Widows received pensions, as the Report recommended, but not till seven years later. Schemes for a National Maternity Service have been prepared, but their realization still hangs fire. For immediate practical results, the War Cabinet Committee on Women in Industry was about as effective as driftwood on the tide which swept the women workers back towards the pre-war mark.

One voice on the Committee, however, was raised in opposition to the assumptions made in the Majority Report : the assumption especially " that industry is normally a function of the male, and that women . . .

are only to be permitted to work for wages " under special conditions. Mrs. Sidney Webb's Minority Report received the attention due to work proceeding from her pen. The argument she put forward carried all the more weight owing to her known sympathy with Trade Unionism, and lack of sympathy with feminism and the Suffrage movement. When the moderate, or timid, proposals of the majority were shelved, it was not to be expected that the bold and consistent recommendations of a solitary adviser would be accepted as a basis of Government action ; but the influence of the Minority Report in shaping opinion about the relation that should be maintained between the wages of men and women was probably greater than that of the Majority Report, the Medical Memorandum, and all the evidence put together.[1]

In so far as they were directly concerned with the economic relationship between men and women, Mrs. Webb's chief proposals were :—

(1) That there should be a National Minimum Wage, which should be equal for men and women ;
(2) That there should be Standard Rates of Remuneration for every Occupation, which should be equal for men and women ;
(3) That the principle of the " vested interest " or prior right of the male to any occupation should be rejected ;
(4) That provision should be made for children from the Exchequer ;
(5) That adult dependents (such as the aged, infirm and sick) should also be provided for as a national obligation, " because it is not desirable that one adult should be dependent on another adult for maintenance ".

The foundation of this scheme for adjusting the economic relationship of men and women in industry was a readjustment of the burden of dependency, planned to ensure that the burden should fall equally (through the medium of the Exchequer) on all wage-earners, irrespective of sex. Thus on levelled ground it was the plan to

---

[1] The Minority Report was afterwards reprinted for the Fabian Society under the title *The Wages of Men and Women : Should they be Equal?*

sow the seed of justice between men and women workers, and of industrial prosperity ; to standardize the pay by the job, without regard of sex, and sweep away at the same time the restrictions imposed by the male workers on women, and the ancient necessity for them.

The weakness in the scheme, as I see it, is that despite the levelling of different burdens, the ground is still not level. There remains a mountain, which Mrs. Webb certainly sees, but describes as a molehill. The mountain is, several million domestic wives attached to male wage-earners. Are they to come in under the National Minimum Wage plan, or to have their needs provided for by the Exchequer " because it is not desirable that one adult should be dependent on another adult for maintenance " ? No, neither ; they inhabit a peculiar economic Limbo of their own.

> " I do not mention the housekeeping wife (among dependents) ", wrote Mrs. Webb, " because I suggest that she should not be counted as a financial burden on the wage-earning husband. The domestic services that the housekeeping wife renders to her husband—important and valuable as they are, do but correspond with those for which the unmarried man has normally to pay in his outlay on board, lodging, washing and mending, and which the woman wage-earner has equally either to pay for, or else to perform herself at no less a cost in efforts and sacrifices. If the homekeeping wife has also children to care for, a portion of her maintenance—in so far as she is not housekeeper and domestic servant to her husband—must be deemed to form part of the cost of maintenance of the children, to be provided in whatever way their food and clothing are paid for." [1]

The wage-earner's nationally-fixed minimum wage, reckoned to cover the expense of keeping one person in board, lodging, washing and mending and such-like domestic services, is therefore deemed sufficient to cover the full expense of maintaining a " housekeeping wife " to perform such work. This means that every wage-earner should receive, for his and her minimum wage, a sum sufficient to cover adequately the joint subsistence

---

[1] *Report of War Cabinet Committee (Minority Report)*, p. 305.

of two persons. But the services in connection with board, lodging, washing, mending, etc., normally required by one wage-earner, should surely not be reckoned to employ the regular full-time labour of another person. Housekeepers could easily be shared between two, three, or probably even half a dozen wage-earners, and such co-operative housekeeping would inevitably result in a reduction of expenditure at the same standard of living. It would seem reasonable to expect that the national *minimum* wage should be based on the lower expenditure, and not on a method of obtaining services which is excessively expensive. But a housekeeping *wife* cannot be thus, from motives of economy, shared, because she is a wife. Not an economic, but a conventional family form of social organization, determines whether the cost of her services is to be shared by several wage-earners (perhaps husband and sons or daughters) or borne by one alone. The financial burden may be very real, when a worker must be retained and maintained full time, for a part-time job, by a wage-earner whose wage is adequate, but only adequate, to cover his own subsistence costs.

The burden, even with all the suggested attempts to attain equality, may be even heavier than this. The wife cannot be dismissed, nor the obligation to maintain her. She may be inefficient, or lazy. She may become, perhaps through no fault of her own, abhorrent to her husband, so that he wishes to leave her, and have the domestic services she might provide, provided in some other way. Even if he does this, he is still under the obligation to maintain her, just as though she were performing for him to the full the services for which a normal outlay has been allowed in reckoning his subsistence wage.

The weakness of Mrs. Webb's scheme is therefore, it seems to me, the disregard of men's obligation to maintain their wives; an obligation not merely customary but legal; definitely differentiating between men and women; taking no account whatever of the rendering of services by the wife to the husband, but holding good whether the wife be indeed a "housekeeping wife", or a wage-earning wife, or a wronged and separated wife, or a lazy slut of a wife. It is an economic obligation, though of an anomalous kind. To find its parallel in money payments for services rendered to the bachelor or spinster, is to disregard the essence of the conjugal economic relationship, which is founded on a bond of a different kind, more difficult to break or modify, persistent even when it is, to the recipient of the service, unprofitable.

The words in which Mrs. Webb advocated the principles of equal pay and equal opportunity for men and women have been repeated on many feminist platforms and pamphlets since. She pointed out that

> " The long-continued exclusion of women from nearly all the better-paid occupations has been largely the result of the assumption that these occupations were the sacred preserve of men." [1]

Without indicating how or why such a practice had arisen, she stated :—

> " There is no ground whatever for any deliberately-imposed exclusion or inclusion with regard to any occupation whatever of a whole class, whether marked out by sex, height, weight, colour, race or creed." [2]

But is there indeed no more ground for the exclusion from well-paid work of a class based on sex than of a class based on, let us say, height or weight ? Men of six foot do not pay a subsidy to men under that height. Men of twelve stone are not legally compelled to keep many of the men lighter than themselves. If they were so compelled, would not the talls and the heavies organize to protect their right to higher wages, and the chance of earning them ?

And since organization is in itself a source of strength, is it not likely that the talls and heavies would soon secure a preference even greater than the liabilities they had incurred for the support of their—shall we say weaker, or merely shorter and lighter—brethren ?

[1] *Report of War Cabinet Committee* (*Minority Report*), p. 265.
[2] *Ibid.*, p. 287.

The "principle of the vested interest of the male " is an attempt to set the scales of Justice—to strike an economic balance. While there is on one side of the scale a weight unrecognized and unascertained (the monies paid by men for the maintenance of women irrespective of economic return) a true setting is impossible. For these monies act as a subsidy to women entering industry, even though a woman individually may receive none.

It is indeed undesirable that the principle should continue to act with its present force on the economic relationships of men and women and to keep women out of the better-paid forms of employment. But the elimination of it would be—or one may more hopefully write, will be—a more difficult matter than was suggested in the Minority Report. Additional suggestions to those of the Report are put forward in the closing chapters of this book (" The Direction of Change ") ; these include in particular, a revisal of our marriage laws, and the further organization of paid work for married women whose domestic work does not occupy their full time or energy.

There was no " housekeeping wife " on the War Cabinet Committee, nor any male or female wage-earner, nor, except for Mrs. Webb herself, any representative of Trade Unionism.

The non-representation of the women chiefly concerned was no new thing. The women workers had been generally unrepresented in the negotiations between employers and operatives at the beginning of the war, when agreements were made as to the pay and rights of workers taking the places of men going on active service. Even more remarkable : the Conference summoned by the Government in March 1915, which drew up the famous Treasury Agreement, was " composed of 33 principal Trade Unions directly concerned in the output of munitions of war. The only important union forgotten was the National Federation of Women Workers, whose 20,000 members already included several branches of women munition workers ".[1] Although this may seem strange procedure

[1] *Women in the Engineering Trades*, p. 17.

to the outside observer nowadays, it did not seem so at the time to eminent women Trade Unionists. Miss Susan Lawrence and Miss Macarthur said :—

> " It must be remembered . . . that the agreement by which women were admitted into the engineering trades was an agreement between the men and the Government. No representative of the women was consulted ; and this was not unreasonable in itself, as the women had at that time no *locus standi* in the matter. The trade belonged to the men and they laid down, in consultation with the Minister, the terms upon which women should be admitted." [1]

The event proved, however, that the non-representation of the women in 1915 was most unfortunate for the men ; for the two sexes had a common interest in the wage paid for the job, during the war, and might have been able to maintain it intact, if they had been able to stand together from the start. The women, who were due at the end of hostilities to suffer by the enforcement of agreements which they had had no hand in making, stood loyally by the men in insisting on those pledges being redeemed. It was the women, who were *not* represented at the Treasury Conference, who pointed out immediately the ambiguities in the agreements, through which so much resentment of injustice afterwards arose, on the part of both men and women workers.

> " The altering position of women " (the Majority Report stated) " is . . . making rarer such omissions. . . . But, even now, representation of women at labour conferences involving their interests is not quite a matter of course, and we have therefore thought it necessary to emphasize the unfortunate consequences of the absence of such representatives at the Treasury Conference in March 1915, and we recommend that whenever industrial questions directly or indirectly affecting the interests of women are discussed under the auspices of a Government Department, that Department should be responsible for seeing that there are women present who can adequately represent these interests." [2]

---

[1] *Women in the Engineering Trades*, p. 112.
[2] *Report of War Cabinet Committee*, pp. 216, 217.

The new national valuation of women's work, which came into being during the war, had its influence on the social and economic position of women, though indirectly, and not through the medium of the committee which investigated and reported on it. Its chief medium was the legislation by which women were ensured representation in Parliament, and by which some of the disqualifications attached to their sex were removed. *Equality* of suffrage, however, took ten more years to achieve, and it was not until 1928 that the majority of women industrial workers were represented in Parliament. Representation in council is in any case only an intermediate step to the securing of desirable conditions. Since the date of the stillborn recommendations of the War Cabinet Committee on Women in Industry, no comprehensive practical plan has been prepared, outlining " the relationship to be desired between the wages and position of men and women in industry, having regard to the interests of both sexes and the progress and prosperity of industry itself ". There is as much need of such a plan to-day as there was at the time these terms of reference were put before the War Cabinet Committee.

CHAPTER VII

TRADE UNIONISM AND WOMEN'S WORK

Industrial Revolution of eighteenth century the genesis of Trade Unionism—its effect on source of family income—competition instead of co-operation within the family—men's wages undercut by women—monopoly of heavy work by men not customary—attempted by male organization in wool, silk, coal industries—monopoly of all factory work by men suggested—opposed by women workers—monopoly proposed on grounds of women's welfare, in coal, pottery, metal, clothing industries—and on various other grounds—improvement of working conditions based on welfare of women—Equal Pay—early attempts to secure it—silk trade, cotton trade, metal trades—Trade Union Congress resolution—organization of women—difficulties—practical obstacles to proposals for equal pay—Trade Board practice—connection of Equal Pay and married women's work—limitation of sex-conflict in industry—by conventional absorption of women in domestic work after marriage and low wage-demands of others—Trade Union restrictions as partial cause of this—summary.

The restrictions which had been suspended by the Trade Unions during the European War, 1914–1918, had a long history; a history, in fact, longer than that of the Unions themselves. In medieval times, girls generally had not practised craft work under the same conditions as boys; they had much less often been regularly apprenticed. Consequently when adult they had less often worked as independent Guild members, since membership was normally reached through the gate of apprenticeship. But in Guild work, craft or commercial, women commonly helped the men of their family, and widows frequently succeeded to their husband's Guild status. It was possible, therefore, for women to acquire high Guild status, both in their own right if, as did sometimes occur, they had been apprenticed as children, or if the Guild right of the husband descended to his widow; but it was more usual for their labour to be subordinate to that of men, and it was normally regarded as casual labour, being in fact particularly important in that respect, since it was the *only* casual labour permitted a Guildsman to employ. A rush of trade orders could not be met by engaging another skilled worker at short notice, since apprentice-ships were of long term, and the number allowed to each master was commonly limited. Wives and daughters therefore had a definite labour value even though their labour was usually subordinate in kind.[1]

The principles and organization of medieval Guilds and of modern Trade Unions differ, however, in many material respects, and to understand the latter, a study of the soil from which the Trade Union movement sprang is prob-ably more valuable than research into the practice of the Guilds.[2] That soil was the new economic organization of society produced by the industrial revolution of the eighteenth century.

English society at this time experienced three simul-taneous revolutions : in manufacturing industry, in agri-culture and land tenure, and in political philosophy. The manufacturer began to use more complicated machines, and more capital. The possession of capital sufficient for effective use for manufacturing became restricted to a smaller proportion of the population, and industry be-came centralized and specialized. Farming developed in a similar way ; more scientific methods demanded larger units under centralized control, and the remaining avail-able common lands were gradually enclosed. Parliament, instead of setting itself to organize the industrial life of the nation with regard for the welfare of the individual and society, as had formerly been considered the func-tion of government, was persuaded that national wealth could be most effectively promoted by the abdication of any such directing power.

One of the manifold effects of this economic revolution

[1] See *English Apprenticeship and Child Labour*, by O. J. Dunlop ; also *Working Life of Women in the Seventeenth Century*, and *Growth of English Industry and Commerce*, p. 352.
[2] In respect of women's labour, however, the problems of Guilds and Unions were in some respects similar, and might provide an interesting comparative study.

was to alter the basis and source of the worker's family income. The greater part of the industry of the country had been located in the worker's home, and in these circumstances even babies in petticoats joined in the work.[1] The proceeds were legally the father's, but it was obvious that the " breadwinning " was not exclusively his province, and that each member of the family above the merest infancy took its share in earning the bread it ate. In industry so conducted, there was no competition between stronger and weaker individuals, between legally-maintained and legal supporter, man or woman as such. Their gains increased progressively with their numbers, or in proportion to their combined strength and industry.

But under the new conditions which arose in the eighteenth century this was changed. With the new centralization of industry, and its departure from the home to the factory, each individual in the family had to seek, compete for, or forfeit, profitable employment.

The effect of this change on family life did not become everywhere immediately apparent. The change occurred at different rates in different industries. Hand labour and individual home capital sometimes competed with factory labour for a considerable period.[2] Consequently, although one or more members of a family might go to the factory, those who could not or would not go, could still earn money while staying at home. Also, during the earlier industrial period, there were still in many places opportunities for independent rural livelihood, not only for the agricultural worker, but even for the factory-hand, and occasionally for the coal-miner. The York-

---

[1] In Yorkshire " there was hardly anything above four Years old but its Hands are sufficient to itself " (Defoe, *Tour through the whole Island of Great Britain*, 1724). In a *Report to the Board of Trade*, in 1697, John Locke urged that children of poor and improvident parents, above the age of *three*, should be sent to working schools to learn and practise spinning and knitting. See *English Social Life in the Eighteenth Century*, M. D. George, p. 9. Textile work was the most usual method of employing poor people's children.

[2] Cotton-weaving, for instance, was carried on by hand-looms to a great extent until the 1830's. See Hammond, *Skilled Labourer*, Chap. IX ; Pinchbeck, *Women Workers and the Industrial Revolution*, Chap. VIII.

shire weaver had been used to keep his cow on his own plot of ground ; the new factories were often placed in rural surroundings, and for a time old customs survived side by side with new.

In the payment of the family wage there was also for some time mutual aid between capitalized agriculture and manufacture. The agricultural labourer's family now sometimes had the chance of supplementing his inadequate individual earnings by doing factory work instead of domestic industrial work, and the capitalist manufacturer was relieved of the necessity to pay each employee a family-subsistence wage, because the rural situation of " the works " provided their families with rural employment, if not independence. Both the farming and the manufacturing employer were thus aided in offering wages reckoned on an individual subsistence basis. Until the reform of the Poor Law in 1834, they derived further encouragement for this procedure (which, it must be remembered, tradition, founded on the earlier economic circumstances of labourers' families, seemed to justify) by the Poor Law practice of assisting from the rates those families in which the earned income was insufficient for the support of the family. This assistance was in certain cases given on a scale in proportion to the number of children in the family.[1] The withdrawal of Poor Law assistance after 1834 did not always result in the raising of the agricultural labourer's wage, but in the more pur-

---

[1] The practice of systematically subsidizing wages from rates, so as to raise them to a constant figure according to the size of the family ; and of assuring the labourer of the receipt of this sum whether he could find work or no ; and of sending each worker out to auction his labour under these circumstances to the highest bidder—was the result in certain parishes of an Act passed in 1782. It kept wages from rising above the level of individual subsistence. The practice of assisting from the rates workers whose families were too large for subsistence on their wages did not begin with this (Speenhamland) system. Locke, in the Report already quoted, wrote : " A great number of children giving a poor man a title to an allowance from the parish, this allowance is given once a week or once a month . . . to the father in money, which he not infrequently spends at the alehouse. . . ." Lecky states that " with the warm approbation of Pitt (in 1796) parochial relief was made proportionate to the number of children in a family " (*History of England in the Eighteenth Century*, Vol. VI, p. 206, ed. 1887).

poseful provision by the farmer of work for the women and children.[1]

The survival of the old system side by side with the new thus concealed for a time the problems which arose from the centralization of labour, and the change from a family-earned to an individually-earned income. But as profitable domestic industries, and the opportunities for independent rural livelihood, were driven out of existence, and after the system of subsidizing wages from rates was abandoned, there seemed to be no way of proportioning the income to the family except for all the members of it to work for the capitalist employer in farm or factory, as they had previously worked independently at home. If they did do this, however, the last state of the workers was usually worse than the first. That factory work could not readily be combined with domestic cares, as domestic work could, was only one of the difficulties. Equally fatal, in its effect on the family's standard of life, was the fact that the members of it were not now co-operating but competing for livelihood. Unless they could effectively combine (and until 1824 the law forbade them to combine at all), their very numbers tended to lower the wages of each ; and besides this, the wage or employment of the man was undercut by the competition of a form of labour customarily supposed to require only a lower reward.

The accepted convention of the lesser need of women was chiefly based on the obligation of the husband to maintain his wife and young children, but it was strengthened by the fact that in the days of family (i.e. domestic) industry, working-class women who did not belong to a family had been at a disadvantage. Spinsters had usually

[1] " In the districts where (after the Poor Law Amendment Act) scales (of rate-allowances supplementary to wages) were abolished, farmers had higher wages to pay. . . . Even so, earnings were still insufficient to maintain a family. There were, therefore, definite attempts to provide regular employment for wives and children, and farmers made it a rule to employ the families of their labourers before taking on extra hands. At Glynde, in Sussex . . . work was found for women . . . and for children . . . throughout the year when the allowance system was abolished " (*Women Workers and the Industrial Revolution*, p. 77).

suffered such a straitened, hand-to-mouth existence that their ilk were unlikely to expect more than a mere subsistence wage in capitalist, centralized industry.[1]

If it was possible for an employer to secure his labour at a comparatively low wage, current industrial ethics, in the eighteenth and early nineteenth century, instructed him to do so. The sex of the employee made no difference to this general rule. Consequently the convention that women needed less favoured the offer of work to women rather than men, as the new methods of industrial organization gained ground. Examples of such "undercutting" of men's employment and wages by women may be found both in connection with agriculture and with manufacturing industry.

" As capitalistic farming developed and with it the desire to lower the cost of production, women's labour was increasingly in demand. Such advocates of new methods as Marshall and Arthur Young frequently pointed out the advantages to be gained from their employment. After pointing out the cost of transplanting, for example, Arthur Young added naïvely : ' This is doing it very cheap . . . from whence it is evident, that transplanting should always be done by women ! ' " [2]

" The cheapness of women's work caused a general depression of wages over the whole country—a result which was observable from the earliest days of their employment as labourers. In 1788 Marshall had pointed out that the employment of women to hoe corn was ' beneficial ' to the farmer, since by it ' the wages for Men are lowered '. As time went on and the employment of women increased the effects were more noticeable, and after 1834 the earnings of women and children allowed married men to be employed for wages on which they could not otherwise have lived, and made it difficult for single and old men to secure employment at all." [3]

---

[1] This seems to be the deduction to be drawn from such evidence as is available. Wages obtainable in the domestic textile processes varied very much from time to time and from place to place, but in general appear to have been barely sufficient to support a single person living alone.

[2] Pinchbeck, *op. cit.*, p. 100, quoting Young, *Eastern Tour* (1771 ed.).

[3] *Ibid.*, p. 102, quoting Marshall, *Rural Economy of Gloucestershire*, 1789.

Nearly seventy years after Arthur Young wrote, an investigator of the West of England textile industry reported :—

"When it becomes needful to lower wages, women are employed, who will readily undertake it at a lower rate than men receive . . . indeed, it appears to be a custom in every trade to pay women at a lower rate than men receive for the same article. I have found it in the broadcloth trade, in the blanket trade, and in the silk-velvet trade." [1]

Factory Inspectors reported in 1843 :—

"The small amount of wages paid to women, acts as a strong inducement to employ them instead of men, and in power-loom shops this has been the case to a great extent." [2]

In some cases the practice was carried one degree further ; the married women undercut the single women. In a speech in 1844 Lord Ashley (afterwards Shaftesbury) quoted a letter giving an instance of this :—

"Mr. E. . . . a manufacturer, informed me that he employs females exclusively at his power looms ; . . . gives a decided preference to married females especially those who have families at home dependent on them for support ; they are attentive, docile, more so than unmarried females, and are compelled to use their utmost exertions to procure the necessities of life." [3]

It became obvious to the workers that if men's wages were to be raised and maintained at a level corresponding to the obligations of many of them, the competition of women must be prevented.

In branches of work too heavy, or in any way considered unsuitable for the employment of women, men had less need to fear their competition, and it was found that wages were not reduced to the same extent as in the trades where they competed. For instance it is recorded that

"in the woollen trade the width of the loom and the corresponding strength required excluded all but a few muscular

[1] Pinchbeck, *op. cit.*, p. 178, quoting *Report on Handloom Weavers,* 1840.
[2] *Ibid.*, p. 188 n., quoting *Factory Inspector's Reports,* 1843.
[3] *Ibid.*, p. 194.

H

women from such branches as broad-cloths, blankets and carpets ".[1]

In the general reduction of wages which afflicted the trade from 1815 onwards, the cloth-weavers suffered less than others. In the cotton trade, on the other hand, the observed sequence of cause and effect was reversed :—

"Disastrous effects were especially noticeable after the power loom was employed for the heavier work in which up to that time men had had the monopoly. Girls as well as boys were put to the trade at an early age, and constant reductions of wages in the nineteenth century made it essential for most women to continue at work after marriage."[2]

Theoretically, therefore, one might expect that in many branches of work which were particularly heavy, wages would be maintained because women were not employed. But in the early industrial period, instances of this were probably very rare, the reason being that it is only in quite modern times that the question whether some kinds of work were too hard for women has been raised at all. Women worked in the mine, at the forge, at the quarry, as well as in factories and fields. In the mines they were chained to trucks weighing as much as 250 lb., which they dragged along the rough, uneven passages. Sometimes these passages were only two to three feet high. Nor was the collier woman the only heavy worker, though she received, later, the most attention. The idyllic occupation of the dairymaid included the handling of cheeses weighing upwards of 140 lb., and labour from summer dawn to dark. Women, and children of both sexes, shared the heaviest work of the farm, driving the three- or four-horsed plough and loading the dung-cart. Women had worked as smith-wives from medieval times, and as late as the 1840's many women were working at domestic forges in the Midlands. In the early days of the Industrial Revolution there was scarcely any industry in which women were not employed, or in which, when individual

---

[1] Pinchbeck, *op., cit.*, p. 166.   Axminster carpets were an exception.
[2] *Ibid.*, p. 167.

earnings superseded family earnings, they did not compete with men to the detriment of wages.

Though the male wage-earners could not, therefore, in the earlier days of capitalist industrialism, secure a higher wage in most trades owing to exclusive demands for male labour, nevertheless they came to realize that if they *could* exclude women, or segregate them in certain branches, they might more effectively unite to put forward a uniform demand based on their own recognized needs, and so secure higher payment than a woman would customarily ask, or be likely to receive. Early instances of such action occurred among a group of Western wool-weavers, and among the London silk-weavers. Mr. and Mrs. Hammond record that in the West Country during the eighteenth and early nineteenth century, light woollen weaving "was done almost entirely by women, 'those who do the work being the wives or daughters of agricultural labourers, of mechanics or others ' ". But

> " There was one curious exception in the case of this trade, at Cullompton, where the men had bound themselves not to allow any woman to learn the trade. This prohibition lasted for nearly a century, till 1825, when the advantages of obtaining help from their own wives and daughters broke down resistance. Nearly fifteen years later there were still 250 men to 62 women, and the prices paid were higher than in other parts of the district." [1]

In the London silk-weaving industry, carried on in Spitalfields, an attempt was made in 1769 to exclude women from the better-paid classes of work. Silk-weaving had been primarily a women's industry as early as the fifteenth century,[2] but now, in the Book of Prices set out as the basis of agreement, the following statement was included :—

> "No woman or girl to be employed in making any kind of work except such works as are herein fixed and settled at 5½d. per ell . . . or . . . per yard or under for the making. . . . And no woman or girl is to be employed in making any sort of handkerchief of above the usual or

---

[1] *Skilled Labourer*, p. 162.
[2] See Clark, *op. cit.*, pp. 139–42, and Pinchbeck, p. 169 n.

settled price of 4s. 6d. per dozen for the making thereof
PROVIDED always . . . that in case it shall hereafter
happen that the Kingdom of Great Britain shall engage in
war . . . that then every manufacturer shall be at liberty
to employ women or girls in the making of any sort of works
as they shall think most fit and convenient without any
restraint whatsoever. . . ." [1]

This attempt at stabilizing wages in the silk industry
was not permanently successful, but the silk-weavers were
peculiarly fortunate in the alternative event. After strikes
and rioting, they managed to procure legislation (in 1773,
only three years before the outlook of politicians was in-
fluenced in the contrary direction by the publication of
Adam Smith's *Wealth of Nations*) by which the local magistrates were empowered to fix their wage-rates. Equal pay
for men and women was secured, presumably at a satisfactory rate. Until this legislation was repealed, the silk
workers' attitude to the questions which agitated their
contemporary Trade Unionists were peculiar to themselves ;
they were content with labour conditions, and refused to
support a petition for the repeal of the Combination Laws,
because they looked upon the law not as an enemy but
a friend. " The law, cling to the law, it will protect us ! "
they exclaimed ; but the law did not cling to them, and
the Spitalfields Acts by which their wages were regulated
were repealed at about the same date as the Combination
Acts.

The Luddite riots, which came to a head in 1811–1812
among the Framework Knitters of Leicester, appear to
have been caused " by the use of a new machine which
enabled the manufacturers to employ women in work in
which men had been before employed ".[3] " The repeated
reductions of wages, the rapid alterations of processes,

---

[1] *London Life in the Eighteenth Century*, by M. D. George, quoting
A List of Prices in . . . Branches of the Weaving Manufactory. . . .
1769.

[2] *History of Trade Unionism*, p. 98 and n. See also pp. 54–5, and
Pinchbeck, *op. cit.*, p. 176 n.

[3] *Skilled Labourer*, p. 257, quoting from the *Annual Register* of 1812
an account of a Report of the Secret Committee of the House of Lords
on the disturbances.

and the substitution of women and children for adult male workers, had gradually reduced the workers to a condition of miserable poverty." [1] Much of the discontent seems to have centred round the employment of women, and the low payment they in particular received. Attempts were made to prevent them from working. On Christmas Day, 1811, a steward wrote to his master describing the activities of Luddites at Pentridge, Derby :—

". . . two men came to this place who called themselves inspectors from the Committee, they went to every stockinger's (i.e. operative's) house and discharged them from working under such prices as they gave them a list of . . . Where they found a frame worked by a person who had not served a regular apprenticeship, or by a Woman, they discharged them from working, and if they promised to do so (i.e. to desist) they stuck a paper upon the frame with these words written upon it : ' Let this frame stand, the colts removed.' Colt is the name given to all those who have not served a regular apprenticeship." [2]

Even among the coal-miners the view began to prevail that the employment of women prevented the man receiving a family subsistence wage. This was the more remarkable because among colliers the old system of family work (though in their case for a capitalist proprietor) survived into the nineteenth century. The men employed their own wives and children as helpers, and in some cases personally received, and personally spent, their wages. [3]
Yet even so

"There were colliers in the West Riding who strongly objected to their (i.e. women's) employment, because ' they

[1] *History of Trade Unionism*, p. 86.
[2] *Skilled Labourer*, p. 263. It is interesting that the only personal violence said to have been done by the Notts Luddites was offered to an employer who had previously received a threatening letter about women's wages. It was represented that a middlewoman in his employ "gives her Girls but half a Crown a week . . . for which they work a great number of Hours. You must be sensible, Sir," the writer continues, "that these unfortunate Girls are under very strong temptations to turn prostitutes, from their extreme Poverty. The Captain (of the Luddites) . . . these People being defenceless he conceives them to be more immediately under his protection as he believes their Wages are the lowest in England. . . ."
[3] "Until the end of the eighteenth century, colliers frequently borrowed money which was repaid out of the labour of their children" (Pinchbeck, *op. cit.*, pp. 257–8).

prevent lads and men getting their proper wages'. In parts of Scotland also it was opposed 'not so much from the soreness of the work as from a notion they have that it cheapens their own labour'; and in accordance with the policy pursued by the Unions to force up wages after 1825, the men themselves had in 1836–1837, excluded women from both coal and ironstone pits. For a time it remained a rule of the Unions that no woman should be allowed underground, but the temptation to employ them proved too strong, and they found their way back again. It is possible that a similar notion of self-interest had its influence in prompting the resolution of 350 Barnsley miners—some of them employers of women—who, in 1841, declared, with only five dissentients, 'that the employment of girls in pits is highly injurious to their morals, that it is not proper work for females, and that it is a scandalous practice'." [1]

All these efforts were limited in extent to the particular industry in which the men in question were employed. But in 1842, a deputation from the Short-Time Committee of the West Riding, representing the male operatives, waited on Peel and Gladstone, and included in their demands "the gradual withdrawal of all females from the factories". Peel, as a manufacturer, interested in the supply of cheap labour, disapproved of the proposal. Gladstone was more sympathetic, and

"thought the object might be achieved by the following regulations: 'First by fixing a higher age for the commencement of infant female labour, than . . . of infant male labour in factories. Secondly, by limiting the number of females in proportion to the number of males in any one factory. Thirdly, by forbidding a female to work in a factory after her marriage, and during the lifetime of her husband'". [2]

Gladstone's proposals cause one to reflect on the strange limitations consistent with a Victorian Liberal's idea of individual liberty.

A proposal similar to that of the Short-Time Committee had been put forward ten years before in the pages

[1] Pinchbeck, *op. cit.*, pp. 264–5,
[2] *Ibid.*, p. 200 n,

of Leigh Hunt's journal, *The Examiner*.[1] All children under fourteen, and " females of any age ", it was suggested, should gradually be excluded from manufactories. This suggestion actually called forth a reply from " The Female Operatives of Todmorden ". It is so unusual to find wage-earning women of that time (1832) speaking for themselves, and they put their case so admirably, that this letter must be quoted as it is given by Miss Pinchbeck :— [2]

" SIR,
Living as we do, in the densely populated manufacturing districts of Lancashire, and most of us belonging to that class of females who earn their bread either directly or indirectly by manufactories, we have looked with no little anxiety for your opinion on the Factory Bill. . . . You are for doing away with our services in manufactories altogether. So much the better, if you had pointed out any other more eligible and practical employment for the surplus female labour, that will want other channels for a subsistence. If our competition were withdrawn, and short hours substituted, we have no doubt but the effects would be as you have stated, ' not to lower wages, as the male branch of the family would be enabled to earn as much as the whole had done ', but for the thousands of females who are employed in manufactories, who have no legitimate claim on any male relative for employment or support, and who have, through a variety of circumstances, been early thrown on their own resources for a livelihood, what is to become of them ?
In this neighbourhood, hand-loom has been almost totally superseded by power-loom weaving, and no inconsiderable number of females, who must depend on their own exertions, or their parishes for support, have been forced, of necessity, into the manufactories, from their total inability to earn a livelihood at home.
It is a lamentable fact, that, in these parts of the country, there is scarcely any other mode of employment for female industry, if we except servitude and dressmaking. Of the former of these, there is no chance of employment for one-twentieth of the candidates that would rush into the field, to say nothing of lowering the wages of our sisters of the same craft ; and of the latter, galling as some of the hard-

---

[1] Pinchbeck, *op. cit.*, p. 199, quoting *The Examiner*, January 29, 1832.
[2] *Ibid.*, p. 199.

ships of manufactories are (of which the indelicacy of mixing with the men is not the least), yet there are few women who have been so employed, that would change conditions with the ill-used genteel little slaves, who have to lose sleep and health, in catering to the whims and frivolities of the butter-flies of fashion.

We see no way of escape from starvation, but to accept the very tempting offers of the newspapers, held out as baits to us, fairly ship ourselves off to Van Diemen's Land, on the very delicate errand of husband-hunting ; and, having safely arrived at the 'Land of Goshen', jump ashore, with a 'Who wants me ? ' Now, then, as we are a class of society who will be materially affected by any alteration of the present laws, we put it seriously to you, whether, as you have deprived us of our means of earning our bread, you are not bound to point out a more eligible and suitable employment for us ?

Waiting with all humility, for your answer to our request, we have the honour to subscribe ourselves, the constant readers of *The Examiner*,

THE FEMALE OPERATIVES OF TODMORDEN."

" In reply," writes Miss Pinchbeck, " the editor of *The Examiner* admitted the cogency of these arguments and as a compromise naïvely suggested that ' the interdiction might be confined to *married* females, and those whose parents are alive, and not in receipt of parish relief ! ' But at the same time, in all seriousness, he advocated emigration as offering the greatest advantages for that large class of young women whose ' parents or other near relatives ' were unable ' to support and protect them '."

Neither the proposals of *The Examiner* nor those of the Short-Time Committee were translated into legislative action at the time, but similar, if less drastic, suggestions continue to be made in the twentieth century. The employment of married women is restricted in certain occupations ; and to the question circulated by the War Cabinet Committee *Is it considered desirable to regulate the employment of married women ?* a number of replies were received in the affirmative.

The policy of exclusion of women's labour, urged by male Trade Unionists in the interests of their own wage-rates, was reinforced by another current in the stream of public opinion. During the nineteenth century the theory became prevalent that certain kinds and conditions of work suitable or inevitable for men, were not suitable or inevitable for women. This view spread rapidly during the reign of Queen Victoria, and found concrete expression in the suggestion that women should not work under sweated conditions in factories, or at all in mines.

There was, indeed, ground for supposing that the conditions of industrial work might lead to rapid race deterioration, and might be more detrimental to the health of women and children than of men. Probably these evils were not new : certainly in the mines, and possibly in many cottage-homes and town tenements where domestic industry had previously been carried on, conditions had been as bad as in early nineteenth-century factories. But there was probably a greater proportion of healthy outdoor work in earlier times, and it may have been easier to adjust burdens to individual strength, under a domestical system of industry ; and even if that were actually seldom done, the pre-existence of evils could hardly justify acquiescence in their continuance, when the concentration of work brought them to public notice.

When proposals for protective legislation first arose, current political philosophy held sacrosanct the freedom of the labourer to contract with his employer untrammelled by legal regulation. This was held to be essential to the economic welfare of both parties. There was, however, so great a tendency to think of " economic man " as an adult male, that to legislate for women and children did not seem so heretical as, according to the orthodox doctrine of *laissez-faire*, it actually was, nor so inimical to their interests as, if that doctrine were true, it certainly would be. Early industrial legislation therefore concerned itself particularly with women and young persons, either being directed exclusively towards amelioration of the conditions of one or both these groups, or differentiating its application in respect of them, or being based on their needs more particularly.

Differential industrial legislation, and the problems

arising from it, will be discussed more fully in the next chapter. We are here concerned with it, and the sentiments which gave rise to it, only as factors influential in determining the actions and attitude of the male Trade Unionist *vis-à-vis* the female worker.

The theory that certain kinds and conditions of work permissible for men, were unsuitable for women, does not seem to have been resented by the men. It would appear that they generally welcomed this point of view, not so much because they shared it—they were probably too conservative for that—but because they desired to limit the competition of women with men on economic grounds. In one trade after another we find the men expressing apprehension for the health, happiness, or morals of women who might have the misfortune to compete with them, and each historian of industry notes that these sentiments do not quite ring true. Thus Miss Pinchbeck surmises that " a notion of self-interest " may have prompted the Barnsley miners in their decision that the employment of girls in pits was highly injurious to their morals, not proper work for females, and a scandalous practice. Mrs. Drake discovers the same motive in the expostulation addressed by the Potters' Unions, in 1845, " to maidens, mothers and wives " newly brought into competition with them owing to the introduction of a new machine.[1] In the Metal Trades many attempts were made to secure the exclusion of women, ostensibly on the grounds of their own welfare. But they followed on previous efforts in which the low wages accepted by the women were the admitted motive, so that their sincerity was suspect.

" In 1866, a single pen factory in Birmingham engages, according to good authority, no less than 2,000 women . . . the competition of ' cheap female labour ' causes the despair of the men's trade unions. Through the 'seventies and 'eighties, the Birmingham Brass Workers, the Nut and Bolt Makers, the Chain Makers, the Nail Makers, raise their voices in protest against the female invasion." [2]

[1] *Women in Trade Unions*, p. 6.
[2] *Women in the Engineering Trades*, p. 7.

The men would not support the women's Trade Union movement in its early days, because by so doing they would be recognizing " those presumptuous females who ' turn at the lathe and file at the vice ' in Birmingham, cutting out their own men-folk ". When the representative of the Midlands Trades Federation moved, in the Trade Union Congress of 1887, " to introduce such amendments to the Factory and Workshops Act as shall prevent the employment of females in the making of chains, nails, rivets, bolts, etc., *such work not being adapted to their constitution* " [1]—the benevolent motive—the kiss, one might call it, or perhaps more aptly, the wag—in the tail of the resolution, could impress only the uninitiated.

When the Journeymen Tailors' Society sought to prevent the competition of women, they had a more difficult case to make out. In the light of history and tradition, it was almost impossible to describe sewing or cutting as work not proper for females, highly injurious to their morals, or ill-adapted to their constitution. If a benevolent motive were required for the exclusion of women from this industry it must be discovered in some hardship of quite general application.

" Have not women," said the Journeymen Tailors, " been unfairly driven from their proper sphere in the social scale, unfeelingly torn from the maternal duties of a parent and unjustly encouraged to compete with men in ruining the money value of labour ? *The Times* lies when it says that the Tailors of the Metropolis have struck against these poor creatures, with whose sufferings and privations the Committee deeply sympathize, and the terms under which they obtain employment are too gross for the public ear." [2]

When organization enabled, or initiative or extreme need impelled the women workers to give public expression to their own views, it is common to find them strongly objecting to such proposals to exclude them from industry, or from particular industries ; and they objected none the less because these proposals were made under a semblance of regard for their welfare. In the Owenite move-

[1] *Women in Trade Unions*, p. 20.
[2] *Ibid.*, p. 4.

ment of the 1830's, when the women were swept into Trade Unionism on the general wave of enthusiasm, " the ' Grand Lodge of Operative Bonnet Makers ' vies in activity with the miscellaneous ' Grand Lodge of the Women of Great Britain and Ireland ' ; and the ' Lodge of Female Tailors ' asks indignantly whether the ' Tailors' Order ' is really going to prohibit women from making waistcoats." [1] The Women's Trade Union League, formed in 1874, constantly opposed the attempts of the men's Metal Unions to exclude women from the Midland trades, and from other industrial work. They were suspicious of every form of restriction, and strongly opposed protection which took the form of prohibiting the employment of the person protected, " even when that person was a mother with young children ". [2]

The most extreme and exclusive form of protection of women, passed into law in 1842, was the complete prohibition of their work underground in mines ; the culmination of the benevolent agitation led by Lord Shaftesbury. It does not seem that the views of either the men or women workers had much influence in bringing this about ; the motives were altruistic, on the part of a group of benevolent philanthropists and the public they aroused. It was strange that the benevolence which prohibited the employment of women underground, did not extend to relieve their sufferings on expulsion. The fear of unemployment—unemployment forced upon them in the name of their own welfare, and social progress—which had aroused the genial but determined opposition of the Lancashire factory women to *The Examiner's* proposals, was brought to realization ten years later among the mining women.

> " The greatest pressure occurred in East Scotland, where 2,400 had been employed, and where the isolation of the mining districts made it exceedingly difficult to get other employment. . . . Numbers of women . . . unable to procure a living any other way, continued to go down the

---

[1] *History of Trade Unionism*, p. 136.
[2] *Women in Trade Unions*, p. 21.

pits by stealth, sometimes disguised as men. And since in Scotland, the law gave them no claim to parish relief, the plight of many, especially those who had parents or children dependent on them, was pitiable in the extreme."[1]

It is perhaps one of the most pathetic episodes in industrial history, though not unique in kind, that after the labour of women was prohibited in mines, the higher wages which owners had to pay the men enforced the introduction of improvements which, if they had been brought in earlier, would have saved the women " frae toil an' pain ayont conceevin' ".

The benevolent objections to the industrial work of women tended to fall under three distinct heads : that the work in question was " not adapted to their constitution ", by which it was usually inferred that it was by its nature beyond the physical strength of a female, or dangerous to them as potential mothers ; that the conditions under which the work was carried on were specially detrimental to women (night work, long hours, etc.) ; or that it was unkind to women to permit them to work anywhere except in their own or someone else's home.

The last position, taken up by *The Examiner*, the Journeymen Tailors, the Short-Time Committee of the West Riding in 1842, and by others from time to time, was so obviously untenable as a policy for industry, the sex, and the nation as a whole, that it requires no serious discussion. It was but a last-ditch argument of those who wished to exclude women for ulterior motives ; or a kite flown by masculine theorists unacquainted with the economic realities of the situation.

Those who opposed the employment of women on work requiring much physical strength, stood on firmer ground ; but their advocacy of exclusion was less needed. The keener appreciation of economy which naturally accompanies division of labour and modern industrial method, would bring about the preferential, if not the exclusive, employment of men rather than women in heavy work requiring a high degree of strength or allied skill, quite

---

[1] Pinchbeck, *op. cit.*, p. 269.

apart from any consideration of special benefit to either sex. This might fail to occur if the unit of labour were divisible, and if the women's wage were disproportionately lower than the men's, so as to make it possible to employ a greater number of them to do the same amount of work at lower cost in wages. But that course had countervailing economic disadvantages; the overhead charges would be higher. It would seem, on the whole, that little pressure from the men, or expression of benevolence on either side, was required to ensure the monopoly by men of heavy manual labour in most industries, after industry had become centralized.

When the monopoly of "heavy" work by men had become more or less a general rule, a certain amount of further ground was consolidated by the men, on the plea that they should not be employed *only* on arduous work; each worker should have an opportunity to take the rough with the smooth. Thus the evidence given before the War Cabinet Committee shows how the men objected, except for the special purposes of the war, to being given a complete monopoly of the heavier or more difficult work, unless they were also allowed to monopolize some of the easier.

" The Amalgamated Society of Engineers were of opinion that (women's) employment tended to concentrate men on work which was either highly skilled, arduous or physically disagreeable. ' That is one of the reasons why men on highly-skilled work . . . are now complaining.' "

" In the Boot and Shoe trade (during the war) . . . some 11,000 (women) were employed in the men's departments, clicking, pressing, lasting, finishing and stitching. Of these processes, however, ' clicking ' was generally held by witnesses to be too dangerous for women, and other processes, except stitching, too heavy. The cutting of the linings, upon which the women were largely employed, was not unsuitable, but the women had not sufficient experience, and the employers preferred the men. Nor were the men prepared to give over, after the war, all the light jobs to women, and had further a sentimental objection to ' mixed ' departments." [1]

[1] *Report of War Cabinet Committee*, p. 85, par. 93, and p. 92, par. 97.

In these later attempts at consolidating an existing exclusion, there was, of course, no expression of benevolence. For although those who benevolently sought to exclude women from particularly heavy work stood on firmer ground than those who sought to exclude them from industrial work altogether, their foothold was ever shrinking, amid the flood of progress and mechanization. Physical strength was less and less needed in industry ; comparison of industrial with domestic work became less and less to the advantage of the latter, and it was difficult to suggest that women had been unfeelingly torn from the home The invention of new machines became the Union man's nightmare, as we find graphically described in the Webbs' account of a typical Trade Unionist's life :—

" The club is . . . a centre for obtaining the latest trade news. Here . . . are to be heard reports of reductions or advance of wages . . . or the first rumour of that bug-bear to the men : the invention of new machines, with its probable displacement of their labour ; or even worse, the introduction of women and boys at reduced prices." [1]

The man's natural monopoly of greater strength had failed to give him its full advantage before the industrial revolution, because, for one thing, the more primitive division of labour prevented the advantage being fully appreciated, and for another, the man and woman co-operated, rather than competed, in many branches of industry. Industrial developments had discovered man's advantage, only again to deprive him of much of it by mechanical inventions which superseded human physical strength altogether, or took little account of the comparatively slight difference between the natural force of male and female.

At the same time as it became more and more difficult to secure the exclusion of women on the grounds of the strength, endurance, or length of training and skill required, in the majority of manufacturing processes, it also became more and more difficult to suggest the same

[1] *History of Trade Unionism*, p. 445.

policy on the ground of unhealthy conditions of work. In this connection, indeed, the men's Trade Unions had, by the end of the nineteenth century, already eaten a large slice of their cake : they had used the special sympathy felt by the Victorian philanthropists for women and children, to improve conditions of work for all. The welfare of the weaklings was the thin end of the wedge driven deep into the trunk of *laissez-faire*. The Trade Unions used it as such, while disregarding with instinctive common sense (as a general rule) the proprietary interest in industrial amenities which philanthropists seemed to claim for the female sex. Thus the special sympathy felt for women and children who had to work long hours, was made full use of by the Cotton Workers' Unions, when they were seeking support for the Eight Hours Bill, in 1872. They even demurred to working openly with the Parliamentary Committee of the Trades Union Congress for the Bill, because they were afraid that by so doing they would lose the support of those who were sympathetic to the women and children, but not to Trade Unions.

"So far as the public and the House of Commons were concerned, the Bill was accordingly . . . ' based upon quite other grounds '. Its provisions were ostensibly restricted, like those of the Ten Hours' Act, to women and children ; and to the support of Trade Union champions . . . was added that of such philanthropists as Lord Shaftesbury and Samuel Morley. But it is scarcely necessary to say that it was not entirely . . . for the sake of the women and children that the skilled leaders of the Lancashire cotton operatives had diverted their ' Short-Time Movement ' from aggressive strikes to Parliamentary agitation. The private minutes of the Factory Acts Reform Association contain no mention of the woes of the women and the children, but reflect throughout the demand of the adult male spinners for a shorter day. And in the circular ' to the factory operatives ' . . . we find the spinners' Secretary combating the fallacy that ' any legislative interference with male adult labour is an economic error ' and demanding ' a legislative enactment largely curtailing the hours of factory labour ' in order that his constituents, who were exclusively adult males, might enjoy . . . ' nine hours per day . . .'

It was, however, neither necessary nor expedient to take this line in public." [1]

The Bill in question provided one of the earliest instances (if not the earliest) of opposition from the leaders of the Suffrage movement, or those in sympathy with them, to industrial legislation differentiating between men and women. In this particular case the cloven hoof was particularly well hidden, because the legislation differentiated in the letter, without any differentiation being intended by its promoters in the eventual practice of the law. But Mr. Fawcett scented brimstone, and danger to women, in the limitation of legislation to one sex, even though the limitation was hypocritical.

The Short-Time battle was fought and won in the Cotton Industry, where women had been entrenched from the infancy of the trade, where they were comparatively well organized, and where, in at least one important branch, they received equal rates of pay. In many industries equal pay and the improvement of conditions for all workers together only became the men's Union policy after the hope of exclusion or segregation of women had been, if not successful, abandoned. The sympathy which was a source of benefit to the women when they shared its effects with men, seldom proved as welcome when directed exclusively towards themselves.

The exclusion of women from certain branches of work by the action of men's organizations has continued to be effective, to a considerable extent, and legislative prohibition of their employment in particular trades or processes has been recently extended, in accordance with the Washington (International Labour Organization) Convention of 1919. Such exclusion has undoubtedly had some effect in stabilizing men's wage-rates in monopolized trades or processes ; but the practicability and success of the policy are limited. The constant changes of industrial processes, the introduction of new machines, and the increasing stringency of supervision and regulation of

[1] *History of Trade Unionism*, pp. 310–11.

I

industry by the State in the interests of all workers, without distinction of sex, make it increasingly difficult for the Trade Unionist to put up a reasoned defence against the introduction, or even substitution of men by women, where the employer wishes to effect this change.

From the earliest days of Trade Unionism it was recognized that an alternative policy existed, to prevent women undercutting men's employment, namely, to organize, and urge women to organize, to secure equal pay. We have seen that the London silk-weavers were among the first to attempt the exclusion of women from the better-paid classes of work, but when their attempts were not successful they secured from Parliament the famous Spitalfields Acts, by which magistrates were empowered to regulate their wages. The wage-regulations which followed were made without regard for sex.[1] Until the Acts were repealed half a century later, the London silk-weavers were comparatively prosperous, in spite of general depression of trade towards the close of the period. After the repeal of the Acts, a very great reduction of wages took place. In 1834 nearly 900 men, women and children of the district (Bethnal Green) were in the workhouse (" chiefly operatives in the silk business "), while over 6,000 persons (mostly weavers and their dependents) were receiving out-door relief.[2]

Among the Lancashire cotton weavers, equal pay between men and women has had a longer trial. In this trade the men for a long time refused to go into the factories, but competed with the manufacturers by working on hand-looms at home. By the time they were forced into centralized industry, the women's right to employment could not be denied, wages had been standardized at the women's level, and competition with the besieged domestic workers had forced the manufacturers to cut

---

[1] See Pinchbeck, *op. cit.*, pp. 177–8, quoting Sholl, *Short History of the Silk Manufacture*. It would seem that until 1811 it was taken for granted that wages as regulated would be paid without distinction of sex, but that on a master refusing then to pay a journeywoman the regular wage, an Amending Act was passed, " enabling women to obtain their price under the same pains and penalties as the men ".

[2] *Ibid.*, pp. 176–7 n.

even these wages as low as possible. But strong organization of the two sexes combined, working on a basis of piece-work rates without distinction of sex, served to raise the cotton-weavers' wage-level until, by the early twentieth century it was, for women, on the average a high one, and probably a fair average for the men employed, as compared with that of men of corresponding skill in other industries.

For the last half-century, however, it is probably the Engineering trades which have been the most important in determining the official Trade Union attitude to women's labour. During the 'eighties, the men's Metal Unions of the Midlands made great efforts to prevent the employment of women altogether, which efforts met with determined opposition from the women's representatives at the Trade Union Congress. As a compromise, a resolution was passed in 1888, to the effect that " where women do the same work as men, they should receive equal pay ". This remains the official policy of Trade Unionism, and similar resolutions were passed by a number of individual Unions, though constantly rejected by others to the present day.

In supporting the resolution a certain Juggins, secretary of the Nut and Bolt Makers, who had been the leader of the party which opposed "the iniquitous system of female labour ", explained "that he had come to the conclusion that nothing but better pay for women could cure the evil, and they had therefore resolved to organize women as soon as possible ".[1]

The resolution was somewhat ambiguous. Trade Unionism is based on the application of the standard rate and the common rule ; its principles demand equal pay according to the job, the time worked, or by uniform piece-rates, irrespective of the capacity or bargaining power of the individual worker. Unless the same principles were intended to be applied to the work of women, the formula could have no useful meaning. But on whatever lines the phrase " the same work " was to be interpreted, it

[1] *Women in Trade Unions*, p. 20.

was obvious that any attempt to put it into practice
would depend for success on the women being organized
on the same lines, and in co-operation with men. The
Trade Union organization of women, which compared
with that of men was little more than embryonic, received
a great impetus. The meteoric and successful strike of
the previously unorganized girl Matchmakers, unexpectedly
brought about by the journalism of Mrs. Annie Besant
in the same year as the Trade Union Congress registered
the resolution on equal pay, added to the impulse. The
movement to bring women into the Trade Union world
merged into the new wave of activity and the new Union
outlook which was sweeping in great numbers of unskilled
workers who had before been (intentionally) untouched
by the gospel of organization.

"The plumber vied with the engineer, the carpenter with
the shipwright, in helping to form Unions among the labourers
who work with or under them. And the struggling Unions
of women workers, which had originally some difficulty in
gaining admittance to Trades Councils and the Trade Union
Congress, gratefully acknowledged a complete change in the
attitude of their male fellow-workers. Not only was every
assistance now given to the formation of special Unions
among women workers, but women were, in some cases,
even welcomed as members by Unions of skilled artisans." [1]

But sometimes the new enthusiasm did not reach as
far as the women, and the old antagonism to their competition remained.

"The whole constitution of the Amalgamated Society of
Engineers was, in 1892, revised for the express purpose of
opening the ranks of this most aristocratic of Unions to
practically all the mechanics in the innumerable branches
of the engineering trade." [2]

But the women remained unrecognized by the Society,
and other Metal Unions took the same line as the A.S.E.
A campaign to enlist women workers in separate craft
Unions, or in a general women's Union (the National
Federation of Women Workers) proved a difficult task.

[1] *History of Trade Unionism*, p. 421.   [2] *Ibid.*, p. 420.

The organization of women in Trade Unions is, in fact, very much more difficult than that of men. The lower average age of the workers ; their attitude to their work (the view that it is not likely to be their permanent source of livelihood) ; the domestic duties they almost all accept as having prior claims to those of public life, and the greater diffidence in public affairs which convention has long imposed, and still to some extent occasions—all these conditions act as a special bar to the enlistment and the strength of women in Trade Unions. Until the establishment of Trade Boards, and still to a great extent afterwards, the extremely low pay received by many women was a further bar to organization, because it pre⁕ vented the expenditure of the most meagre amount on contributions.

Substantial results have followed unremitting efforts of the last half-century to organize women workers. The Trade Union movement has been served in this field by some of its most able, sympathetic and forceful leaders —Miss Mary Macarthur, Mrs. Margaret MacDonald, Miss Margaret Bondfield, Miss Susan Lawrence, Miss Gertrude Tuckwell, and others who are following in their footsteps. The establishment of Trade Boards in the worst " sweated " industries has raised many women's wages sufficiently to permit them to contribute a few pence a week without the difficulties of earlier times. There was a great increase of enthusiasm and numbers of women Trade Unionists during the war period. Nevertheless, the proportion of women organized in Trade Unions remains low compared with the proportion of men.

Many of the important Unions, including the Metal Unions whose opposition to the labour of women led to the Congress resolution, remained exclusively men's organizations, and the attempts to organize women so as to secure equal pay when on " the same work ", had to be directed to the formation of separate Unions, or recruitment to a general Women's Union. The Union of Women Chain-makers at Cradley Heath was one of the separate Unions in the Metal Industry. But the wages of women chain-makers remained scandalously low despite their organization, until they were covered by the 1909 Trade Boards Act.

The wages of unskilled or semi-skilled workers in general have risen compared with those of skilled men, during the last half-century ; and women, who are mostly semi-skilled workers in industry, have benefited in the general lift. But the Congress resolution on equal pay has been little more than a dead letter. If no other policy had been possible—if there had been no tradition or alternative of attempted exclusion—the men might have invited the women workers into joint Unions throughout industry, organized them in the manner of the large amalgamated Textile Unions, and secured equal pay with their co-operation. But where the demand for equal pay was to depend on the organization of the women, acting separately though in co-operation with the men, it had rarely a hope of success, for the organized strength of the women, proportionately to their numbers, was much less.

Even in those industries where the men and women are jointly organized, it frequently occurs that lip-service only is paid to the ideal of Equal Pay, and in practice little attempt is made to secure it. The Trade Union negotiator who represents his members is out for the best he can get for them. He is not prepared to sacrifice pounds to principles ; he may *reculer pour mieux sauter*, but only when he can see where the last leap is likely to land him. The aggregate cash benefit of equal pay, to the workers, seems highly problematical ; whereas the average employer, even if he employs men, recognizes a social obligation to pay a man more than a woman, of the same grade of life, or doing the same work. What, in terms of cash, is the workers' representative to demand : that the employer should pay all his employees the amount he is (perhaps reluctantly) willing to pay the men, or that he should scale the men down and the women up to an intermediate level—a level less than that on which the men have been saying they can fulfil their minimum (standard) obligations ?

The National Union of Shop Assistants, Clerks and Warehousemen offers a case in point. Large numbers of men and women are organized in this Union. The difficulties, such as undercutting of wages, which would be obviated by the payment of equal rates for similar work, are recognized by the Union, which has adopted in its programme the policy of Equal Pay; but in practice the officers find they can but accept a minimum weekly wage, for Shop Assistants, which differentiates between adult men and women to the extent of about £1 a week. Reserves of unorganized labour, male and female, willing to accept lower rates respectively, make it sufficiently hard work for the Union to secure the standards set, and they see little hope of general advantage for their members in objecting to sex-differentiation.

It would be easy, but futile, to condemn such action as hypocritical; to point to the Equal Pay resolution on the Union's programme, and compare the demands actually put forward in negotiation. Before taking this line, however, let us consider the action of the Trade Boards when faced with this same problem of the relation between men's and women's rates. Each Board is a body consisting of representatives of employers, workers (who before the establishment of the Board have been only poorly, if at all, organized) and impartial members, appointed by the Minister of Labour. Though the members of the Board have little reason to take account of the Trade Union Congress resolution in favour of Equal Pay, they may be supposed to hold in respect the similar principle laid down in the International Labour Convention of Versailles, 1919.

"One of the fundamental problems which issues from attempts at rate fixing," writes Miss Sells, in her book on *The British Trade Boards System*, "is the relation between the prescribed rates of wages for men and women. *No underlying principle is evident in the determinations of the Boards as a whole.* Although it cannot be said that in either case wages have always been prescribed which actually meet the money requirements of a living wage for a man with a family to support, or of a single woman living alone, it is these two ideas which Trade Boards, since 1918, seem to have had in mind as a foundation upon which to fix men's and women's wages, respectively. However, the compromise which is incident to collective bargaining in the Board Meetings, the economic conditions of a particular trade or other circumstances, may so alter the original wage scheme that some of the rates are thrown entirely out of plumb with these ideas. In several trades where men's and women's work is clearly differentiated, for instance, it appears that the men workers have compromised by allowing the women's rates to be set at a low figure in order to keep their own wages up.[1] Employers in a number of trades where women workers are predominant are willing to agree to such an arrangement, because it reduces their total wages bill.

The principles of equal pay for the job and equal pay for equal work have been brought up again and again, but for the most part it has seemed an impractical basis for wage adjustment for the reason that women seldom do exactly the same work as men. In the case of four trades, viz. Boot and Shoe Repairing, Brush and Broom-making, Fur-dressing, and Sugar Confectionery manufacture, the same time rates of wages have been prescribed for both men and women who are engaged upon certain jobs where the work is the same. In two of these trades the object in fixing the same rates for both men and women is generally believed to have been to protect the male workers, and thus far the operation of the rates in one trade, at least, appears to have led to a readjustment of the work in the trade as between men and women. The object of the Sugar Confectionery Board in prescribing the same rates of wages for women as for men who are engaged in . . . occupations . . . which are ordinarily known as men's occupations . . . was honestly to apply the principle of equal pay for the job.

The principle of equal pay for equal output is recognized by those Boards . . . which have fixed the same piece rates for women as for men. Relatively speaking, there are fewer men than women engaged upon a piece basis, and even piece tasks are usually different for the two sexes, so that it is not often feasible even to prescribe like piece prices for men and women.

Equal pay for equal value, which is the principle incorporated in the recommendations regarding International Labour Standards of the Treaty of Versailles, is sometimes

[1] A woman Trade Union officer comments on this, that the women's representatives may have made similar suggestions to maintain the women's wage-levels at the expense of the men's.

stated by persons connected with Trade Boards to be the general principle upon which Trade Boards endeavour to work. If this general principle is to be applied in fixing time-rates, presuming that it means equal value in quality and quantity, it should be preceded by job analysis and tests for the purpose of discovering just what are the relative values of male and female workers on a given job. In no case known to the writer has such a scientific inquiry been undertaken by a Trade Board.[1]

When the application of any one of these principles has seemed inexpedient or has failed, it is customary for the workers' side to demand four-fifths . . . or five-sixths . . . of the male time-rate for female workers upon the basis of the cost of living for a woman living alone, but this has not often been granted.

An analysis of the relation between the male and female general minimum time-rates shows that female rates most nearly approximate to male rates in Boot and Shoe Repairing, e.g. 70 per cent. . . . the lowest of all being Coffin Furniture, at 49·1 per cent. The average of these percentages is 57·6 per cent., and the average weekly wage of women is 29s. as opposed to 52s. for men. . . . If we compare these results with the average for all trades in 1914, given by the War Cabinet Committee on Women in Industry as rather less than 50 per cent., some progress seems to have been made over pre-War days, though the percentage is not so high . . . as in 1918, when the women's wage stood at rather more than 66·3 per cent. of the men's."[2]

So one finds that the relation between men's and women's wages under Trade Board regulation is very similar to their relation under conditions of collective bargaining. Equal Pay for men and women is recognized, in a somewhat hazy, ambiguous way, as an ideal ; there are exceptional instances of its practice ; but the pressure of other economic interests in most cases prevents its realization.

It has already been noted that in the Cotton-weaving branch of the Lancashire textile industry, an important exception is found to the general rule ; men and women are employed on similar work, and remunerated according to identical piece-work rates. It is significant that

---

[1] Nor are instances reported of men's wage-rates being fixed, or there being any suggestion that they should be fixed, lower than women's in industries where the woman's output is suspected to be higher.

[2] *The British Trade Boards System*, by D. Sells, pp. 153–5.

in this district, and especially in this industry, it is customary for women to remain at or return to work after marriage.

The more commonly accepted convention that women retire from work after marriage, to be maintained on their husband's wages, is among the most important factors preventing the application of the widely accepted ideal of equal pay, or its substitution as a practical policy alternative to restriction of admission or training of women for well-paid work. Those who desire equal pay have a very direct concern in the customs and laws of marriage. The possibility of some practical reconciliation between the conflicting ideals of Equal Pay and the Wife's Personal Care of her Home is considered in later chapters.

It is significant that in spite of considerable strain, the Trade Union movement maintains its solidarity, and does not irrevocably split along the line of sex. The women workers, as daughters often partially dependent, and prospectively dependent wives, sympathize with the men's demand for preferential employment and/or higher pay. The division of their sympathies is an important element in mitigating the shock of conflict. It increases the difficulty of securing representation of the point of view of the woman worker *qua* worker, and so tends to make women's wage-rates and opportunities dependent on the men's demand or permission, rather than on the women's organization.

The conventions of civil marriage are thus in yet another way an important factor within the Trade Union movement in standardizing low wages for women. Professor Sargent Florence, in a recent article in the *Economic Journal* (March 1931) has developed the view that they are the most important factor, and that the importance of Trade Union or other " artificial " limitations on the occupational field open to women has been over-estimated.

Briefly, his argument is as follows : the generally accepted theory that the low wages of women are due to the restricted occupational field open to them, offers an insufficient explanation. The restrictions imposed by men's Trade Unions on women's employment would soon be overridden by employers, at least to a much greater extent than they now are, if there were not other influences at work. For the cheapness of women's work (the lowness of their " efficiency wage ") is in many instances real enough, and appreciated as such by employers. The main class of work in which both men and women are employed is, broadly speaking, semi-skilled work, for which the period of training is short, so that a comparatively quick labour-turnover, such as occurs especially with women workers, is not of very great importance. In the general wages system ruling in most industrial countries, semi-skilled women's wages are, in fact, below unskilled men's wages, and probably only 50–70 per cent. of the wages of similarly skilled men.

But the women's " supply-price curve " is peculiar. There are a considerable number of women readily available for industrial employment at this comparatively low wage, but the supply is definitely limited, and when the limit is reached, women are only obtainable at a price higher than any " likely to be thought reasonable in business circles ". The women willing to accept low wages are (in general) the unmarried women ; the latter are (in general) the married women. There is a wide gulf fixed between the price which each of these groups set upon their labour, and in consequence only the former group is actually called into the labour market under anything like normal conditions.

The conflict between the economic interests of the man and woman worker in industry certainly exists, and may be severe, but is limited in extent by the limited effective supply of female labour, and may therefore be much exaggerated by observers who note the comparative cheapness of the women's wages, and the restrictions imposed by men's Trade Unions.

" It is usually assumed that the economic forces of supply and demand act antagonistically to the male Trade Unionist position ; that the demand for women's labour, based on women's apparently superior efficiency in relation to wage, will inevitably undermine the attempt to restrict women's employment. Within limits this assumption is, I think, valid. A certain supply of women can be obtained cheap, and the men's Trade Union wage will be undercut—but only up to a point. And if this point were not soon reached I do not think Trade Union restrictions on the employment of women would avail. In fact, however, once a certain number of women is absorbed by industry, the remainder do not clamour to overcome Trade Union barriers.

For the supply of women available for employment cheap in any one area is strictly limited by certain institutional factors. This . . . in the last resort is perhaps the most important factor in the situation."

With this explanation of the economic situation, in its general outline, I find myself in agreement. But I think any analysis of the problem which treats it as though the psychological element were essentially static, leads to an underestimate of the effect of Trade Union and other " artificial " restrictions on women's work. Professor Sargent Florence infers a comparison between the influence of such restrictions and the influence of " institutional factors " (such as the working-class convention of marriage-retirement for women) on the low wages of women, and concludes that the former are of less importance than the latter. But these forces do not act independently. Marriage, for natural, sentimental, and conventional reasons, raises the value of a woman's domestic work. Restrictions on women's industrial employment prevent them from fitting themselves for, or having any expectation of securing, the better-paid industrial jobs. Women cannot therefore expect to secure work at what would be, from *their* point of view, and that of their family, a reasonable wage, after marriage. This fact has considerable influence on the orientation of their life, and on their upbringing. They prepare their minds for a non-industrial adult life, take less interest in industrial employment while they are engaged in it, and are inclined to demand less from it, individually and collectively, than they would if they were presented with more opportunities for rising to well-paid work, and if retirement were consequently less taken for granted.

Thus the gulf which inevitably separates the supply price of the unmarried woman from that of the wife is artificially widened as a result of the restrictions placed upon the latter's opportunity to qualify for good wages, and these restrictions have a certain indirect effect on women's wage-rates over and above the very limited direct effect Professor Sargent Florence seems to attribute to them.

The conflict between the interests of men and women in industry, in its modern form, arose in consequence of the centralization and capitalization of industry which was a part of the Industrial Revolution. The Trade Union movement, which until about 1870 was almost exclusively a male activity, arose as a result of the same developments. Since the earliest days of the movement the undercutting of men's wages and employment by women has been recognized as one of the chief menaces to the working-class standard of life. Attempts have been made to counteract it in various ways. Many of the Unions have, at one time or another, sought to prevent the employment of women in their particular industry altogether, and the suggestion has been made that they should be prohibited all industrial employment. Or the Unions have sought to exclude women from the better-paid branches of work ; or they have sought to secure, through joint or co-operating organization, equal wages for men and women so that the women should have no preference in employment. At the least, higher wages, if still unequal, have been sought for the women. In all these methods some successes can be registered. With the aid of other social forces, women have been entirely excluded from some branches of industry in which they were formerly occupied ; in many industries or factories the better-paid work is not considered " women's work " ; and instances exist of adult women's wages being fixed and maintained on an equal level with men's, and of the joint efforts of men and women securing a rise in the woman's wage-level.

The struggle has been a constant feature of the Trade

Union movement. At no time has the menace ceased. The extent and severity of the conflict is at normal times limited, but it continues to exist as a drag on the workers' standard of life. Men's wages are maintained at the expense of the women's, but the conventionally low wages of women are a danger to the men. They are an especial danger to the general standard of life in times of depression, when the lowness of a man's wages or unemployment pay may force domestic women into industry at equally low or lower wages, thus flooding the market with cheap labour over and above the normal supply, and further delaying wage-recovery. (This aspect of the question has not been discussed in the present chapter, but is deferred to Chapter XII.)

The existence of this menace is not due to the Trade Unions. Although the effect of action taken by men's organizations for the past century and more has probably been, on the whole, to depress the price of women's work, the primary inequality of price between women's work and their own, which is the cause of the conflict, arises independently of their actions, through the survival of an older economic relationship between the sexes, into an era of industrial civilization.

CHAPTER VIII

INDUSTRIAL LEGISLATION AND WOMEN'S WORK

Industrial legislation differentiating between men and women—its paternal character—genuinely or hypocritically benevolent—international scope—conventions and recommendations of I.L.O.—differential legislation in Great Britain—differentiation in law but not in practice—effect of such legislation on women's employment —pros and cons of differentiation—conclusions.

It has been recorded in the last chapter that men's Trade Unions have in the past occasionally made attempts to preserve their members' standard of life from the danger of competition with cheap female labour by means of legislation ostensibly framed in the interests of the women workers themselves. It would, however, be a mistake to suppose that the workers' organizations have been the chief instruments in securing differences in industrial legislation as between men and women. Public sentiment, informed and led by disinterested men of the upper and middle classes, was the primary force which, early in the nineteenth century, began to break down the barriers set up by the *laissez-faire* principle against administrative interference with industry. There is no doubt that Lord Shaftesbury and others who worked with him genuinely believed, and many men and women still believe, that it is important in the interests of the women workers, and of the race, that women should be protected from the evils of unfettered industrial competition.

In the 1840's, when some of the most notable differential legislation was passed, excluding or exempting women from the evils known to men to exist in the conditions of work in factories and mines, very little indeed was being done to secure their life and health, or their children's, in their alternative work-place, the home. The tale of the birth-rate and conditions of birth, the infant mortality rate and conditions of death, and the housing conditions in industrial towns, up till 1870 and later, will paint for future generations a picture of domestic misery of this period, beside which the tale of long factory hours and foul ventilation in workrooms will sound only as a recognized Hell set down beside an unrecognized Inferno. To realize this, however, is not to deny the genuine goodwill towards women workers, and the real concern for the future of the race, which provided the incentive for early industrial legislation differentiating between the sexes. Victorian laws might be sincerely devised for, but never by, women.

There is now on the Statute book a considerable body of legislation, and there exist a large number of Home Office regulations, discriminating between men and women as workers. Some of the legislation dates from the days when Government interference with industry was considered only permissible, if at all, in the case of women and children ; some is more recent, subsequent to the abandonment of this view, and some is subsequent to the enfranchisement of women in 1918. No woman under 30 years of age, however, had a vote in Great Britain until 1928. As a very high proportion of the women employed in industry at any one time are under 30, industrial legislation has always been, so far as women are concerned, paternal, or at best (or worst) elder-sisterly, in character. The laws have been made to deal with a group of persons not represented in the legislature when they were made.

From the careful and intentional limitations of its beginnings, Factory Legislation has grown to include within its scope every manual worker in every manufacturing industry. Already in 1910, Mr. Sidney Webb (now Lord Passfield) wrote :

" The range of Factory Legislation has, in fact, in one country or another, become co-extensive with the conditions of industrial employment . . . and the advantage of Factory Legislation is now as soundly ' orthodox ' among the present

generation of English, German and American professors as
'laissez-faire' was to their predecessors." [1]

The original principle which forbade the inclusion of
men in the scope of Factory Legislation has been abandoned, but the practice of legislating specifically for women
has not. It has, in fact, been given renewed impetus in
this country by international action, which originated on
the initiative of the Swiss and German Governments in
1890. It was a matter of importance for nations engaged
in commercial rivalry, and yet desirous of safeguarding
the recruitment of their population, that no commercial
loss should be suffered by a nation which ceased to ex-
ploit its women workers. At the Conference which met
at Berlin in 1890, the industrial protection of women
occupied the foremost place on the agenda. When the
permanent International Labour Organization of the
League of Nations was established by the Treaty of Versailles (Part XIII) in 1919, it was stated in the Preamble
to that Part, that "an improvement . . . is urgently
required" in the conditions of work of "children, young
persons and women".

Among the nine General Principles enumerated for the
guidance of the I.L.O., the following are specially relevant to women's work :—

"Men and women should receive equal remuneration for
work of equal value." (Seventh.)

"The standard set by law in each country with respect
to the conditions of labour should have due regard to
the equitable economic treatment of all workers lawfully
resident therein." (Eighth.)

"Each State should make provision for a system of
inspection in which women should take part, in order to
ensure the enforcement of the laws and regulations for the
protection of the employed." (Ninth.)

Among the Conventions and Recommendations adopted
at Conferences of the I.L.O., which particularly refer to
women workers, are the following :—

[1] Webb, Sidney, Preface to Hutchins and Harrison, *History of Factory
Legislation*, p. viii.

K

1. *Maternity Convention,* adopted at Washington, 1919. Making provision for a woman to be absent from commercial or industrial work for six weeks after confinement (compulsorily), and six weeks before confinement is expected, and laying down that during the whole period of such absence adequate benefits shall be paid for the maintenance of mother and child. *Ratified by eleven States, not including Great Britain.*

2. *Night Work Convention,* adopted at Washington, 1919. Prohibiting the employment of women at night (10 p.m. to 5 a.m., plus four hours in addition, all taken consecutively) in industrial undertakings. *Ratified by nineteen States, including Great Britain.*

3. *Employment in Unhealthy Processes.* A Recommendation adopted at Washington, 1919, referred to the prohibition of the employment of women in any industry dealing with lead oxide. The *White Lead Convention,* adopted in 1921, regulated the use of paint containing white lead or lead compounds, and prohibited the employment of women on work in which such paint was used. *Ratified by nineteen States, not including Great Britain ; but Great Britain, by the* Lead Paint (Protection against Poisoning) Act (1926), *gave effect to the Convention so far as concerned the prohibition of women's work.*

The following Conventions do not particularly refer to women, but, owing to the conditions of women's work, affect them especially :—

4. *Hours Convention,* adopted at Washington, 1919. Limiting hours of work in industrial undertakings (with certain specified exceptions) to 8 per day and 48 per week. *Ratified unconditionally by nine countries, not including Great Britain ;* and by France and Italy, conditionally on ratification by Great Britain, Germany and Switzerland.

5. *Minimum Wage Convention,* adopted in 1928. Requiring that in industries poorly organized, and in which wages are exceptionally low, the minimum wage paid should be adequate to maintain a reasonable standard of living, as this is understood in the time and country in question. Home work (industrial) is particularly referred to. The final paragraph of a Recommendation accompanying the Convention states that the Conference " thinks it right to call the attention of Governments to the principle . . . that men and women should receive equal remuneration for work of equal value ".[1]

[1] *The International Labour Organization, The First Decade,* 1931 (I.L.O.). See especially Part II, Chap. I, and Part III.

In Great Britain legislation differentiating between men and women does not follow exactly the lines of the Conventions and Recommendations of the I.L.O. Much of our industrial legislation preceded the establishment of the International Organization, some by as much as a century, and some of the most important by thirty years and more. In some respects it is more far-reaching, both for all workers and for women exclusively.

Reference has already been made to the prohibition of women's work underground in mines (which, however, does not apply to the Indian Empire). The length of the working-day or week, overtime, and night-work, are limited for women under the Factory Acts, and under these Acts the Home Secretary may also make orders with regard to the welfare of workers in dangerous trades, and may regulate or prohibit the employment of women exclusively in such trades. Under the Police, Factories (Miscellaneous) Provisions Act (1916), orders may also be made in respect of trades other than those scheduled as dangerous. Under these Acts women are excluded by Orders from a number of industrial processes, many of such processes being concerned with the use of lead in some form, and in addition their employment is further regulated or prohibited under the Women and Young Persons (Employment in Lead Processes) Acts of 1920 and 1926, and the Lead Paint (Protection against Poisoning) Act (1926).[1]

The provisions of our Trade Boards Acts are in many respects similar to the requirements of the I.L.O. Minimum Wage Convention.

The limitation set by law to the number of hours a woman may work per day or per week in factories is (in Great Britain at the present time) so wide, compared with current practice, that it does not seem to result in actual differentiation between the sexes. The hours legally permitted to women are 72 per week (except in certain classes of work in which regulation of hours—not always

---

[1] *The Woman Worker and Restrictive Legislation*, by J. Blainey, provides a useful summary of this type of legislation.

identical for men and women—has been made for all workers). The working week recognized as normal is 48 hours, so that the hours allowed to women permit of them working for time which is reckoned as overtime in the trade, though not by law. The limitation of their overtime therefore is not in practice an occasion of differentiation between them and male workers.

A Factories Bill presented to Parliament in 1926 proposed the limitation of a 48-hour week for women only. This distinction between the sexes is not in accordance with the Washington Hours Convention. If it were carried, it might result in a certain amount of practical differentiation between men and women workers, and would at the same time set a seal on the non-ratification of the Convention by other European powers which have made their ratification dependent on our own.

Acute difference of opinion has arisen in this country as to the effect of differential industrial legislation on the general welfare of women as workers. The early history of these differences has been touched upon in the previous chapter. Briefly, it may be said that there have always been bodies, some composed chiefly of women, which have opposed differentiation between men and women in industrial laws, either with reference to industrial employment in general or to certain employments in particular.

In the past on a number of occasions women workers, organized and unorganized, have initiated or joined in such opposition. The present official view of the Industrial Women's Organizations (as expressed through their Standing Joint Committee [1]) is, however, that protective legislation is a good thing, whether applied exclusively to one group of workers or to all ; and that differences in industrial legislation for men and women have not had any harmful effect on the economic position of women workers, although if enacted without good reason such differential legislation might have such effect. The Com-

---

[1] *Protective Legislation and Women Workers*, by the Standing Joint Committee of Industrial Women's Organizations.

mittee considers that good reasons for supporting such legislation are (a) that the law would be beneficial for all workers, but owing to the state of public opinion can only be obtained for women at the present time ; (b) that the regulation in question is more needed for women than for men owing to differences in the constitution of the sexes ; (c) that the regulation in question is necessary for the protection of the functions of motherhood.

In 1930 the Home Office published a White Paper [1] in answer to objections to the system of making distinctions in industrial legislation as between men and women. The distribution of women in industry was discussed with reference to the allegation that such legislation restricted women's opportunities of employment, and some interesting statistics were presented of the growth or decline of male and female employment in a selected group of industries. These statistics showed an increase of female employment (and in some cases an increase in the proportion of females employed) in a number of these industries since 1890. The conclusion inferred was that differential legislation had not resulted in restriction or diminution of the employment of women compared with that of men.

The facts presented, though valuable in themselves to students of the economic position of women, could not, however, be considered as conclusive of the effect of differential legislation on women's employment or economic position in general. No reliable general conclusion could be reached by a study of selected industries exclusively. No estimate was or could be made of the effect of total prohibition of women's work (as in mines underground, and in lead processes) on their opportunities for employment, and thus on the relation between demand and supply of women's labour, and thence on their wage-rates. This factor is of varying importance in different localities, and of great importance in some ; and in this

[1] *A Study of the Factors . . . operating . . . to Determine the Distribution of Women in Industry*, Home Office, 1930, Cmd. 3508, H.M.S.O., pp. 20, 23 ; 11, 18.

connection the limited mobility of women's labour must be taken into account. No account was taken of the effect of fluctuations in trade-prosperity on the proportionate employment of the sexes in industry (a subject discussed later, in Chapter XI), which might result in a student reaching quite different conclusions according to the years taken for comparison. Finally, no comparison was or could be made of the actual figures of female employment under the present system, and those which would have prevailed if legislation differentiating between men and women workers had not existed.

Some of the evidence pointed to a certain loss of employment on the part of women workers owing to the prohibition of their work at night. Instances were given of the employment of men on night-shifts in work customarily carried on by women, in the hosiery and artificial silk trades. In the flax and jute trade, and the tinplate industry, instances were given of the complete substitution of male for female workers in work which is carried on by both day- and night-shifts.

The chief motives for enacting or maintaining industrial legislation differentiating between men and women at the present time fall under three heads :—(a) that the legislature is under special obligation to protect one sex rather than the other ; (b) that regulation is more necessary for one sex than the other owing to differences in their constitution ; (c) that regulation is necessary so as to give protection to the function of motherhood. And behind all these premises lies the major premise that the economic strength of the worker, and particularly of the woman worker, is not sufficient to ensure her securing individual or social welfare through the free play of economic forces.

Arguments in favour of legislating for women specially, may be advanced under all these heads, with reference to industries in general or in particular. It may be pointed out (a) that the economic position of women bequeathed to us by the ages is so inferior to that of men, and the Trade Union organization of women is as a rule also so inferior, that it is necessary for them to be additionally protected from exploitation. In the words of the late

Professor Knowles, " The unions were the masculine side of the Factory Acts." [1]

With regard to (b) (the greater harmfulness of certain kinds of work for women than for men), the Standing Joint Committee of Industrial Women's Organizations state that " under this heading comes the exemption of women from all forms of active service ; [2] their prohibition in dangerous industrial processes, such as work in underground mines, outside window cleaning, the cleaning of dangerous machinery ; also . . . the lifting of heavy weights, exposure to excessive heat, and the handling of poisonous substances which may be specially injurious to women. The prohibition of night-work, in so far as night-work is necessary, may be placed in the same category."

Under the third head (c) fall some of the most powerful arguments in favour of differential legislation. The effect of certain kinds of employment on the boy and man as potential parent are little known, but there can be no doubt that some occupations have a harmful effect on the potential, and the expectant, mother. In general, it seems probable that long hours of sedentary work, or work underground, or perhaps even in poor or artificial light indoors, especially during adolescence, may be expected to have a deleterious effect on the maternal function. Certain particular processes are also supposed to have especially evil results for mother and offspring, and also employment of the mother too soon after childbirth.

The prohibition of women's work underground in mines may be justified under this head, and could be the more justified in the days when it was first enacted, when conditions were much worse than they are now. The prohibition of long hours of indoor work (e.g. more than the 72 per week now allowed under the Factories Acts, or

---

[1] *The Industrial and Commercial Revolutions in Great Britain during the Nineteenth Century*, by L. C. A. Knowles.

[2] The view of the Industrial Women's Organizations is here recorded. To the author it appears doubtful, however, whether legal differentiation between the employment of men and women is indeed to be justified, or ever need be based, on this ground. The inclusion of active service under this head seems particularly questionable. Death or mutilation are as harmful to men, individually, as to women : it is the greater danger to racial survival through exposure of the latter to risk which is the deciding factor.

the 74 per week under the Shop Acts) may also be justified by reference to the woman's function of motherhood, more especially because many " women " in industry are still, or still should be, growing. But there is no need in this case to put forward this special justification, or any justification that differentiates between men and women. For the men's Trade Unions ("the masculine side of the Factory Acts") have secured a working-day in most industries short enough to suit the needs of womanhood, under present standards, and much shorter than the day permitted to women by law.

The history of the Short-Time movement thus suggests a method of avoiding differentiation without relinquishing necessary protection of the worker ; a method already advocated by some opponents of differentiation. By enacting legislation which, for men, might sometimes be unnecessary—because they could obtain as good conditions by Trade Union action—differentiation might be avoided. It is not generally thought necessary, and if not necessary, inadvisable, to enact in legal form regulations which men's Trade Unions could secure for themselves by collective bargaining. But there are now strong arguments in favour of such a course :—(1) discrimination between men and women workers then becomes impossible by law, and does not depend upon the varying strength or will of the men's organizations ; (2) international legislation for the protection of all workers is facilitated.

This aspect of the problem of differentiation may also be studied in connection with the Trade Boards Acts. The agitation which led to the establishment of Trade Boards was almost entirely based on public disapproval of the conditions of women's work in "sweated" industries, but neither the Acts nor the administration of them have dealt with women exclusively.

Much legislation (though not all) which now differentiates between men and women might well be applied to both sexes, and it is a strong reason for doing this if differentiation be considered unfortunate in itself. There are many reasons for considering it to be so—

for considering that differentiation between men and women as workers is an attempt to treat a social disease by mitigating the effect of its symptoms only, while the ill itself remains untouched by such treatment, or even stimulated to increased activity.

The Washington Convention prohibiting the employment of women at night has been ratified by a great many States, including Great Britain. Prohibition of night-work for women is based on the view that it is more harmful to the health of women than of men to work at night. It is not easy to determine, however, from the views expressed by medical experts, whether this difference between the sexes is to be assigned to physiological causes, or should be attributed to social conventions which provide a different environment for the woman night-worker during the daytime from that which a man usually enjoys. It seems probable that women certain of returning home to a cooked meal, a bed prepared for them, and complete lack of responsibility for domestic chores, might be employed on night-work as harmlessly to themselves and as efficiently as industrial men and professional nurses are now. There are doubtless wide divergencies in individual adaptability for night work, but under circumstances admitting of scientific comparison, it might be found that the sex-correlation was not high.

Other prohibitions relating to women's industrial work present similar problems. It is not easy to disentangle the effect of social conventions from the consequences of different physique or function ; and it may be suggested that if the social environment were less dissimilar there would be less call for differential treatment in industry. For instance, British legislation nearly a century old prohibits women from cleaning machinery while it is in motion. One of the reasons originally given for this enactment was that " the customary dress of girls and women made them especially liable to be caught by the machinery, and perhaps killed or seriously injured ".[1]

[1] *History of Factory Legislation*, p. 85.

That was an instance of genuine difference of ability between the sexes arising from, or being much increased by, not an innate difference of their constitution, but superficial conventions. Circumstances more intricately inherent in our present economic system, but nevertheless ultimately due rather to convention than nature, may similarly be responsible for the conditions which have led to the prohibition of women's work in many unhealthy processes. The most notable of these refer to the use of, or exposure to, lead and allied compounds. The prohibition of women's work in this connection is based on the view that women are specially susceptible to lead poisoning, and also that exposure to lead makes a woman liable to suffer miscarriage or stillbirth of children. But the view that women " exhibit a sexual proclivity of plumbism " is disputed by some of the highest experts on industrial medicine.[1] It is suggested that the supposition arose because, when early observations were made, the women employed were being paid very low wages, and were undernourished—a condition which renders both men and women susceptible to the disease. Apart from special proclivity to individual suffering, however, the effect of plumbism in causing miscarriage and stillbirth would seem a sufficient reason for prohibiting the employment of women in lead processes, but for the doubt whether lead poisoning of the father has not a similarly dangerous effect on the unborn child as poisoning through the mother. There is some evidence to show that the wives of men who work or worked in lead processes, as well as the women who (before prohibition) did so, suffer a high proportion of miscarriages and stillbirths.[2]

It may therefore be suggested with some reason that much differential legislation has been based on differences not inherent in the nature of the sexes, but arising from superficial features of civilized life which themselves might

[1] Collis and Greenwood, *Health of the Industrial Worker*, 1926, quoted by Blainey, *op. cit.*, p. 36.

[2] *Women and the Lead Paint (Protection against Poisoning) Bill*, pamphlet published by National Union of Societies for Equal Citizenship, 1926, p. 4.

have been, and perhaps were crying out to be, more fundamentally regulated. The long skirts and hair of the nineteenth-century female, the comparatively low wages and undernourishment of the woman worker, both nowadays and more especially before the 1914–1918 war, are not essential to womanhood, nor desirable accompaniments of female industry.

But, it may be replied, administration is a practical art, which cannot wait for the findings of science, or legislate for peoples living under hypothetical conditions. It must deal with them according to their sheep-like habits, even if those habits regard not social justice, uniformity, nor common sense. Machinery may hold out special dangers for women because they go to work in unsuitable clothes, or with long hair, but if it is the administrator's duty to protect the woman's safety equally with the man's, he is hardly to be blamed if he prohibit her tampering with the machinery, rather than insist that she should adopt the use of male attire. She might have preferred to die. If women workers in lead processes, being underpaid and undernourished, unable by social circumstances to procure adequate domestic service and consequently under-rested, submit to disease at a higher rate than men, it might be more logical to award them higher wages and draft a corps of general servants and infant nurses into their homes, or to organize communal homes and crèches for them, but such procedure scarcely falls within the bounds of practical politics.

But if administration is anything more than a practical art, the slow findings of science must be eventually used, and social habits gradually moulded, to make practicable a more desirable future. The physician must pay some attention to the disease, as well as to the symptoms. The weaknesses inherent in measures which differentiate between men and women in industry, if there be such weakness—the transitory nature of the circumstances on which they are based, if they be indeed based on transitory things rather than innate sexual constitutions—must be diagnosed, so that a more desirable state of affairs may be gradually brought about, or recognized when by social evolution it arrives.

Disadvantages inherent in the practice of excluding women from dangerous or unhealthy processes have been summarized by the International Labour Organization in a Report prepared for the Washington Conference—and they may well be applied also to the prohibition of night-work :—

> "There is . . . the way of . . . absolute prohibition of the employment of women in the (dangerous or unhealthy) process. This affords complete protection for the women who might otherwise have entered the industry to their hurt, and is so far satisfactory, but it is not without serious drawbacks. By its adoption, a number of avenues of employment, otherwise suitable for them, are closed to women ; manufacture loses a valuable potential supply of labour ; and—most unfortunate in its general effects—the unhealthiness of the trade or process is perhaps accepted as incurable, and its conditions are apt to become stereotyped for lack of incentive to improve them, with grievous results to the health of the men (and in some cases the boys) by whom they are exclusively staffed." [1]

Each of these three objections provides a forcible reason against differentiation. The restriction of women's opportunities of employment is without doubt one of the causes of their economic weakness (many economists have held that it is the chief cause of it) and leads to their industrial exploitation. Thus if any action promoted by national or international regulation further restricts such opportunities, it tends to increase the very condition which it is or should be its object to remove. [2]

The loss to manufacture of a valuable potential supply of labour may be recognized even by those who have scant sympathy with the individual manufacturer who has profited from the exploitation of female labour. Mrs.

---

[1] Report III of the League of Nations, on *The Employment of Women and Children and the Berne Conventions of* 1906, prepared for the International Labour Conference, Washington, 1919, p. 40.

[2] "The protection of the weak, and therefore of women as well as of children and young persons, is one of the fundamental principles underlying the movement which led to the creation of the I.L.O." (*Studies and Reports, Series I, No.* 1, I.L.O., 1921, p. 1.)

Webb, who will not be accused of lack of sympathy with the worker's point of view, has stated this consideration clearly :—

> " It is imperative, if we are to get the maximum production out of any given generation, that those who are responsible for the selection of workers, whether by hand or brain, for the several occupational grades, should be under no temptation to deviate from the rule of getting every task performed by the workers who are, in all respects, the most efficient for the purpose. (She therefore argues in favour of equal pay for men and women on similar work.) The same argument, in my opinion, condemns the idea of differentiating in the prescribed conditions of employment, notably as regards sanitation, amenity, and hours of labour, between men as such and women as such."

> . . . . .

> " I note with concern (she continues) that my colleagues . . . advocate the extension and elaboration of the regulations of the Factory Acts in the case of women only. . . . I think, on the contrary, that the consolidation of the Factory Acts should be made the occasion of sweeping away all special provisions differentiating men from women." [1]

A third disadvantage of differential industrial legislation, observed in the I.L.O. Report quoted, is the acceptance of bad conditions of work for the men and sometimes also the boys who continue to work in the industry or process from which women have been excluded. Unless the greater susceptibility or danger of women can be definitely proved (or the greater danger to the race through women), it is therefore a false chivalry which is satisfied with the exclusion of one sex, rather than a reduction of a common danger.

> " The officials of the men's Trade Unions often represent that such and such an occupation is ' unfit for women ' merely on the ground of its danger. Medical practitioners, usually men, have sometimes put forward a similar plea. But unless it can be shown that the danger is inherently and universally greater for women than for men, there seems no reason why any sex restriction should be imposed. What

[1] *Report of War Cabinet Committee on Women in Industry* (*Minority Report*), pp. 282–3. Mrs. Webb's advocacy of the abolition of differential legislation was closely linked with her proposals for equal pay per occupation.

the community has to do for dangerous occupations is to take care that all possible means are employed to reduce the danger to a minimum, and to provide full compensation for the victims—leaving then the occupation open so far as the law is concerned to such individuals of either sex as chose to engage in it.

There may conceivably be processes which are specially injurious to persons of the female sex, warranting some special provisions with regard to them. The chief case is that of working in lead, where it is said that women are specially susceptible to lead poisoning. I do not feel sure that what has been proved is a special susceptibility of the female sex. . . . The experience during the war . . . leads me to the inference—and this is the suggestion of women doctors who have served as medical officers of factories—that what is called for is not the exclusion from work of all persons of one sex, or even the subjecting of them to special restrictions, but the minute, careful and persistent observation . . . of the health and diathesis of the individual workers irrespective, of sex, and the application of such special precautions . . . as may be called for by the proved susceptibility of the several individuals affected, whether they are men or women." [1]

In addition to these admitted drawbacks to legislation discriminating between men and women workers there are dangers less direct which may arise from a policy based on statements referring in general terms to the weakness of women. The lessons of the war, and much of the experience of those concerned with women's health, tend to be overlooked unless this " weakness " of the woman worker is analysed. Before the war it was commonly accepted in England that light, sedentary, indoor work was most suitable for females. In the light of war-time experience, however, Dr. Janet Campbell reported :—

" The results of employment of women under war conditions emphasized the importance to health of the good food, clothing and domestic comfort which can be obtained when the wages represent a reasonably adequate recompense for labour. They have also proved that properly nourished women have a much greater reserve of energy than they have usually been credited with, and that under suitable conditions they can properly and advantageously be em-

[1] *Report of War Cabinet Committee on Women in Industry* (*Minority Report*), pp. 283-4,

ployed upon more arduous occupations than has been considered desirable in the past even when these involve considerable activity, physical strain, exposure to weather, etc. Light, sedentary occupations are not necessarily healthy occupations."[1]

Dr. Rhoda Adamson, Medical Officer of the Maternity Hospital in Leeds, gave evidence in 1919 (and I have heard her make a similar statement in 1930) :—

"There is no industrial work as heavy as charing, and women should not be prevented from doing any work they think they are fit for, including foundry work, shipbuilding, heavy engineering, and heavy chemical work. . . . Work involving standing or being jolted does not injure healthy women, and they stand high temperatures and bad weather conditions as well as men. Night-work is not found to be more disadvantageous to women, even to young women, than to men, and they should not be prevented from doing it. Women should be left free in their competition with men. Employers would probably select men for the heavier jobs, and women for the lighter ones. . . ."[2]

Dr. Elizabeth Butler, Medical Officer at a Munition Factory, stated :—

"Very severe and continuous physical work, whether outdoor or indoor, such as charing or even some forms of domestic work, aged women prematurely, and on the heaviest kinds of work women should not be employed. But the work which women would be well advised to avoid, if physical health were the main consideration, was sedentary indoor occupation such as that of sempstresses and clerks. In the shops (i.e. industrial establishments) of Georgetown, however, there had been no authenticated cases of injury arising from heavy lifting and other heavy strain, though some women had been engaged on this work continuously for the past three years. For work with poisonous substances, such as T.N.T., women were more useful than men by reason of their cleaner habits and more careful observance of regulations."[3]

Dr. Fulton, having a Nottingham panel practice of over four thousand patients of whom about half were women, testified to his belief that

[1] *Report of War Cabinet Committee on Women in Industry: Memo. on Health*), pp. 251–2.
[2] *Ibid. (Appendices, etc.)*, p. 203. [3] *Ibid. (Appendices, etc.)*, p. 202.

"if men and women were brought up on the same food, the present difference in weight of the average man and woman would probably not decrease, though their physical strength would approximate ".[1]

Such evidence tends to show that the " weakness " of the woman worker as compared with the man is largely due not to innate physical constitution but to circumstances determined by economic considerations. If the " weakness " is treated as purely a matter of natural physique, methods of cure may be entered upon which actually increase women's " weakness " though increasing their economic disadvantages.

The references made by several women doctors to the heaviness of much domestic work, which is an alternative for most women to industrial work, suggest that dangers to female and, through women, to racial health arising from the conditions of women's employment, may be more deeply engrained in our civilization than we yet recognize, and that our present attempts to improve matters by industrial legislation for women merely scratch the surface, doing on the whole as much harm as good. Dr. Kathleen Vaughan, with wide experience of medical work among women in Europe and India, has pointed out that our alarmingly high rates of maternal mortality, stillbirth and mental deficiency are largely due, perhaps chiefly due, to maldevelopments of the female pelvis resulting from lack of outdoor exercise and occupation, and too much sedentary work, on the part of growing girls and young women.[2] In this connection it is notable that 96 per cent. of women gainfully employed, as against 46·6 per cent. of men, are engaged in indoor occupations —and the majority of these women are young.[3] If women non-gainfully employed were considered, the proportion occupied indoors would probably be higher still.

[1] *Report of War Cabinet Committee on Women in Industry* (*Appendices, etc.*), p. 199.
[2] *Maternal Mortality and its Relation to the Shape of the Female Pelvis* (*Proceedings of the Royal Society of Medicine*, December, 1929), and *The Shape of the Pelvic Brim as the Determining Factor in Childbirth* (*British Medical Journal*, November 21, 1931), by Dr. K. Vaughan.
[3] See Chapter II, p. 19 (Table IV).

In considering the case for and against legislation which differentiates between men and women workers, it is therefore necessary to consider not only the work which it is proposed to regulate or prohibit to women, but also the alternatives open to them if regulation limits or prohibition diverts their employment. To legislate in such a way as to drive more women into light, sedentary, indoor work, or into domestic work carried on under conditions often far harder and less congenial than those of factories ; to restrict their opportunities for gainful employment, and so lower still further their economic status, which in itself is their chief source of weakness and danger to health ; to examine closely the effect of exposure to lead in causing abortion and stillbirth, while shutting the eyes to the number of intentional abortions procured among women who pursue a domestic career without adequate income, strength or hope—such procedure as this offers little chance of increased happiness to women or final benefit to the community.

While, therefore, the " practical politician " may feel on occasion justified in supporting differential legislation at the present day, the statesman with a longer view is committed to act so as to eliminate wherever possible the necessity for it.

This can only be done by equalizing as far as possible the economic circumstances of men and women. Some necessity for differential legislation might then still arise owing to the fact that the physical functions of men and women are not the same ; but if other conditions were equal, right selection of worker for job would tend to be more nearly automatic ; sex in itself would provide no cause for special exploitation, and the need for sex-differences in legislation would be less likely to occur. Its present necessity arises for the most part from the social conventions and economic circumstances which create *artificial* distinctions between men and women workers ; it is these which demand the chief force of our attack.

L

CHAPTER IX

THE WORK NOT PAID WITH WAGES

The work of home-making defined—its characteristics—the quantity
of work—the details—the national cost of home-making labour
—peculiar economic treatment of it—results of this treatment:
restriction of demand for industrial goods and services—effect on
wages—and on industry in general. Working-hours and efficiency
of home-maker—results of inefficiency—(a) on industry; (b) on
children's health and intelligence. Health of home-maker neglected
nationally—and individually. Need for new social-industrial policy
respecting home-making.

Thousands of women retire from the labour market
every year, or refrain from entering it, to devote themselves to work for which they receive maintenance, but
no wages. What is this work they do and what is its
relationship to other national industry?

The work is home-making—a hybrid occupation, concerned with the re-creation of the energy, mental and
physical, of human beings by means of a variety of services designed to provide them individually with rest and
refreshment.[1] It may be considered a branch of Personal
Service. In practice a clear distinction can be made between the two : Personal Service is the recognized title of
a gainful occupation classified in the Census Occupational
List, while Home-making is not recognized as a gainful
occupation, and is not included in Occupational surveys.

In fact, so much sentiment attaches to it that many
people dislike the suggestion of classification : they fear
" to brush the dust from off its wings "—though one does
not suggest that Registrar-Generals have been affected
in this way. Yet butterflies appear each spring, in spite
of schoolboys and lepidopterists, and homes are not likely

---

[1] And concerned also with the provision of a suitable environment
for the production and care of new units of human energy, i.e. babies.

to become extinct because one discusses the analogies between home-making and other labour.

Like other occupations, home-making offers a supply of work which can be performed in the last resort only by the application of human energy, mental or physical. This work is of constantly recurring demand : much of it inevitably recurs every day. It has the peculiarity that the worker is usually specially attached to the persons she serves, either by kinship or by marriage. And, as a still more essential peculiarity, that a certain relationship exists between the surroundings where the work is done and the mentality of those for whom it is done. The re-creation of energy is a psychological as well as a physical experience. The home is the place where this experience is most constantly sought, and one important element in the home-experience of the common man is a sense of special property or familiarity [1] in his surroundings, animate and inanimate. Catullus expressed this marvellously well :—

> " O, quid solutis est beatius curis,
>   cum mens onus reponit, ac peregrino
>   labore fessi venimus larem ad nostrum
>   desideratoque acquiescimus lecto !
>   hoc est, quod unumst pro laboribus tantis."

" O, what is happier than the moment when, all care laid aside, the mind puts down its burden, and tired with toil and travel we come to our own home and rest in the bed we have longed for ! This is the one thing which makes such great toil worth while."

So home-making is not just work which happens to be done in a certain house ; it is a service which must essentially be performed at that place, with those particular properties that we know—" *larem nostrum, desideratoque lecto* "—our own hearth, our household gods, the bed remembered and desired.

This necessary localization of home-services in the home

---

[1] The idea of home has become so closely associated with the idea of the family that this word " familiarity " now expresses more nearly a meaning of " homeyness ", without necessarily any properly *family* (i.e. human relationship) significance, than any other word in the language.

depends, however, to a great extent on individual psychology, and is more marked in the old and middle-aged (and perhaps the child) than the adolescent and the young adult. For some rare spirits, a single piece of portable property—a picture, an ash-tray, a tea-pot—may be sufficient to provide the psychological experience of home in an otherwise strange environment. For others, a large circle of familiar faces, in surroundings which their ancestors knew, seem necessary for the fulfilment of the idea of home. Most men to-day are grouped between these extremes.

Young people, especially those to whom the experience of independence is new and attractive, are commonly unconscious of any demand within themselves for this psychological experience of home. Their parents frequently accuse them of " using the house as an hotel ". If indeed the whole rising generation of mankind continued throughout life regardless of the psychological element in home-services, and really used homes as hotels, or hotels as homes, economic problems would very soon be immensely simplified. But usually the attitude of young people changes when they acquire a house or room of their own, and they then join, in this respect, the rest of mankind.

There is, however, wide difference of opinion in different communities as to which services are essentially of the home, and which may be suitably provided elsewhere. Frenchmen eat a family meal in public more happily than the English ; and I believe it was a Frenchman who, on the death of his wife, decided not to marry his mistress because he would have nowhere to spend the evenings. The English home is more accessible to friends, and more apt to entertain them, than the average French one, which remains the sanctuary of the family. When my husband and I were recently being hospitably received amidst a large family in South Germany, we were told that they were able to dispense altogether with expenditure on cinemas because they enjoyed themselves in the evenings singing part-songs. (There were seven children

at home.)   An American writer considers that privacy is
the essential quality of a home :—

> " All day this crowded existence is destroying our identity,
> breaking down our personality. The new home must be
> the place where we can re-create our personality. . . . And
> creation is a solitary undertaking. The new home must
> offer solitude and quiet and privacy. It must be a place
> of trust and of few, very few, demands. If it is the safe
> refuge where we can go about this re-creating of our person-
> ality . . . it does not matter who does the cooking or where
> the laundry is done. The new home can be a vitally signi-
> ficant element in society, with all its vocational aspects
> gone, with the women as well as the men finding the major
> occupation outside." [1]

The German home certainly would not have suited the
American lady, nor would her ideal have seemed in the
least like a satisfactory home to them.   The home retains
different services in different communities and in different ages, but some everywhere, and it infuses into these
services which it retains a quality as necessary to our
mental health as vitamins to our body.

So long as we need individual homes, there will always
be a residue of localized home-work, but it is in process
of shrinking *in variety* with the advance of industrial
civilization.   Indeed, considered from the angle of industrial history, present-day home-making represents simply
a residue of work which society has not as yet found it
feasible to accomplish by centralized management.   Almost
every modern industry, national or local, was originally a
function of the home.   The student, observing this fact,
concludes that the domestic work remaining can hardly
be sufficient to claim in genuine labour more than a
fraction of the time originally spent.   But in judging the
home-maker's work to be reduced *in quantity*, certain
aspects of modern life are often forgotten.

Firstly, the standard of work has been raised, in the
average home.   Miss Eleanor Rathbone has drawn atten-

---

[1] *The Annals of the American Academy of Political and Social Science,*
Vol. CXLIII, May, 1929, *Women in The Modern World* ; *The Married
Woman and the Part-Time Job,* by Lorine Pruette, p. 306.

tion to " the steadily increasing strain on housewives'
resources and endurance caused by the rising standard
of educational and social requirements " :—

> " Through medical inspection at school, the visits of a
> health visitor when a baby is born, her own attendance
> at a child-welfare centre, her attention is continually being
> called to some fresh requirement said, perhaps with truth,
> to be essential to a healthy home, but involving on her part
> more labour in cooking, washing, scrubbing, sewing and
> contriving, and demanding better utensils and materials
> than she has money to buy." [1]

The same tale is told by observers of rural life :—

> " While economic and social changes appear to reduce
> the agricultural and domestic work of rural home-makers
> in some respects, they add to it in others. For instance,
> reduction of work in butter-making . . . may be counter-
> balanced by these increasing exactions in respect of clean-
> milk production in which the women of the farms must
> play a foremost part." [2]

Secondly, it is more difficult to secure help for house-
work than it used to be when a greater variety of labour
was performed at home. Not only work but workers
too, *qua* workers, have left the home. It is impossible
to determine whether the one departure is in proportion
to the other—whether the woman in the home has now
more or less work than she had before many industries
were centralized. Probably some have more—those in
rural homes and those with young children—and others
less, than in former days. Yet this " less " may still be
equal, or may even exceed the normal working day of
the modern industrial worker, whose hours have during
the last century progressively decreased. No figures are
available of the working-hours of English housewives, but

---

[1] *The Disinherited Family*, pp. 69, 70. The late Miss Lina Eckenstein
once told me that, within her own time, the German peasant housewife
only washed her linen once or twice a year ; if observed to do so more
frequently she was scorned by her neighbours for her shortage of supply.

[2] *Report of Ministry of Agriculture on the Practical Education of
Women for Rural Life*, p. 13. The Report continues as follows :—
" . . . and such lessening of household work as may be effected by
purchase of commodities at shops, instead of their manufacture at home,
is more than offset by the growing difficulty of finding paid household
assistance. It would probably be more true to say that the volume of
women's work in the rural home is, on the whole, tending to expand. . . ."

in a study recently made by the American Bureau of
Home Economics (a branch of the United States Agricultural Department) of the work of over one thousand
housewives, more than half of them were found to spend
over forty-eight hours a week in their home-making, and
one-third spent over fifty-six hours. There was little
variation in the records of the urban and the rural homes ;
the latter average was a little higher, but for both small-
town and country housewives the time spent in home-
making averaged approximately 51 hours a week, and in
large towns the average was over 48 hours.[1] If these
are the American figures, there is little likelihood that
the unaided English housewife spends less, or even so
little, time over her work, for it is generally recognized
that the conditions of English home-life and work are
less adapted to labour-saving than the urban American.

It should also be realized that the smaller home organization is less well adapted than the older home to
meet labour emergencies. When sickness, disablement,
or the incidence of child-birth which is so normal a feature of her occupation, now occurs for the home-maker,
it is very much more difficult to provide a temporary
re-organization of service to meet the special need of the
time, than it can have been when industry proper was
also a branch of domesticity. This difficulty in finding
anyone to act as substitute or temporarily to supplement
her labour, is without doubt a case of additional work for
the individual home-maker, and a strain upon her, peculiar
to modern life.

Thirdly, it may well be a delusion to suppose that the
home has been relieved of labour in proportion to the
centralization of industry, because this very centralization has in many other ways made homework more difficult. Of these modern difficulties, it is sufficient to mention smoke alone. The difference in labour between keeping a house clean in, say, Wigan, and in rural Sussex, is

---

[1] *Journal of Home Economics*, March, 1929. See also *Annals of
American Academy, op. cit.* ; *The Woman Administrator in the Modern
Home*, by Anna E. Richardson, p. 22 ; and *Woman's Economic Contri-
bution in the Home*, by Hildegarde Kneeland, pp. 34 ff.

indicative of a difference between medieval and modern times.

The work that still remains in the average English home includes the processes of food-provision—catering, marketing, cooking, dish-washing—the care of the house and furniture, the washing and mending of clothes, and usually of house-linen, and sometimes the care of children, the sick and the aged. Many housewives perform at home work which competes with centralized industry, such as making jam, preserving fruit, making clothes, house-painting ; and in the north-country it is the custom, even in small houses in large towns, for bread to be baked at home.

Considered in detail, the work of home-making seems infinitely laborious and petty. Considered as a national concern it seems honourable and important. One has to bear in mind both aspects.

Although home-making is not a gainful occupation, so far as the worker is concerned, it is evident that the labour concerned in it has to be rewarded in some form. It is paid for in the form of maintenance of the worker, usually according to the standard of living of those served. This may or may not be an economic bargain from the view-point of the latter (apart from considerations of personal relationship). That depends, firstly on the standard of maintenance, secondly on whether the home-maker is fully employed and efficient. In the average working-class home it is probably an economic bargain for any family in which there is a young child, since one finds it generally acknowledged that a working man whose wife dies leaving young children is forced by that circumstance to marry again if he wishes to keep the family together. He cannot keep and pay a housekeeper. This is partly because of difficulties connected with housing accommo-dation and social proprieties, but the economic motive is also of great importance.

Whether, for the worker, her reward makes home-making a profitable transaction, depends on the standard of living at which she is maintained, the energy and time she expends at work, and the degree of economic independence she receives. Her position will be more fully discussed in the next chapter.

From the point of view of the community, there are many reasons for supposing that the present method of providing and paying for home-making services is not economical. It is scarcely possible to make any estimate of the *economic value of the amount* nationally expended in the form of maintenance-reward for home-making at any one time : the reasons for supposing that the system is not economical are chiefly based on the results of the peculiar *method* of reward. It may be noted, however, that the decreasing birth-rate is a factor tending to the decrease of the total amount of work performed in return for total maintenance expenditure, or becomes so when infant mortality ceases to decline at a similar rate. As the proportion of live children decreases compared with the adult population, it is probable that an increasing number of homes, and especially urban homes, do not provide sufficient work to make the maintenance of a full-time worker an economic proposition. If at the same time the number of married women, and of non-gainfully occupied married women, increases in proportion to the total population (as we have seen on page 12 that it has recently been increasing), then the community spends more on maintenance for the purpose of home-making services than it used to do, and receives in return either less service, or services of less vital value to the community.[1]

---

[1] The question of the value of home-making services in modern communities has been provocatively and philosophically discussed by Thorstein Veblen (*The Theory of the Leisure Class*). But the distinction he makes between services to man's physical and psychological nature, and the classification of the former services as *work* or *effort*, and the latter as *vicarious leisure* or *wasted effort*, seems to me a fallacy. If a non-domestic worker likes to keep twenty photographs on a pigeon-hole mantelpiece, and see this paraphernalia kept clean, it is not wasted effort on the part of a domestic worker to dust the structure daily. The employer's taste may be deprecated, but the gratification of it is not to be classed as waste until all such industries as Tobacco Manufacture, the Theatre, and the Fine Arts are so classed. Such services and industries are, however, luxuries ; and if through mere force of habit an individual or nation indulges in them without receiving gratification, or gratification equivalent to their cost, Veblen's description may be justified.

The treatment of home-making labour is in two important respects peculiar. One peculiarity is the method of reward, by maintenance, without wage or money profit ; the other is the lack of freedom in the labour-market. Home-making labour is the field of work open to married women, and other fields of labour are commonly closed to them on marriage.

This peculiar treatment has certain economic results. The reward for work has little relation to the amount or efficiency of the work performed. Lack of incentive to work, which might be expected to result from this under other conditions, is, in home-making work, usually counteracted by the fact that the profit accrues to the worker's own family. But other disadvantages remain. No reckoning of the comparative value of labour is possible.

The non-valuation of home labour has far-reaching effects. When labour is not evaluated, there is no way of judging at what point it is an economy to use power other than human, or a new machine rather than an old one. No reckoning can be made of the saving to be effected, because no money saving is effected at all. The human labour is not paid for in proportion to the work done, or the time spent ; it costs the same anyhow ; that is, for practical purposes of comparison, nothing. Even a slave whose continued labour is desired must be maintained. When labour is given no value, innovation has to carry the whole dead weight of additional expenditure.

It has been constantly found in industry that comparatively high labour costs encourage invention and final economy. The history of slave labour systems, such as that of the Southern States before the American Civil War, seems to show a sapping of the impulse to economic progress. The history of the two branches of our own Cotton Industry in Glasgow and Lancashire may offer an example of the same influences at work. Wages in Glasgow ruled much lower than in Lancashire, during the nineteenth century. Strikes, which in the main ended disastrously for the Scottish workers, were a means of

securing comparatively high wages for the English operatives. Yet prosperity gradually deserted Glasgow, while
the Lancashire industry, until 1914, throve, and became
a model of efficiency both as regards labour organization
and mechanical equipment. Henry Ford has preached
the doctrine, and practised it in the automobile trade :
cheap labour does not pay. The originality of Ford lay
not so much in his enunciation of the doctrine as in the
fact that, as an employer, he practised it, independently.
The House of Commons Select Committee on Home Work
had stated in 1908 :—

"Low-priced labour is a great obstacle to improvement.
It discourages invention and removes or prevents the growth
of a great stimulus to progress and efficiency." [1]

The principle applies also to *unpriced* labour—to the
domestic work of the home. The conventional method
of reward is a drag on the industry itself, and by discouraging labour-saving it is also a drag on the development of all the industries subsidiary to it, which should
find in it a more ready market for goods and services,
both new-fashioned and long-tested.

To realize the effect on subsidiary industries, one must
think not only in terms of electric vacuum-cleaners, but
also of the humble brush, knife and saucepan. The
former, more expensive, type of labour appeals to those
who employ, or wish to attract, paid labour, or are suddenly faced with the problem of performing work for which
they have been accustomed to engage paid domestics.
Small as the English demand may appear to the manufacturer of these comparatively expensive articles, it is
nevertheless among the class who might afford them that
economies in money and effort are most readily appreciated. But in the homes all over the country where the
home-maker " does her own work ", old apparatus is used,
and compensated by extra labour-time and energy. Who
can afford the new broom that sweeps clean, the aluminium
saucepan that is light to lift ? These are comparatively

[1] *Report of Select Committee on Home-Work*, 1908, p. xiv.

small expenses, but many women add an extra hour to their day's work, and extra fatigue per hour, for lack of such expenditure, which represents a mere fraction of the real value of their extra labour per week. This is false economy, from the point of view of the home, and it results, for industry, in a reduced consumption of goods which are in no sense luxuries, but would satisfy a legitimate, though suppressed, demand. It raises questions in connection with the comparative effective demand in different industries, which are of great importance.

The connection between the rate at which home-labour is valued, and the size of the market for industrial goods, may be exemplified by a comparison between England and the United States. We in England are far behind the United States in our consumption of labour-saving inventions and domestic machines, and probably also in our regular consumption of ordinary domestic tools. The position of the wife, with regard to maintenance as reward for domestic work, is practically the same in the two countries, but paid domestic service is harder to obtain in America. Consequently the home-maker more often belongs to a class in which frequent demands are made for her leisure society, or the tradition of whose family leads her to demand more leisure. Her time and energy are therefore more appreciated, and roughly assessable at money-value. This attitude tends to spread within the community with the spread of wealth.

The reduction of demand for industrial *goods* through under-valuation of the home-maker's labour applies also to industrial *services*. The question arises in America, for instance, whether the use of elaborate machines in the home is industrially economical. It is considered that the multiplication of such machines for individual use might reasonably be superseded by an increase in the tendency to perform " domestic " work under centralized industrial conditions.[1] Laundry is a case in point. An electrical washing-machine may lighten the labour of the weekly wash—a point to be appreciated by those who

[1] See *Middletown*, by R. S. and H. M. Lynd, p. 174 n. 31.

realize what a strain this branch of domestic labour is to many women—but probably it is a more desirable development both for centralized industry and the home that the washing should be sent out to a laundry where a large number of processes can be performed by efficient machines and specialized workers.

Such increases in industrial markets are, however, prevented or retarded, not only by non-valuation and undervaluation of the home-maker's labour, but also by the discouragement or restriction of her work outside the home. So long as women are discouraged from undertaking outside work, they are the more encouraged to compete with " industrial " work domestically. If they are forced to stay in, they will not send the work out. At the best they will buy efficient tools. When trade is good and a little capital is available for household expenses, or hire-purchase of other than immediate necessities may be ventured upon, a sewing-machine, washing-machine or preserving-pan may be bought, and then when trade is bad and wages are low, the wife by working harder than ever, unlimited by any 48-hour week, may make the family's clothes or jam instead of buying them ; or she may undertake the family wash instead of sending it out.[1] In any case, if the wife must be at home employed domestically rather than industrially or professionally, she will usually attempt to save the family income by engrossing into domestic work as much potentially industrial work as she can. The more valuable money seems to her and her family, in comparison with her time and energy, the more she is likely to do this.

Thus the policy of prohibiting or discouraging the employment of married women, practised in most branches of the Civil Service in England, by a number of Local Authorities in respect of teachers, and often also by in-

[1] Work *may* be performed domestically not only because it is cheaper to do so, but because a quality is thus obtained which is commercially unobtainable. In this case the competition of the home, though no less restrictive of commercial markets, has a definite value, and one hopes such competition will persist at least until a consumers' organization becomes sufficiently effective to secure the commercial provision of these special demands.

dustrial management, tends to restrict the demand for
goods and services produced by centralized industry, particularly in periods of depression of trade. The domestic
worker confined to her home unwittingly retaliates upon
the industries from which she is excluded, hits the dog
when it is down, and increases industrial unemployment
by working overtime. Neither her work-time nor overtime appear in national labour statistics. If they did,
the latter would afford no ground for satisfaction.

Such competition has an effect also on wages, which
may be most clearly seen in the clothing, catering and
laundry trades. The manufacturer, or industrial employer,
has certain advantages over the home-worker, such as the
saving of labour-time brought about by division of labour
and use of machinery, the saving of cost brought about
by wholesale buying, and the saving of fuel brought about
by more continuous use, but he has to compete with a
system—that of the home—in which overhead charges
and labour-costs are entirely left out of account, and there
is no legislative interference or sound tradition as regards
time worked, conditions of work, or health insurance. It
is one consequence of this, that in these three trades the
workers have had great struggles, scarcely yet successful, to rise above the " sweated " level. Attempts to
secure better wages and conditions through Trade Union
organization alone have not availed. Both the Clothing
and Laundry industries have been covered by Trade
Boards, and the delay in the establishment of a Trade
Board for the Catering trade is due not to lack of evidence of the low wage-rates of employees, but to opposition from capital interests. All these trades tend to be
" manned " by women workers (except in those branches
which rise above competition with the average home and
its standard of work) and tend also to be extremely difficult to organize.

The drag on industrial development and wages occasioned by the treatment of home-making labour is most
obvious in respect of trades where the competition is
most direct ; but when one realizes that the demand for

services, such as clothes-making, laundry, catering, food-preserving and cooking, and also for goods such as domestic dwellings, furniture and tools (composed of an almost innumerable variety of materials), is restricted in the same way, it becomes clear that there are few branches of national industry which are not affected by the obsolete conditions of home-labour and its method of reward. Few branches of industry escape, except those concerned with the manufacture of luxury goods. The blight of undervalued domestic labour reaches all the rest. Articles not worth the toil of an hour are repaired at home—soldered, tinkered, darned or scrubbed ; hours are spent patching pillow-cases and turning sheets " sides to middle ", as in the days before Lancashire knew the use of mechanical power. An immense amount of unnecessary energy is spent in performing almost every domestic operation in the majority of households, owing to the survival of antiquated domestic architecture and fittings, whose industrial prototype would be condemned unhesitatingly and effectively by any wage-paying, profit-making concern.[1]

It may be suggested that the bogey of domestic competition with industry has been over-blackened by an exaggeration of the extent of the home-maker's energy. The average home-maker, it may be said, does not work as hard or as long as all that.

We have no means of judging how long or how hard or how effectively she works, except by piece-meal observation of fact, and record of the conventional standards to which she is expected to conform. These suggest a day which, in most working-class homes, begins before the industrial worker's, and ends considerably later, sometimes with, quite often without, rest-periods in the afternoon. Five a.m. to ten p.m., with perhaps an hour off from 2 to 3 p.m., seem to be the working hours of many working-class women with small children. If there is

---

[1] See *The Uses of Costing*, by Mrs. C. S. Peel, for some calculations of waste of energy in the performance of domestic operations in the average house.

no baby to be nursed, bedtime may be an hour earlier, especially in winter, when it is necessary to save fuel and light ; but the time of rising is determined by the necessity of preparing breakfast for a husband who has to begin work probably at latest by eight o'clock, and possibly (among Londoners) some distance away. The doors of the London Underground railways open at 5 a.m. ; between 6 and 7 a.m. over 34,000 people travel on the trains, and nearly 106,000 between 7 and 8 a.m.[1] That is the peak of the whole morning ; the later crush familiar to business and professional men is less extreme. There is probably not more than one in ten of these travellers who has not had his breakfast prepared by a home-worker, and will not be greeted by a cooked meal on his return. London's daily life begins no earlier than that of the country, or of provincial towns.

As for idleness in the meantime, it is certainly much more rare for the housewife than lack of method in labour. Many working-class women hardly ever seem to sit down in their own homes, except for a brief, occasional cup of tea ; and gossip over the teapot or at the door is less common in English cities nowadays than the supposed virtue of " keeping oneself to oneself ".

The mother with a small baby, or with a member of the family ill, is on duty day and night. A young woman of my acquaintance, living not penuriously in a working-class district of Glasgow in 1931, lay down to bear her second child while her husband lay seriously ill in the same room. She said how thankful she was to have a reason for lying down.

There are no half-days off in the home-maker's week, no weekly Day of Rest, nor, in most cases, any annual holiday.

Certainly there are many women, mothers of young or large families, who would seem to have little time to compete with the industrialist. But very often they do so nevertheless, partly because of their greater need to save

[1] These figures were obtained and published by the Underground Railways in 1928.

expenditure, and partly from the tradition that a woman's work never *ought* to be done. This last consideration equally applies to social strata distinctly above what is usually termed working-class. Such was a mother of six children who told me yesterday : " After I have got baby (aged four) to bed, I like to sit down with my knitting *and have a rest.* I make all his socks, and his grand-mother makes his other things. She's always at her machine."

The degree of every home-maker's energy and achieve-ment are, however, obviously extremely varied. They may be exaggerated. But where they fail, industry seldom reaps the benefit in larger orders, and may lose seriously in other ways. Though the home-worker labours less, or is incapable single-handed of doing all that is to be done in her home, no money becomes directly available for alternative expenditure on goods and services industrially produced, since her economic reward has no relation to the work she does. The more likely result of her ineffi-ciency (a word to be used without prejudice, for the cause may be character, or ill-health, or too large a family for her strength) is the ill-health or comparative inefficiency of those she works for.

This, however, is a result as unfortunate as possible. Every year the public is staggered afresh at the record presented by the Ministry of Health, of work-time lost and money expended through ill-health of industrial workers. The latest record (for 1930) is of 26½ million weeks' work lost in the year, or an equivalent of 12 months' work of over half a million persons.

" Moreover, it must be remembered," writes the Chief Medical Officer of the Ministry of Health, " that it is not only the working equivalent of 510,000 persons that was involved, but also the labour and expense entailed in their care during the period of incapacity." [1]

Undoubtedly much of this sickness is due to conditions of home life, contemporary or previous—perhaps long pre-

[1] *Annual Report of the Chief Medical Officer of the Ministry of Health* for 1930, p. 13.

vious—to the date of invalidity. No one can exactly apportion the responsibility for this burden, and say how much is due to the conditions of home life, how much to personal habits, how much to unfortunate heredity, how much to conditions of work. In the words of one of the chief authorities on Industrial Fatigue :—

" It is a matter of great difficulty to determine how far, if at all, the sickness and mortality experienced by industrial workers are due to fatigue, and how far to other causes. There can be little doubt that in many cases fatigue is a predisposing cause of sickness, even if it is not the direct and immediate cause. . . . Sickness may be due to poor factory conditions, such as bad heating . . . inadequate lighting . . . and so on. More frequently it is due to poor conditions of home life, such as inadequate food and housing." [1]

In connection with the health and nutrition of children, Professor Cathcart and his colleagues have made studies of the importance of various conditional factors, and they conclude that the quality of home-service given to the children is the most important factor.

" The only factor which really counts in the average household is the capacity of the mother and the amount of time and intelligence she gives to the running of the home." [2]

In earlier studies by the same workers the factor of maternal intelligence was over-stressed, as compared with the size of the family income—partly owing to the fact that " in about 90 per cent. of the cases a good mother is associated with a good father ". But even so, the observers consider that the mother " must bear the preponderating rôle " in providing the conditions that make for the health and growth, through nutrition, of her children.

On the home-services so given the intelligence as well as the physique of the nation to a great extent depend.

[1] *Industrial Fatigue and Efficiency*, by H. M. Vernon (1921), p. 161.
[2] *Report of the Medical Research Council. A Study in Nutrition*, by Cathcart and Murray, 1931, p. 40.

"Progressive improvement in home conditions may be expected to react favourably not only on the health but also on the intelligence of school children." [1]

The devotion and intelligence, the health and resources of the home-worker, are shown to have a direct, a preponderating effect, on the health and capability of those she serves. There can be little doubt that her services are of as great importance to the industrial worker as to the child, and that their quality consequently affects the amount of money expended in any year by the State and other organizations on Health Insurance benefits, and on other subsidies to national health.

Yet the health, fatigue, and working conditions of the home-maker are commonly neglected. Her health is not insured under the National Health Insurance Scheme. Enlightened employers, and the State, spend considerable sums investigating industrial efficiency and fatigue ; factories are built and rebuilt with the object of minimizing the strain of work. Meanwhile, one of the most important factors in the causation of industrial (as of other) fatigue and sickness—the inefficiency and fatigue of the home-maker—remains neglected.

It is definitely a secondary consideration in the health organization of the State, and in the individual home as well. The latter fact has been noted by many observers of home conditions. Among those families whose small income per head makes any preferential care a matter of vital importance to health, the necessity of maintaining the strength of the man, because of his earnings, means that the woman, and often the children, must take a secondary place, and may actually have to go short of food.

"There is reason to believe that the quantity of food obtained by the wife, and also by the children at the period of rapid growth, is in many cases, in almost every county (among agricultural labourers) deficient."

These words occur in a report on "The Conditions of Nourishment of the poorer Labouring Classes in England"

[1] *Report of the Medical Research Council. On the Relation between Home Conditions and the Intelligence of School Children* (1923).

presented to the Local Government Board in 1863. In 1925 Mr. A. B. Hill, after studying the diets of rural workers in Essex, stated that the same conclusions " in the main apply equally well to the county of Essex to-day ".[1] Rowntree and Kendall observed in 1913 that the diet of the agricultural population usually did not " contain the nutriment necessary for physical efficiency ", and that " the women and children suffer from underfeeding to a much greater extent than the men ".[2] The same conditions are found among urban families.

> "Extraordinary expenditure, such as the purchase of a piece of furniture, is met by reducing the sum spent on food. As a rule, in such cases, it is the wife and sometimes the children who have to forgo a portion of their food— the importance of maintaining the strength of the wage-earner is recognized, and he obtains his ordinary share." [3]

In *The Third Winter of Unemployment* it is reported that in Glasgow

> "the midwives say they have to get more medical assistance now because the women are not as strong as they used to be. Our opinion is that this is due to under-nourishment. The mothers always are the first to suffer ".[4]

The mothers are the first to suffer, but as there is no medical inspection of the home-maker's health as of the schoolchild's, it is only the child's suffering which usually receives public notice. Medical reports show that such undernourishment continues to occur. It was reported

[1] *Journal of Hygiene*, October, 1925, A. B. Hill, *A Physiological and Economic Study of the Diets of Workers in Rural Areas as compared with those of Workers Resident in Urban Districts.* The quotation from the 1863 Report is made by Mr. Hill (p. 205) and provides also a summary of his own conclusions. One of his own most interesting discoveries is the close correspondence between the amount of money available for the housewife to spend on food per head, and the diet value obtained from it. " As the income per man per week increases, the calorific value of the diet steadily increases likewise." In the cases which showed this correspondence so clearly, the diet was (in varying degree) below the family's physical requirements. This perhaps indicates that the instinct of hunger, rather than the mother's intelligence, is the first safeguard of the family's health *below a certain income-level.*
[2] *How the Labourer Lives*, Rowntree and Kendall (1913–1918), p. 309.
[3] *Poverty, A Study of Town Life*, B. Seebohm Rowntree (1901), p. 54.
[4] *The Third Winter of Unemployment* (1923), p. 202, quoted by E. F. Rathbone, *The Disinherited Family*, p. 73 n.

in *The Times* of August 14, 1931, under the heading *Malnutrition in West Suffolk*, as follows :—

"Dr. A. M. Critchley, Acting School Medical Officer for West Suffolk, commenting in his annual report on the increased number of children in the elementary schools of the county who have in the last two years been found to be showing definite signs of malnutrition, says : ' It is impossible to propound one cause for all these cases, as each individual varies in his powers of assimilating food. The agricultural depression now current undoubtedly reacts unfavourably on the children of the farm labourers, who receive food which may not be deficient in quantity, but certainly is in quality, as it contains an excessive proportion of carbohydrates, these being the cheapest foods.' "

Schoolchildren found to be suffering from malnutrition are provided with meals at school, if it is found that the parents are necessitous ; but the mother who is undernourished has no such resource, except when she is expecting or nursing an infant. Then, if she (or her husband) is not in receipt of Poor Law Relief, and if she requires the additional food " solely on medical grounds ", it may be provided for her at less than cost price through the Public Assistance authority.[1] But many a mother will be found to consider the production of a child under conditions of poverty quite sufficiently unpleasant, without the added indignity of such partial and qualified assistance ; and many undernourished mothers are not expecting or nursing babies, though they may do so again later, with undermined physique.

The custom of giving the husband-father the preference of nourishment and care in the home is not to be traced primarily to male selfishness or wifely altruism or subservience, though it may encourage such sex distinctions. It is a necessity which arises out of the economic organi-

[1] *Annual Report of the Ministry of Health*, 1927-1928 :—" In connection with the estimates of Local Authorities of their expenditure during the year 1928-1929, it was found desirable to draw the attention of certain Authorities . . . to the importance of reviewing their procedure so as to secure the limitation of the supply at less than cost price to persons who are not in receipt of Poor Law Relief and who require additional milk or food solely on medical grounds " (p. 66).

zation of modern life. This organization makes the family directly dependent on the money earned by the man, and only indirectly dependent on the non-gainful work of the woman, and so enforces a preferential care of his health and strength, and preferential undernourishment for her, despite the need of society that mothers should be physically fit. It is one of the many disadvantages for society and the individual woman arising out of the present antique method of rewarding the home-maker.

It may be suggested that this disability could be cured by higher incomes for all, or for all family men. Without entering into the discussion of the feasibility of the general raising or even maintenance of real-wages, or the practicability of an effective redistribution of wealth within the present structure of society, it may be pointed out that such a solution of the difficulty is really no solution, but simply an inversion of the problem. There is a close connection between the undervaluation of home-labour and the restriction and uncertainty of industrial markets for necessity-goods and services. So long as these markets remain restricted and liable to extreme fluctuation, the industrial development which would make high real-wages permanently possible is prevented. Expert study of the economic conditions of home-making labour in relation to centralized industry is a necessary preliminary to the achievement of wide markets and high wages—expert study which, it is suggested, would lead to an attempt to secure for married women and all home-makers (1) the maximum of freedom to engage in non-domestic work, (2) a reward more definitely related to the occupation of home-work, (3) health care similar to that provided for other workers, and also specifically related to special health-problems of the home-maker.

Such a policy, co-ordinated and based on a definite conception of the right position of the home-maker in the social organization of an industrial community, would prove of immense value to industry, the home, and society of the future. It would point the way simultaneously to an increase of wealth and welfare.

CHAPTER X

THE HOME-MAKER

Dissatisfaction with economic position—social significance of dissatisfaction—effect of economic position on health—health of married
women gainfully occupied—of domestic women—maternal mortality rate—causes of maternal mortality—connection with economic position of women in general and of home-maker in particular.

The present methods of organizing and financing domestic services have unfortunate results for industry, society
and the home. They have become a drag on industrial
development, restricting the market for industrially produced goods and services, depressing wages, and providing a lower standard of industrial efficiency and national
health than might and should be attained. What of their
effect on the home-maker herself?

Marriage, which is the usual gate to home-making service, still brings with it to the woman a certain conventional rise in social status. This has its foundation in
a mental attitude older than Christianity, and probably
older than formal marriage itself. Respect for fertility
and for sexual activity that promotes it, and a certain
contempt for adult virginity and sterility, are deeply
rooted in human psychology.

There are also more superficial reasons for this rise in
status. The married woman has usually more money at
her disposal than the single one. Her importance as a
buyer of goods is increased, and is reflected in the eyes
of the tradesmen with whom she deals, and in the eyes
of those men and women whose minds fall into the shop-
keeper pattern.

But the satisfaction this occasions to the woman is
frequently followed by a deep dissatisfaction at the lack

of economic independence which accompanies the change. " It's horrid for a girl who's been earning her own living to have to ask her husband for the money every time she wants to buy a pair of shoes ! " This remark was recently made by a young married woman, during the discussion that followed a meeting of the local Women Citizens' Association. Such sentiments are constantly expressed in different form by women of all classes who have no settled income and no chance to earn. The domestic servant or factory girl who, after a short experience of married life, returns to paid work, is not always impelled by need or lack of occupation. The woman whose husband's wage is insufficient for their needs, or whose husband is unemployed, does not always regret the opportunity of supplementing their income, unless a young family have prior claims on her energy. As the knowledge of contraception spreads, the young woman's demand for some degree of economic independence after marriage adds an incentive to family limitation. The longing to have " some money of one's own " is not limited to wage-earners' wives. One may hear it expressed, more hopelessly, by women whose husbands' incomes run to four figures and are not ungenerously spent.

To the women who share this feeling, it is such an accepted factor in their mental outlook that it scarcely needs stating to another woman, and certainly no explaining. But one may meet men, young and old, to whom it seems inexplicable. They cannot understand the difference in satisfaction between having the right to spend someone else's money without definite limit, and the use of a certain sum of one's own for which one need render no account. Or they feel that a husband is not " someone else ", though money is certainly money when it is spent.

Two cases of the husband's incomprehension of the wife's point of view come to my mind, both of recent occurrence. A middle-aged business man, of considerable income, and a most kind and generous nature, explained how he had never set any limit to his wife's personal expenditure, and yet for some reason she was unhappy about this financial arrangement. At last, at the request of a friend (whose interference he distinctly resented), he decided instead to place a sum to her credit quarterly at the bank and give her her own cheque book. She then proceeded, according to her husband, to act in an absurd way, spending large sums on a picture or book at the beginning of the quarter, and lunching on a meagre bun at the end of it. Under the old system her expenditure was unrestricted ; under the new she was sometimes almost penniless for weeks ; but she found the new system far more satisfactory. He could never understand it.

The other instance is of a younger man of quite different character. He was educated by his comparatively well-to-do family at a co-educational public school with distinctly modern views of the relationship between men and women. Yet when he married, on a small income, he required his wife to render him an account of every penny, quite literally, that she spent. The wife was young and docile, but after she had a baby to care for, without sufficient domestic help, the irritation of this lack of freedom in every movement of her daily life became intense. A friend was begged to intervene, for really, said the wife, life was not bearable if, when she paid one penny to enter a lavatory, she had to present her husband with a record of the transaction ! Yet her own objections had no effect whatever on his view of the correct economic relationship between them.

These were not cases of marriage consciously or completely unhappy on both sides, or indeed on either side. But there are many marriages in which the consciousness of economic dependence of one partner on the other is a cause of estrangements which make married life a continual misery, though they provide no motive for the husband to bring the marriage to an end, and deprive the wife of any power to do so.

Such dissatisfaction is not likely to become conscious where the total amount of the family income is seriously insufficient for its needs. The wife has then little thought to spare for any grief less urgent than inadequate defences against hunger, weather and criticism.

In many families somewhat above this level, where the breadwinner's earnings seem to leave but a minimum margin for free personal expenditure by either partner, the demand for some degree of economic independence may take the form of resentment at ignorance of the amount of the husband's earnings. For such ignorance is in itself an element and sign of the dependence of the one partner on the other. But it is not peculiar to working-class homes, or to those who live by weekly incomes. How well I know that middle-class, business-man's home, where the wife has not the least idea what her husband is making, but when at the breakfast table she asks him for ten shillings for the day's expenses, he requires to know before handing it over what it is to be spent on!

Dissatisfaction at economic dependence is not a matter of the amount of money in hand, or the extent of the family income. Not money itself is required, or the things it can buy, so much as the spiritual freedom implied in the personal possession or the acknowledged right to it. To have to ask her husband or her father for the cash to buy him a birthday present, or to " save it from the housekeeping ", or to send him a bill for it afterwards, may give a woman far more annoyance, unless her sense of humour is particularly strong, than any gift from him can give her pleasure. She does not need to be taught that it is more blessed to give than to receive. That is the very reason for requiring the wherewithal. When elementary physical needs have been satisfied, better the right to two shillings or two pounds which one may, if one chooses, throw into the Thames, or blow in an hour at the Ritz or its chosen equivalent, than a thousand a year to be spent as others choose, gaily, sensibly or foolishly.

That those who will not work should lack this freedom of spirit, is commonly agreed, though of course it is often they who secure it. That the unemployed who cannot find work should receive this freedom only in the most scanty degree, is usually assumed. The dissatisfaction of the home-maker is increased by the fact that she is neither of these. She may work hard and regularly, but her work wins none of the customary reward : the freedom put into the worker's hand with his money wage or profit.

Her dissatisfaction is not a purely personal affair ; it has significance for society. From the point of view of society, material wealth has a double function to perform. It has not only to register and facilitate the exchange of goods and services ; it has also to provide a means for the expression of individual personality—to strengthen, as it were, the muscles of each man's spirit, creating in him that individual independence which is the foundation of democracy. The ownership of cultivable land may fulfil the same function, or of a mind that is fertile territory, and of itself can make a Heaven of Hell, a Hell of Heaven. But the majority have not these. Like Blake, they have reason to pray for riches at the Throne of God and protest that it is indeed His Throne, and not that of Mammon.

The housewife has even more need than most of this source of mental health and strength, because of the confinement and lack of social stimulus of her daily work. For her own sake, and for the sake of the young children on whom her influence is so especially profound, it is socially important that she should not be in a position of peculiar economic impotence and dependence.

The total of the moneys nationally expended on providing home-making services must be considerable. It has been estimated that in this country nearly 8½ million women are maintained to do this work. But most of the wealth expended in paying for home-making services is, from the communal point of view, unproductive in respect of one half of its dual function. The home-maker is given, with her material reward for work, too little of the dignity and exercise of independence which the State needs all its responsible members to possess. The money spent is half wasted.

The present methods of organizing and rewarding domestic services have other unfortunate effects for the home-maker, less of the mind, more of the body. She suffers in physical health because of her peculiar economic position.

When the National Health Insurance Act was passed in 1911, the health of married women gainfully employed did not receive any special consideration. It was not taken into account that many of these women were carrying on not one occupation but two, or at the least one and a half, and that such a strain was likely to be reflected in the state of their health. Even the fact that married women frequently produce children, and that this occasionally affects their health, was overlooked.

For the societies with which a large number of married women were insured, this oversight had serious consequences. Mrs. Barbara Drake records that the National Federation of Women Workers

" had been registered as an Approved Society under the Act, counting in 1914 . . . 20,000 insured members. A large number of these were married women, upon whom the defects of the Act pressed with unusual severity. By an oversight of the Government, which apparently had seen no reason to take women's advice, the 'incapacity' due to pregnancy or to the after-effects of confinement had been ignored in the estimates for sickness. The result was a false actuarial basis, which threatened with early insolvency all societies composed of married women." [1]

After an agitation led by the Federation, the Act of 1912 amended the defect.

But " abnormal " claims for sickness benefit from married women workers have continued to trouble those concerned with the administration of National Health Insurance. Nor have they even remained at a constant high level. While all types of claim have increased alarmingly during recent years, the claims of married women have increased out of proportion to those of other groups of workers.

A general increase of claims suggests either (a) a rising standard of health on the part of panel doctors as applied

[1] *Women in Trade Unions*, p. 60.

to their patients and greater laxity in granting certificates ; or (b) a real decline in the existing standard of health ; or (c) the making of claims by persons who previously waived claims capable of substantiation. A worker in receipt of good wages may go on working " till he drops " rather than report sick and receive a lesser amount than his wages in benefit. If he is unemployed, or in receipt of low wages, he is less likely to do so. Under such circumstances he is also more likely to become ill.

A disproportionate increase of claims from one group, such as has occurred in the case of married women, cannot be explained in terms of laxity of medical practitioners ; nor does it seem that married women's wages have fallen disproportionately to those of other workers. The indication is towards a decline in the average health of that particular group especially. The circumstances offer some explanation of this.

Owing to the shortage of domestic service (actually far more acute, though less vocal, in the manufacturing districts of the north than among the more leisured classes of the south) there are many women, married and single, who at normal periods of trade undertake what may be considered part-time domestic work and full-time industrial work as well. They undertake it voluntarily ; they consider it inevitable if they are to earn money at all.

This would be one cause of the comparatively high claims of women for sickness benefit at normal times. But at periods of trade depression, women are driven into the labour-market whose domestic work already demands the whole of their time or energy, if it is to be accomplished without lowering the family standard of health and hygiene. They are even more likely than the former group to break down under the strain. Claims for sickness benefit therefore rise higher still, proportionately to the numbers employed.

The unemployment of men, or low wages in relation to family needs, tend to drive into the labour-market women who are at the same time shouldering the burden of home-making work, and who would at other times not expect to find the strength, energy, or time, nor would wish, to undertake both. They are driven away from home-making, and skimp the time given to what they themselves consider their more important labours, because those labours are so unvalued that they cannot afford the time to carry them on properly. If they can find other, paid, work, and their menfolk cannot, find it they must. One reason they can find it is, that the wages they receive are often lower than men would obtain for the same amount of time spent, and are insufficient to permit payment to anyone else to do their domestic work.

The State disburses much of the difference between the man's and woman's wages in sickness benefits and unemployment benefit to the man.

Though the strain on the health of the married woman who undertakes industrial work was unrecognized before the establishment of National Health Insurance, it has since become a matter of tangible proof and national concern. But the married *domestic* woman's health is not insured under the National Scheme, and there is therefore no way of testing by statistics the condition of her general health.

Although we have no general health records for the home-maker as for other workers, we have a mass of statistical material referring to what may almost be considered an Occupational Mortality of the home-maker—that is, the mortality associated with motherhood.

The maternal mortality rate is very high. That is to say, the general rate is far above that which occurs among large, representative groups of mothers who are known to receive reasonably sound care ; and it has not decreased in the last twenty years, as the general and infant mortality rates have declined, in response to the improvement in Public Health practice, and the spread of popular education. The late Minister of Health stated in 1930 :—

" The death-rate among mothers is higher than that in any other calling. . . . The lot of the miner is the hardest and most dangerous of industrial occupations, but the most dangerous vocation of all undoubtedly is that of mother-hood." [1]

Sir George Newman, Chief Medical Officer of the Ministry of Health, refers to the maternal mortality and morbidity rate with the same gravity in his lectures on *Citizenship and the Survival of Civilization* :—

" England thus loses approximately 3,000 mothers a year, and America approximately 18,000, and 85 per cent. of these mothers die under the age of 40. Then associated with this physiological issue of maternity, there is a vast burden of invalidism, suffering and incapacity which, though unrecorded in the national statistics, is exerting a serious effect upon the well-being of the community. A large number of women are made invalids for life, or lose part of their economic value, or become sterile, or die prematurely from injuries received or disease acquired while fulfilling or attempting to fulfil their function of motherhood. How great and widespread is this kind of physical and social disability was brought to light by the excessive and unexpected sickness returns of women claiming maternity and medical benefits under the National Insurance Acts . . . and further evidence is obtainable in the overcrowded women's departments of the general and special hospitals of Europe and America."

Yet maternity is a natural function, more normal for mankind than coal-mining, or going down to the sea in ships. Its dangers should be less than these, not more. Although even among primitive peoples child-birth contains an element of danger to the life of mother and child, yet civilized life has not so increased those dangers that the death-rate we now experience in Great Britain is unavoidable. In fact, at least half these deaths are preventable ; so much is stated in the recent Report of the Ministry of Health on the subject. [2]

The general maternal death-rate approaches 5 per 1,000 births. At the East End Maternity Hospital (London) the rate for 1921–1928, counting hospital and district (i.e.

[1] Speech of the Rt. Hon. Arthur Greenwood, Minister of Health, reported in *The Woman's Leader*, December 12, 1930.
[2] *Interim Report of Ministry of Health on Maternal Mortality and Morbidity*, 1930.

home) cases, was 0·68. The Queen's Nurses (qualified midwives) who in the latter year attended over 65,000 cases on district all over the country, recorded a mortality rate of 1·9.[1] Neither in the cases attended by the Hospital or the Nurses was there any selection in favour of expected simple delivery or favourable home conditions. The hospital would tend to admit complicated cases and first births ; if a nurse had to call in a doctor owing to complications of labour, the case would still be recorded as hers.

There seems no adequate reason why, if all patients were given the same reasonable degree of care as these mothers received, the average death-rate all over the country should not be reduced to 2 per 1,000 births.

Why is the maternal death-rate more than double what it need be ? why does it remain the same when other death-rates steadily decline ? Why does the home-maker —for it is the home-maker primarily—suffer this tremendous disadvantage ? is it in any way connected with the fact of her domesticity, and the peculiar economic organization of her life ?

The Reports published by the Ministry of Health [2] indicate that the main causes of the high maternal death-rate are (a) inadequate training and low standard of practice of medical practitioners in gynæcology and obstetrics ; (b) low pay and status of midwives ; (c) lack of facilities for care of the mother before, during and after the birth (such as provision for ante-natal care, institutional accommodation for difficult cases, etc.) ; (d) negligence on the part of the mother and those concerned for her to take sufficient care of her health.

Of these four basic reasons for the high maternal death-rate, the two former appear to be closely connected with

[1] *Interim Report of Ministry of Health on Maternal Mortality and Morbidity*, 1930, p. 106.

[2] *Report of Ministry of Health on Maternal Mortality*, by Dame Janet Campbell (1924 and 1928) ; *Report of Ministry of Health on the Protection of Motherhood*, by Dame Janet Campbell (1927) ; *Report of Ministry of Health on the Training and Supply of Midwives* (1929) ; *Report of Ministry of Health (Interim) on Maternal Mortality and Morbidity* (1930).

the economic position of women in general, the latter with that of the domestic woman in particular.

For the last fifty years the great medical organizations themselves have been drawing attention to the poor standard of training of students in Midwifery and Obstetrics, so that at first sight it is difficult to understand the persistence of a state of affairs which one would suppose that they, either collectively or through the influence of their individual constituent members, were competent to alter.

But the neglect of Midwifery is perhaps due to a sentiment too deep-rooted in the individual man to respond to the recommendations of these august bodies. It may be that Midwifery is despised because it is also women's work. It is associated with lesser skill, and with the drudgery and penury which is in England the usual lot of the independent practising midwife, rather than with the well-carpeted rooms and shining car typical of the specialist surgeon.

Perhaps also the dead hand of the past reaches a stranglehold into the present ; it may be that the insufficient attention given to these subjects by medical student and teacher is to be traced to old jealousies between midwives and physicians. The scientific training and incorporation of physicians and surgeons, which began in the seventeenth century, was rigidly confined to men. Up till that time Midwifery had been a skilled women's profession. Although women were excluded from the new learning, the practice of midwifery continued to be shared between the newly-trained male accoucheurs and the midwives with their traditional methods. It may well be that for this reason Midwifery failed to acquire among medical men the honour which became associated with the other *mysteries* of surgery and physic, and so has always seemed less worthy of attention than these.

If the drudgery and poverty so commonly associated with the work of Midwifery have affected the medical man's view of the importance of the study of it, they have had an effect more direct and equally unfortunate

N

in lowering the quality of the midwife's own work. On an average the results of this work are good; at least, they compare favourably with the results of cases for which general medical practitioners are primarily responsible. But there is no doubt that the work of midwives might be much better than it is, if the ordinary midwife, even trained only as she is in England at present and working under the same conditions, could be assured of a higher fee for each case she attends, and a pension when she has become too old to carry on such exacting work efficiently. So long as the midwife "finds the utmost difficulty in eking out a precarious existence" although in full-time work; so long as "midwives feel the urge to undertake more cases than they can properly attend" because only so can they make ends meet;[1] so long as midwives can barely manage to supply themselves with a telephone for their work or comforts for their leisure, it will remain difficult for them to give to their patients the best service of which they are capable, and so reduce the preventable maternal deaths which disgrace the national records.

There seems little sign that the low status and pay of midwives arise from a mental attitude found among certain peoples of somewhat primitive religious outlook, who associate a ritual uncleanness with child-birth, and despise the midwife because of her connection with it. Despite certain passages in the Bible, this train of thought seems to be practically negligible in the social history of English Midwifery. The midwife's low status and pay are merely typical of the woman worker's general economic position, in a profession which has not benefited by any special influence of the movement for women's emancipation.

The low economic position of the woman worker has thus, through its effect on the standard of practice of both medical men and midwives themselves, proved an element in the causation of thousands of maternal and infant deaths yearly for many years past, and is one still to-day.

[1] *Report on Training . . . of Midwives*, p. 39.

The economic position of the mother herself has also had a disastrous influence. The social system which forces the family to make the health of the wage-earner its first care, encourages that negligence of the mother's health which has been officially noted as one of the causes of preventable mortality at child-birth. The health of the wage-earner is, furthermore, nationally insured, which makes it a matter of continuous concern to the State. A State Medical Service is provided for the schoolchild. But the health of the domestic woman is neglected, except during the period of her life when she is expecting or has just borne a baby. A custom of carelessness for her health is enforced by the organization of society and encouraged by the practice of the State ; there can be no surprise if the custom sometimes bears fatal fruit when the crisis of maternity occurs.

A system of insurance or a State Medical Service which would protect the general health of the domestic woman apart from childbearing activities, would undoubtedly help to lower the maternal mortality rate. This mortality is increased by about 25 per cent. from deaths due to causes not directly arising from the maternal condition. In some cases the causes themselves might have been completely eliminated if the woman's health had been properly cared for before pregnancy ; in other cases, such as those where lung disease, heart disease or tuberculosis were already present, contraceptive advice would prevent disaster.

Seeing how successfully the Health Insurance of the major part of the adult working population has been fitted into the organization of society, it seems undeniable that it is the domesticity and dependence of the married woman, her peculiar position within that organization, which has exposed her to special danger.

Besides the dangers that arise for the mother from the low standard of Midwifery practice and the general neglect of her health, there are the dangers arising from obvious causes such as lack of sufficient hospital accommodation for difficult cases, lack of clinic-accommodation for ante-natal supervision, and the many other facilities for maternal care which depend primarily on the provision of public funds.

This lack of funds for the care of maternity is not a matter of the present economic crisis : it is a permanent condition. The amount annually spent on Maternity and Child Welfare in this country under the Public Health Acts is under £2 million—approximately the same as the amount expended on public baths and wash-houses, and about two-thirds of that spent on hospitals and sanatoria for tuberculosis. It represents about $\frac{3}{4}d$. in the £ of our annual budget.[1]

Under the National Insurance scheme maternity benefits are granted to insured women and the wives of insured men, but this system, valuable as it is to the individual beneficiaries, is limited in range, it only deals with maternity as a kind of by-activity of industry. Many child-bearing mothers receive no benefits under the scheme, because they themselves have not been recently insured, or their husbands are not contributors.

The Committee which recently reported on Maternal Mortality outlined a scheme for a National Maternity Service by which it was hoped that the high death-rate of mothers might be reduced. But there has been no sign of their proposals being presented to Parliament in the form of a Government measure. It seems as though $\frac{3}{4}d$. in the £ is about all we can afford as a public contribution towards saving the lives of women and babies in child-birth.

Yet this is a minute fraction of our bill for Defence. A mad world indeed, for what do we wish to defend ? It cannot be the lives of the most defenceless, for we cannot afford to spend money on *them*.

Such anomalies of our civilization are not due to considered plan ; they are due to the survival of conven-

---

[1] Actually less than half this proportion of the Budget is devoted to Maternity and Child Welfare *under the heading of Public Health*, the remainder of the amount thus spent from public funds being raised locally from rates. The Exchequer, however, contributes to maternal welfare also under the head of National Health Insurance.

tions which blind us. Of all members of society, those whose health most needs to be studied and safeguarded are the mothers, who receive it least. The ultimate reason for this absurdity is to be found in the survival of antique marriage conventions. Centuries before members of society insured their health with each other, the childbearing woman alone was ensured against the danger of suffering from sickness without present aid and support, by giving her a legal claim on one man's labour or wealth whether she was or was not at the time repaying him by personal service or sharing his work. Now that the average man's opportunities for labour are so uncertain, and the number whom society permits to amass wealth comparatively so small, those very opportunities must also be insured. The original insurance of the child-bearing woman is rendered valueless when the man's opportunities for profitable labour are so problematic.

As a result of the customs which thus in former times safeguarded the childbearing woman, it has happened in modern times that most mothers are non-gainfully occupied. Because they are not gainfully occupied it has seemed impossible to find the finance for insuring their health along the same lines as that of other workers— to have a truly national health insurance scheme, or a general State medical service.

It is no wonder that Mr. Greenwood when Minister of Health described the maternal mortality rate as a nightmare. But it is also something other than a nightmare. It is a rational indictment of our social organization. The fundamental purpose of society is the protection of the childbearing woman and the infant. " Women and children first " was originally no meaningless phrase ; it expressed recognition of the fact that those whose life was most essential for the continuance of the community should be secured the first chances of survival. The massacre of men in the last war has made us perhaps rather impatient of such suggestion. But except during a war, we now organize civil society in such a way that mothers and unborn children are left last. The time when we shall safeguard *their* health is indefinitely postponed. It is more dangerous to be a woman carrying an unborn child than to follow any other business whatever.

Such are now the results of the special cherishing promised by Christian marriage.

CHAPTER XI

THE DIRECTION OF CHANGE

New views of marriage—the Woman's Movement—the philosophy of political freedom—Programme for Change.

In previous chapters an attempt has been made to show that the economic position of women in modern industrial society is peculiar and unfortunate ; unfortunate for industry, for society as a whole and for many women as individuals. But the society which is to persist adapts itself, consciously and subconsciously. How can we consciously seek, then, to change this present maladjustment ? In what present tendencies of change is hope of adjustment to be discovered ?

It is the former question which here calls more immediately for an answer, and for some suggestion of a programme which, achieved, might tend to solve the misfortunes and problems outlined. An answer to the latter would involve an analysis of the whole psychological evolution of society far beyond the scope of this book, and this analysis would but lead us back to the concrete question of how best to harness reason in the service of these subconscious vital forces. Yet the importance of what may be called our social sub-consciousness—of changes which are due to the general trend of social outlook, unbased on definite plan—must not be forgotten. The present direction of evolution is pointing towards a solution of these difficulties—towards a state of society in which the position of women will be different from what it is now. The forces seeming to make towards this end are many, and defy complete enumeration or analysis. When the movement was in progress to free negro slaves, Wordsworth wrote to their leader in prison :—

183

" Live and take comfort. Thou hast left behind
Powers that will work for thee ; air, earth, and skies ;
There's not a breathing of the common wind
That will forget thee ; thou hast great allies ;
Thy friends are exultations, agonies,
And love, and man's unconquerable mind."

So with our present problems. And before turning to
the formulation of a programme, it is worth while to
consider the reinforcements for it to be found all round
us in the mental air we breathe.

The troubles in question are rooted in marriage laws
and conventions which have survived from older times,
when ways of life were different from ours. But notable
changes are taking place in the modern attitude to marriage
and family life, and in the acceptance of those very conventions. Marriage does not, to the modern man and
woman, convey the same significance as it did to their
fathers. Its significance is not necessarily less ; it is
different. A change of view has occurred, most conscious
among those who read H. G. Wells, Bernard Shaw and
Havelock Ellis ten or twenty years ago, and those who
study Bertrand Russell (and many others) now, but not
confined to these comparatively leisured members of the
population. It has also affected those whose mothers
brought up ten or fifteen children in slums, but who
themselves limit their families ; among those women who
go out to work not, as in many districts of the North
Country, from inherited tradition, but in a spirit of social
revolution, when their husbands are unemployed.

These diverse changing views to marriage and family
life are receiving much attention, sympathetic and de-
nunciatory, as they find increasing expression in action.
They run contrary to orthodox opinion, and sometimes
favour action contrary not only to convention but to
law.

The conventional English and American view is that
marriage should be a permanent bond, within which alone
sexual intercourse should take place ; within this bond
law and custom give the husband certain rights (such as

determination of nationality and domicile) which are not granted to the wife. The force and extent of such laws and customs vary in different English-speaking countries. The acceptance of genuine monogamy for the husband as a practicable ideal is comparatively recent in English society, and coincides or has only slightly preceded the emergence of a school of thought which favours a greater laxity of sexual intercourse for both partners. The tendency in favour of equality for the sexes is the significant factor in both these trends.

Among those who take less conventional views, many regard without disfavour a lesser permanence of marriage ; others consider that while permanence of the bond has great value, especially for unions which produce children, it should be combined with less insistence on monogamy. Many demand a social relationship between man and wife different from that imposed by the laws and customs of their country—by which new relationship, for instance, the wife should be recognized as an equal partner with her husband, should be secured economic independence, equal rights as regards choice of nationality, domicile, divorce, guardianship of children, etc. (the details of such demands depending on the situation of the parties and the laws and customs of the society in which they live).

There are some men and women of modern outlook, not over-ruled by passion, who are so impressed by the disadvantages of conventional marriage that quite soberly they follow the ancient advice of Mr. Punch, whose joke it was to suggest to those about to marry, *Don't !* Others attempt to circumvent these disadvantages by some previous agreement, often informal, enlarging and defining the freedom recognized by each as the other's right, above that permitted by law or custom ; or settling on a division of income to ensure an equal or sufficient independence for each.

Marriage agreements additional to those of the legal contract itself are of course no new thing. It is the custom in the Roman Church, when a Catholic marries a Protestant, to require an agreement as to the religious education of the children. Persons of considerable wealth have for centuries past made legal marriage settlements, but of a kind quite different in spirit from the type here described as modern. Settlements in this traditional form are an affair to be arranged between the bridegroom and his family, and the bride's family. The bride herself is expected to take no interest in the economic aspect of her transference.

New views of marriage tend to act as solvents to the old conventions, but they act slowly. Those who hold the new views are often prevented from testing and practising them by the crushing force of the economic organization which surrounds them, based though this force be on the very system they distrust and question. They perhaps desire an equal economic freedom for man and wife, feeling that love is not love where there is inevitable dependence ; yet if efforts to secure this equal freedom end in failure, they do not always see that the cause may be, not an inherently dependent spirit in woman, but the handicap placed upon her efforts by a social organization which presupposes her dependence.

This makes it the more necessary to plan separately the economic changes without which these new ideals cannot be realized.

The changing attitude to marriage which is so marked a feature of contemporary thought, is one force working towards an alteration in the economic position of women. The force described as the Woman's Movement is another ; indeed the two are closely interlinked. The Woman's Movement is no longer, as it was before the war of 1914, a " Movement " in the sense of having a single and clear aim. But as it existed in the minds of Mary Wollstonecraft, Charlotte Brontë, and countless others, before John Stuart Mill and Mrs. Fawcett arose to inspire and lead it, so it survives among hundreds of men and women whose convictions are courageous and deep-rooted, and springs up constantly afresh in the minds and actions of the young.

Last of these immeasurable and intangible reinforcements working towards change in the position of women in society, may be mentioned the spirit of Liberalism— not in the sense which attaches to the word as a designation of one political party, but as a principle which has inspired Englishmen, and men of other countries, for centuries before the word was used : the belief that freedom and justice that has no respect for persons, have essential value for men, nourishing their healthy development, and that it is the right part of Government to secure for every individual man, woman and child the maximum of mental, moral and physical freedom consistent with the general and increasing welfare of society as a whole. Granted this view of the strategy of government, the adjustment of the claims of the individual and of society are a matter of tactics : between the principles that inspire Individualism and Socialism there is no essential discord. Both are elements of this fundamental Liberalism. Historic English Liberalism, which may count Gladstone, Byron and Milton among its exponents, commonly forgot to apply its principles to women. They are being more justly applied, in this respect, by the Communists in Russia to-day.

It is, in fact, not to any one of these trends of thought alone that one looks for the dominant force which will bring about a change in the economic position of women in modern society, but to the simultaneous action of them all, and of others unnoted. In some countries they may merge, perhaps, into new and revolutionary forms of social activity ; in others they may bring about similar results by gradual means. Those who believe in the inevitability or the preferability of gradualness will welcome suggestions focusing the separate changes by which the new position may be reached. The final outcome will be brought about by many previous interlinked changes which will not occur simultaneously, and will interact on one another according to their time-sequence in ways impossible to foresee. But the attempt to focus future change in one coherent forward view is not therefore futile, for by providing a Programme it may harness afresh a definite conscious impulse towards the new way of life.

That payment for work done should be made without reference to the worker's sex, is of fundamental importance. This would be at the present time impracticable over a large part of the field of gainful occupation, and also unjust to many of those both gainfully and non-gainfully occupied ; yet it is a principle which we must find the right and smooth way to practise if the wrongs and difficulties of the present system are ever to be resolved.

Indeed something more is needed than payment without reference to sex. The need may for the moment be summarized as *Equal Pay for Equal Work*—a phrase to be further defined later, when separate items of this Outline-programme are more fully considered. The formula implies equal opportunity and conditions of work as well as equal pay.

The achievement of Equal Pay is dependent upon a number of other social changes or reforms. When Mrs. Sidney Webb advocated it in 1919,[1] she postulated as necessary preliminaries to its establishment (i) the establishment of a National Minimum Wage ; (ii) a system of Old Age Pensions ; (iii) National Provision for all infirm and sick ; (iv) a State system of Children's Allowances ; and (v) an adequate, subsidized National Maternity Service. Of these services, only the second and a part of the third were in existence at the time. The provision of Old Age Pensions has since been extended, but (except for developments in connection with Children's Allowances, especially under the Widows' and Orphans' Pensions Acts) the other services then non-existent have not yet materialized.

In so far as the domestic wife was occupied with the care of children, the proposed Children's Allowances were to be considered as in part paying for her maintenance in respect of this service. (It is therefore to be noted that they were envisaged as a fully adequate cash payment.)

[1] *Report of War Cabinet Committee on Women in Industry (Minority Report)*.

But wives who have no dependent children may frequently find that they have only a part-time job at home. If they are occupied in no paid work, the husband then carries a burden of dependence unequal to that of his fellow-workers, which condition of things it was intended to avoid. But part-time gainful work for the wife, except of a casual or "sweated" kind, is difficult to get ; and if the wife enters the ordinary labour-market for full-time work without securing domestic assistance for her home, she suffers, the Health Insurance Funds suffer, her home suffers, and the principle of equal pay is endangered.

The solution of this difficulty may lie along the lines of a suggestion made by Miss Van den Plas (of Belgium) at the time of the establishment of the International Labour Organization. She requested, on behalf of the Conference of Allied Women Suffragists, that the question of half-time work for married women should be placed on the agenda of the First International Labour Conference, on the ground that the provision of half-time work would make it possible for many a married woman to work "without abandoning her household . . . and without . . . being subjected to the low wages which were given . . . on the pretext that she only needed a nominal wage ".[1]

Such organization of women's work, besides helping to smooth the road for the establishment of Equal Pay, would have great value in improving the economic position of the domestic and semi-domestic worker, and might, by providing organization, encouragement, and some standard of pay and conditions for part-time domestic work, do much to secure for full-time women workers the domestic assistance which they now so often fail to obtain, or even to seek.

The tradition, now some centuries old, of non-valuation and undervaluation of home-making work, and the ills that arise from this tradition, would probably not be

[1] As reported in *Studies and Reports of the I.L.O.*, Geneva, 1921, No. 1, Series 1 : *The International Protection of Women Workers*, p. 6.

completely overthrown even by the establishment of *Equal Pay, Family Allowances, adequate Health and Maternity Services,* or the *Organization of Part-time Work for Women.* All these would be needed, but also a good deal more.

Wider change must come about through the agency both of law and of new custom—through the statesman and through the man in the street. Oliver Goldsmith wrote, with a political pessimism common enough in our time as well as his own :—

"How small, of all that human hearts endure,
That part which laws or kings can cause or cure!"

But laws may be the final expression of a new view of life among a large number of people, exercising a force without which the dead hand of tradition cannot be unloosened. Change in human hearts may be the only cure for human ills, but law announces, seals, implements the change.

A higher valuation of the business of home-making, once learnt, could readily be expressed in legislative and administrative action along lines already laid down, and might lead to new developments as well. The care of Public Health, the State regulation of utility services, and other Social Services of comparatively recent growth, already provide some necessary extra weightage on the consumer's, or home-maker's, side of the industrial balance, and mitigate the effects of that neglect of human, non-exchangeable values which is a feature of modern industrialism. Housing and Town-planning schemes are vitally necessary State activities, even apart from the subsidies with which they are generally associated, since they provide not only assistance to home-making, but also co-ordination and control for an industry composed of comparatively small, independent units apt in seeking their own ends to defeat them, and achieve ugliness, over-crowding, and waste of health and labour, through the ill-advised search for private profit or amenity. Consumers' Councils, which now exist only on paper, might become realities and acquire effective power, if the consumer as such were to enjoy greater importance and political weight in the social scheme. Such weight, and some such means of exercising it, it is essential that the consumer should possess, if the competition of domestic with centralized labour is not to be encouraged; for distrust of industrial methods and of inordinate industrial and commercial profits provides a valid reason for domestic competition at the present time. In branches of industry in which the home-maker can no longer compete with the producer or manufacturer, the need for him to secure a fair share of the advantages gained from modern methods of manufacture and sale is all the more.

A remodelling of the junior branches of the educational system, to include the provision (at any rate in towns) of Nursery Schools for children under the present Elementary School age, might not only benefit the children admitted, but also leave overburdened mothers freer to cope adequately with other home-making work and the care of still younger infants.

In the United States the Bureau of Home Economics carries out research and educational work without counterpart in this country. It is a stimulus to the best type of home-making, urban and rural. The moral of our own deficiency in this respect has been pressed specially with reference to country home-makers, by advisers to the Ministry of Agriculture. In consideration of the special needs and interests of the agricultural home-maker

. . . " France, Belgium, Holland, Switzerland, Germany, Denmark, Norway, Finland and the United States must be regarded as definitely in advance of England."

" In the U.S.A. . . . the inauguration of that great service known as Extension Work in Rural Home Economics . . . was the first official recognition that ' the value of farm life could not be estimated by the numbers of its flocks and herds or by the value of its crops alone, but must also consider the kind of life maintained in the farm home '. The service . . . now absorbs 25 per cent. of the total funds allocated for agricultural extension work in America." [1]

[1] *Report on the Practical Education of Women for Rural Life*, pp. 14, 15.

The recommendation to our own Government, in the Report quoted, necessarily refers only to the farm-home ; but the same type of educational work is going on all over America, aiming at the encouragement, and providing the support of centralized organization, for high standards of home-making in every home.

This same Report which remarks on the deficient attention paid to the needs of the English rural home-maker, also refers to another aspect of the matter which has a wider reference ; namely, the inadequate representation of women's interests " on the machinery controlling the system ".

> " Women's chance of serving . . . on County Education and County Agricultural Committees . . . is very small. . . . It is possible for an Agricultural Education Sub-Committee . . . to include no woman members. The average representation of women . . . bears little relation to their importance in the industry. . . . The women who serve in these minorities find it a practical impossibility to secure many improvements they desire ; e.g. the throwing open of county appointments to free competition by men and women. . . .
>
> A mixed agricultural college catering for residential women students . . . and now developing a branch of work of particular concern to women, has no woman on the governing body." [1]

This kind of criticism is not peculiar to investigators of agricultural conditions. A similar tale was told by the War Cabinet Committee on Women in Industry nine years previously. There is a marked shortage of women in responsible public work and responsible administrative positions, which results in neglect of the needs and interests of women. The provisions of the Local Government Act, however theoretically irreproachable, seem to have increased this difficulty. While the tradition against women undertaking public work is still widely diffused, it might be wise for the sake of public need to arrange for compulsory co-option of women to many bodies on which they are often, at the present time, unrepresented,

---

[1] *Report on the Practical Education of Women for Rural Life*, pp. 25, 26.

or to reserve places for the election of a woman only. Of course this is fundamentally an unsatisfactory procedure. It is much more desirable that the need for the representation of women should be more widely recognized, and that they should secure regular election in closer proportion to the need for their services than they do at present.

So the need for representation of women on Central or Local Authorities, and action by these Authorities, leads back again to the need for change in individual mental view.

Individual mentality is also the primary factor in the solution of the outstanding problem of securing economic independence for the wife. Some observers seem to believe that the future of the family in industrial society lies along the lines of independently (and approximately equally) earning man and wife, with young children communally reared on State funds. I rather believe that the home-making wife will continue to exist, and that the general problem of her dependence will be solved along the lines of an agreed pooling of income, with recognition of the rights of the joint household and of each partner in the pool. When such a system had secured a considerable degree of voluntary adherence, legislation might proceed satisfactorily on a foundation of new practice, and with due regard for new legislation on similar lines already enacted in other European States.

Such in mere outline is the programme of social and political developments by which, it is suggested, the dislocated joint of Womanhood might be set in proper position in the body corporate. Certain major points to which only brief reference has been made, await fuller consideration. Many of these proposals are not new. Several have already been the subject of Royal Commissions and official Reports ; most have attracted attention from social students and political thinkers. The *pros* and *cons*, the practicability, and the relevance to our subject, of each item, can only be outlined ; for their full development they would fill (and in some cases have filled) separate volumes.

o

CHAPTER XII

EQUAL PAY FOR EQUAL WORK

The meaning of the phrase—opposition disguised under similar titles —the effect of differential rates on industry—aggravation of evil effect during periods of depression—effect on national expenditure through Unemployment Insurance Fund.

If Equal Pay for Equal Work is to be one of the foundations of the future economic position of women, the phrase demands further definition, and it concerns us to consider both the advantages that might be secured by Equal Pay in the future, and the disadvantages attaching to Differential Pay according to Sex at the present time.

The phrase *Equal Pay for Equal Work* is capable of many interpretations. It is obvious that instances in which exactly equal reward is rendered for exactly equal service are rare, and cannot be proven. In fact, equality can here have no exact meaning, but must refer to some rough, accepted measure of approximation.

Such a measure is discoverable in the common rule of industry, as that principle is applied by Trade Unionism, and generally accepted by employers' organizations. A job of work is defined, being measured either by product or by time, and a price is affixed to the performance of it. It is the fundamental principle of Trade Unionism that, by whomsoever that work is performed, so long as the conditions under which the agreement was made remain approximately the same, the price paid for the job shall be the same.

Trade Union practice, in securing Equal Pay, lays upon the employer the onus of completing the equation. The necessity of paying the same wage for a job, irrespective of output or its equivalent, under a time-rate system,

or of time taken, under a piece-work system, impels the
employer to engage the most efficient worker obtainable
at the agreed wage, and so, in a free labour market, results
in the greatest possible equality of labour-return for the
wage offered.

It follows that Equal Pay is not just to the employer,
nor consistent with maximum national productiveness, if
restrictions are imposed on the right or opportunity of
any worker to apply or qualify for any type of work, or
on the employer's right of engaging service. *Equal Pay
for Equal Work* essentially implies not merely payment
for work done irrespective of sex, marriage, family obligations, or any other individual idiosyncrasy of the worker,
but also the equal liberty of citizens to apply for work,
or for the preliminary training necessary to secure it.

The phrase has, however, been given another interpretation which is in effect contrary to the above. The onus
of completing the equation, it is suggested, should be
reversed. The employer should decide what is equal
work, and it should remain with the employees to secure
equal pay.

After the war, employers in the Metal, Chemical, Woollen
and Clothing Industries separately stated that they
favoured Equal Pay for men and women, interpreted as
Equal Pay for Equal Output, Value, Profit, or " Advantageousness " to the employer, and this view was taken
in the Majority Report of the War Cabinet Committee
on Women in Industry.[1] The MacDonnell Commission
on the Civil Service (1912–1915) had also supported Equal
Pay so interpreted.[2]

Whatever advantages such a system might offer, it
must not be supposed that payment irrespective of sex
would be one of them. What is, in practice, suggested,
is that women should receive lower wage-rates than men,

[1] Employers' views :—*Report of War Cabinet Committee* (*Appendices, etc.*), pp. 50, 54, 62 (Metals) ; p. 69 (Chemicals) ; p. 88 (Woollen
Industry, etc.) ; pp. 99, 101 (Clothing).
[2] The relevant passages from the MacDonnell Report are quoted in
the *Report of the Royal Commission on the Civil Service*, 1929-1931,
pp. 126-7.

on the grounds that their output is less, or that their output, though equal or more than the average man's, is burdened with higher overhead charges. Lesser muscular strength, lesser availability in emergency, higher labour turnover owing to marriage-retirement, higher sickness and absence rates, are among the stated causes of women's lesser " net advantageousness " to their employer.

It was not suggested that men should receive lower wage-rates than women in occupations in which *their* output is less—where their lesser dexterity or docility, greater susceptibility to adverse conditions of work,[1] or lesser availability in the emergencies most likely to arise,[2] make them of lesser " net advantageousness " to their employer.

Actually the phrase *Equal Pay for Equal Output (or Value)* is a euphemism for the payment of differential occupational wage-rates to men and women, which rates are always to be lower for the women. If it were consistently applied, without regard to sex—if each employee were to receive a reward proportional to his value to his employer—it would be the negation of the fundamental principles of Trade Unionism, and would signify the complete abandonment of all standard rates, and a return to individual bargaining.

Differential wage-rates based on sex have been justified on the ground that otherwise (under a system of *Equal Pay for Equal Work* in the sense here accepted) women would not be employed at all in certain occupations. But if this were true, it would be rather a condemnation than a justification of differential rates, and would be less than ever valid now that over two million men are unemployed in this country alone. The employment of one class of

---

[1] For an instance of greater susceptibility of men to adverse conditions of industrial work, see *Report on Sickness among Operatives in Lancashire Cotton Spinning Mills*, by A. B. Hill, Industrial Health Research Board, 1930, pp. 55, 78.

[2] For instance a male obstetrician might be less useful in a crisis of domestic management than a female, just as a female lift-worker might be less useful in a crisis of mechanics than a male. In unforeseeable crises masculinity is not, in fact, an invariable asset, any more than femininity. In the history of England it seems probable that the femininity of Queen Elizabeth was as important a factor in securing our national independence and prosperity as the masculinity of her father.

workers on work at which they are less efficient than others who are available, is to the disadvantage of the community, and the disadvantage is made no less by the fact that the less efficient are being paid less than the agreed standard rate.

" There is no public advantage, but actually a sheer national loss in bribing the employer by permitting him to pay lower wages, or to make special deductions from the occupational rate to get his work done by workers industrially less efficient—whether women or men—so long as any more efficient workers for the task required are available. It is imperative, if we are to get the maximum production out of any given generation, that those who are responsible for the selection of workers, whether by hand or brain . . . should be under no temptation to deviate from the rule of getting every task performed by the workers who are, in all respects, the most efficient for the purpose. Only after he has taken on all the less costly workers who can perform the work with the lower expenditure of efforts and sacrifices, and with the least incidental expenses, and with the greater net efficiency, is the employer warranted in resorting to the more costly and less efficient workers, male or female ; and then only to the extent that he finds their employment . . . positively advantageous to him. If their employment is thus advantageous . . . there is no reason why the particular individuals last engaged . . . should be penalized by deductions which will never be proportionate to their individual shortcomings, which inevitably tend to tempt the employer actually to prefer this less efficient labour, and which cannot fail to imperil the maintenance of the occupational rate itself. . . . The existence . . . of identical occupational rates . . . is therefore absolutely a condition of maximum production." [1]

Since such differential wage-rates based on sex are sometimes justified as being in the interests of women workers, it is interesting to note that many women workers themselves, whether organized jointly with men or in separate federations, do not support them.

(The witness) " was of the opinion that at equal rates of wages women would still continue to be employed . . . (but) if it should prove that at equal rates employers preferred men the Society's view was that they would rather

[1] *Report of War Cabinet Committee (Minority Report)*, p. 282.

fight for the equal rate than undercut their men colleagues by accepting a lower rate." (*The Society of Women Welders*.)[1]

" It is in the interest of both sexes that men and women should be paid the same rates for the same job." (*Miss Carlin ; Dock, Wharf, etc., and General Workers' Union*.) [2]

" The National Federation of Women Workers claim that the rate of wages . . . should be fixed for the job, and without regard to the sex of the worker. . . . That (this) means the exclusion of women from certain trades is irrefutable, but . . . it cannot be said that this is in itself either good or bad. . . . Anything less than this would make the position of women in industry intolerable. . . . Under this system, women can demand an equal opportunity of entry into any trade. . . . The women will seek and secure a permanent footing in trades that are suited to them. In other trades, only exceptional women will find employment, and the result of this natural distribution, based upon suitability for work rather than cheapness, will certainly contribute to increased national efficiency." [3]

The MacDonnell Commission on the Civil Service, taking a contrary view to these, reported that

" To make the rates for men and women equal, in disregard of economic considerations, would ultimately have the effect of impeding or precluding the employment of women in the Public Service. It would be found less costly in the long run to employ men." [4]

Yet among the keenest protagonists of Equal Pay in the Civil Service are the women Civil Servants themselves. They are more willing than those who thus advised their employers, that they and their fellows in the future should run the risk of unemployment under conditions of a fair field and no favour.[5]

In fact, it may be said that the interpretation of Equal Pay for Equal Work in the sense of Equal Output or Value to the employer is a formula designed to defend and perpetuate present conditions of arbitrary inequality

[1] *Report of War Cabinet Committee* (*Appendices, etc.*), p. 60.
[2] *Ibid.,* p. 42.
[3] *Ibid.,* p. 16.
[4] See reference, p. 195, note 2.
[5] See publications of the Federation of Women Civil Servants.

of pay. At the best it could but serve to raise women's wages in isolated cases, or to increase their opportunities for cheap employment, without providing any of the ground for equal opportunities, the hope of increased national efficiency, or the cessation of male workers' opposition to female labour, which is offered by a system of equal pay for the job, defined by time, " piece ", or service irrespective of the worker or class of workers engaged. It might perpetuate the preferential employment of women in work 'for which they were not on the whole so well suited as men ; but there seems little ground for the suggestion that under a system of equal pay irrespective of sex women would be excluded from a large number of occupations in which they are at present employed. Women teachers would still be required though their pay were equal to men's. In periods of normal employment men have not ousted women from those branches of the textile industry where equal pay is the rule. Women doctors, journalists, scientific workers, find employment at the same fees as men. In industrial work requiring especial manipulative dexterity it seems likely that women would always receive the preference of employment, and the same applies to telephone operation.

Exceptions may be found in such work as requires a considerable degree of technical skill, knowledge, or adaptability, not acquirable in a short period of training, but in which the training is not normally undertaken at the worker's expense. Here the quicker labour-turnover of women owing to marriage-retirement is a great disadvantage to which consideration must be given. But any difficulty or unequal value arising from the differential retirement rate would more reasonably be met by a system of low-wage apprenticeship for both sexes, than by differential rates for trained workers. Women as a sex would then suffer lower wages, or unemployment in this more-skilled work, in proportion to their higher labour turnover, but the wages of individual men and women would still be equal for the standard job, and there would be no danger of the one sex undercutting the other, or being prohibited from a branch of employment so as to secure the wage-rate.

The advantages and disadvantages of *Equal Pay* have been frequently debated by men and women workers with reference to their own earnings and employment, and by employers of labour with reference to profits. Less consideration seems to have been given to the actual effect of artificial segregation of labour, and unequal group-efficiency wages, on national industry and employment.

It is one of the functions of wages to bear a part in measuring the changes in demand for services and goods. High wages offered for a certain kind of service, relatively to the skill required, indicate an increased demand for that service, and vice-versa. (Mrs. Barbara Wootton has criticized Mr. Bernard Shaw's proposals, outlined in *The Intelligent Woman's Guide to Socialism*, that every citizen should receive an equal wage, on the ground that this function of wages would thereby be destroyed.)

But obviously it is only possible for wages to perform this function of measuring genuine changes in demand, when wages are comparatively elastic, and the mobility and aggregation (as opposed to segregation) of labour are sufficient to ensure a similar reward being obtained for similar degrees of skill or of scarcity in relation to demand. When the efficiency-wage of one group of workers is lower than that of another, and is maintained at the lower level by artificial segregation, the comparative cheapness of production by the former group may stimulate, or even artificially create, a demand for their services.

We see this happening as between the same industry in different countries, and regret, for instance, the languishing of our own textile trade under stress of competition with the Japanese, whose workers are comparatively poorly paid. A similar form of undercutting competition may occur between different industries within the same country. All incomes between maximum and minimum offer the recipient a certain elasticity of expenditure, as between different things. One may choose between books and golf, a blanket and a hot-water bottle, between soap and scent, or silk underclothes and beads.

"In the all-pervading competition of the modern world-market, each industry is perpetually struggling against every other industry to maintain and to improve its position . . . tempting the consumer by cheapness continually to increase his demand for its commodities, inducing the investor by swollen profits to divert more and more of the nation's capital in its direction, and attracting, by large salaries, more and more of the nation's brains to its service. In the competition for the foreign market, in particular, product jostles with product in a manner that can scarcely be overlooked. The mere fact that we import foreign produce compels a certain though varying total amount of export sales, but which articles the foreigner will buy depends on their relative cheapness to him. Hence the development of an increased export trade in slop clothing may well have something to do with the check to our export sales of textiles or machinery. The diminution in the Northumberland coal shipments may be ultimately caused by a contemporary expansion in the foreign sales of East End boots and shoes."[1]

Mr. Sidney Webb (Lord Passfield), writing the above in 1910, was particularly referring to "sweated industries". But "sweated labour" is merely an extreme form of inequality of wage-reward per efficiency-unit. The same argument applies in proportionate degree to all industries employing labour at a rate below that paid in other industries where similar skill is required ; the former tend to attract undue custom and capital to the extent that they undercut costs. Nationally and internationally there is "artificial" cultivation of those industries which, owing to segregation of labour and payment of one group at a lower efficiency wage-rate than the other group, secure their labour (or a large proportion of it) at comparatively low cost.

There are, of course, certain conditions under which the advantage of employing cheap labour are lost (even when "cheap labour" is cheap actually in relation to efficiency and skill, not only on the reckoning of money wages). If material equipment or scientific organization

---

[1] *History of Factory Legislation*, Preface by Sidney Webb, p. xii.

are neglected because human power is cheap, an industry
blessed with cheap labour may find itself beaten in the
market by another paying high wages but more scientifically equipped.

It follows that the advantages of cheap labour are
most likely to be reaped in periods of industrial depression, when there is in general less incentive to employ
capital in improved material equipment. In periods of
adversity such as the present, industries mainly employing men (whose labour is normally paid at a higher rate
per efficiency-unit) are likely to suffer more and cause
more unemployment than those in which women are
largely occupied. The proportion of women compared
with men who are gainfully employed is then likely to
increase, above that of normal times. This is the case
at present, as shown in the chart on page 205.

In 1920, before the post-war trade depression began,
there were more women than men registered as unemployed, proportionately to the total numbers of each
registered as insured against unemployment. Since mid-
1921, when the period of abnormal unemployment began,
there have consistently been more men than women unemployed, on the same reckoning. The male and female
unemployment percentages each year since 1921 are given
in Table VI (p. 204), and the variation in the ratio of these
rates from year to year is represented by curve (c) of
the accompanying chart.

What are the reasons for the disproportion between
male and female unemployment rates? Three possible
reasons will suggest themselves :—(1) that unemployed
women can be to some extent drafted to domestic service, which is non-insurable employment, in which case
even if they later become unemployed they are not
generally eligible for benefit, or inclusion in the unemployment figures ; (2) that women have been "taking
men's jobs" ; (3) that trade depression has been especially severe in the industries which mainly employ men.

Each of these is a partial explanation ; none is alone
sufficient. Women's greater opportunities for obtaining

non-insurable employment when unable to obtain insurable work, is not a sufficient explanation of the problem, since it appears that at the same time as women's unemployment rates have been *low* compared with men's, the number of women insured workers as a whole has been *high* compared with that of men. Women have not, comparatively, been leaving industry during the period of depression ; on the contrary, their numbers have actually increased compared with those of men. And there has been a close correspondence year by year between this increase, and the depression of trade.

The numbers of insured workers of each sex, and the ratio between them annually, 1921–1930, are given in Table VI. The variation in the ratio is represented by curve (*b*) on the chart, which may be compared with curve (*a*), representing the total unemployment rate. It will be seen that, disregarding the year of the General Strike, the curves move in the same direction for every year from 1921 to 1930, with the exception of 1928–1929.

This seems to indicate a preference, or comparatively greater advantageousness, of women's industrial employment during the period of depression, and suggests that their lower unemployment rates are not to be completely explained by their greater facilities for obtaining non-insurable employment.

The second explanation also appears inadequate. One is in general aware that employers are reluctant to dismiss men and substitute women at the present time, even where some financial advantage might be expected from the change, because of their view of their responsibilities during the crisis.[1] In a recent review of this problem Mr. Rhys Davies concluded that purposeful substitution of men by women workers had not been an important factor in causing the high unemployment rate of men compared with women, and the higher proportion of women insured workers during the period of depression.[2]

[1] On this point some observations were made by Professor Sargent Florence, *op. cit.*

[2] In an article in *The Political Quarterly*, March 1931, entitled *Are Women Taking Men's Jobs ?*

TABLE VI

STATISTICAL BASIS OF CHART, p. 205 [1]

	Curve (a) Insured workers unemployed, 1920–30. Total percentage rate [2]	Curve (b) Adult workers insured against unemployment; numbers of each sex, and percentage of women to men [3]			Curve (c) Insured workers unem- ployed, 1920–30; per- centage rates of each sex, and percentage of male to female rate [4]		
Year		M	W	W : M per cent.	M	F	M : F rate per cent.
		('000s)					
1920 . (Dec.)	7·8	—	—	—	7·1	9·4	75
1921 . (July 1)	21·9	7,444	2,720	36·5	22·3	21·0	106
1922 .	13·5	7,645	2,619	34·3	15·9	6·8	234
1923 .	11·2	7,794	2,517	32·3	12·0	8·7	138
1924 .	9·2	7,873	2,597	32·1	9·7	7·5	129
1925 .	11·6	7,983	2,672	33·5	12·8	8·0	160
1926 .	14·3	8,112	2,690	33·2	15·2	11·8	129
1927 .	8·8	8,171	2,720	33·3	10·0	5·3	189
1928 .	10·5	7,907	2,748	34·7	12·1	6·4	189
1929 .	9·5	8,010	2,799	34·9	10·7	6·5	165
1930 .	15·2	8,174	2,920	35·7	15·5	14·5	107

When due weight is given to both these partial causes, the third suggestion remains to bear the brunt of the explanation—namely, that depression has been specially severe in the industries which mainly employ men. But this " explanation " is in itself scarcely worthy of the name, unless either some further reason is to be found in the conditions of men-employing industries in general, as compared with women-employing industries, or unless there is a causal connection between the facts, and the

[1] In references to the Chart and this Table in the text, the unemployment rate (curve a) has been taken as an indication of the state of trade. Changes in administration and law with regard to Unemployment Insurance, however, prevent uniformity in this method of presenting the picture of trade conditions. The record for 1928–9 is probably for this reason somewhat distorted.

[2] *Abstract of Labour Statistics for* 1930, p. 46. H.M.S.O.

[3] *Ibid.*, p. 33. (Numbers only.) The choice of midsummer for all the statistics given in this table, for every year except 1920, was determined by the fact that those for curve (b) are only given for early July in the Abstract. The summer rate of unemployment tends to be lower than the average for the year.

[4] *Ibid.*, pp. 46–7. (Male and female percentages, but not Male : female percentage.)

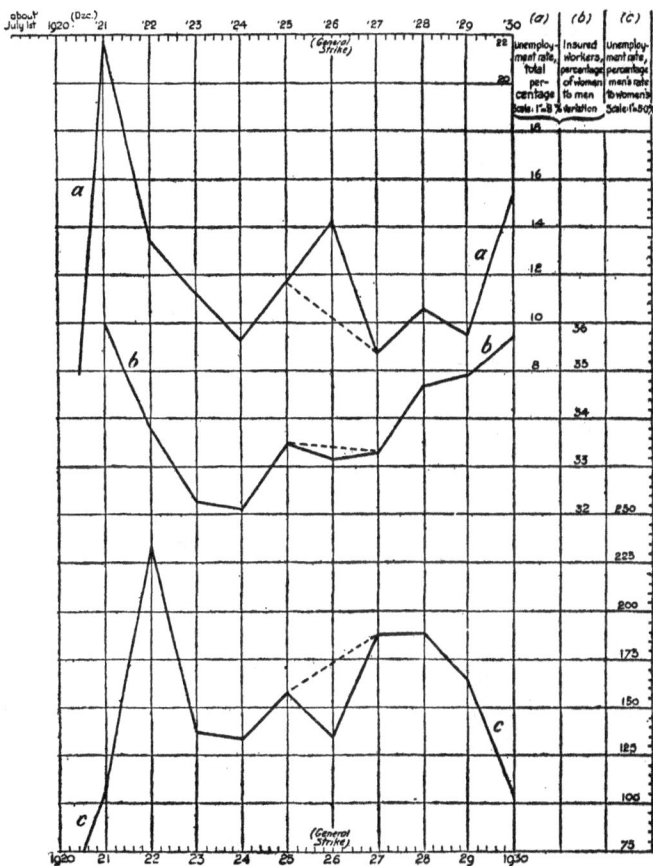

Chart showing the correspondence between depression of trade (a) and the proportion of men and women employed in industry (b and c) as evidenced by (a) general unemployment rate, (b) proportion of each sex insured against unemployment, (c) the proportion of each sex unemployed. 1921-1930.

very fact of mainly employing men is apt to cause depression in a trade.

In the first Report of the Royal Commission on Unemployment Insurance (1931) the causes of depression in industries of exceptional unemployment are attributed to (1) war-time expansion of the industry to a degree excessive for peace-time demand ; (2) the special difficulties suffered during recent years by trades hitherto dependent on export-markets ; (3) poor organization of labour within the industry itself.

In addition, for many industries suffering from specially severe unemployment special reasons for depression may be discovered. Thus the British coal industry has gradually lost advantages enjoyed by this country over others in earlier times, and has also suffered in common with the coal trade of other countries from the increasing use of other forms of fuel and power. The cotton industry is affected by conditions in India.

But neither general nor special causes seem adequate to account for the phenomenon, throughout the period of depression, of a low proportion of men employed, as compared with women, and the correspondence between the movement of this proportion, and the degree of the depression. The war-time expansion of industry increased the volume of female rather than male labour at first. Many industries so expanded had substituted male labour for female after the war, before the contraction of employment set in, but the previous dismissals of female labour had caused a certain amount of disproportionate unemployment among women, and the substitution was not entirely complete, so that a number of women as well as men have been thrown on the labour market by the contraction of industries over-expanded during the war. The export trades do not depend exclusively on male labour. The industries especially ill-organized internally, to which special reference is made in the Report, are Dock Labour and Public Works Contracting, which are almost exclusively " manned " by men ; but in general the organization of male labour is better than that of female, so that poor

internal organization of trades should not provide a sufficient reason for the higher unemployment rates of men
in general as compared with women.

After general and special causes for depression have
been taken into account, there still remain " a residue "
of industries " in which the significance of the high level
of unemployment is not so readily apparent " ; and neither
the general nor special causes seem quite sufficient to explain the movement of men's and women's employment
and unemployment rates in relation to each other, and
in relation to the varying state of trade.

It would appear that the employment of a high proportion of men at recognized rates of men's wages imposes, or
at critical times recently has imposed, burdens heavier than
industry in Great Britain can bear, and that the employment of women relieves an industry of part of this burden.

There is a high percentage of women employees in those
industries which have suffered less from unemployment
in the last ten years.   In many new industries which are
comparatively prosperous a large proportion of women
are employed.

The influence of real-wage rates in general on the unemployment rates has recently received much attention.
The influence of the differential sex wage-rate, however, has
so far as I know received very little, and is rarely mentioned by expert writers on the crisis.[1]   If it is a factor

[1] The point has, however, been studied by Mr. A. R. Burnett-Hurst.
In 1929 he made the following comments on a paper read by Dr. E. C.
Snow before the Royal Statistical Society :—
" Dr. Snow . . . states that ' the figures do not indicate that increase
of employment of women in manufacturing work has had any serious
effect upon the problem of the unemployment of men.' . . . But did
not the position change after 1921 ? . . . After 1921, industry and
commerce were faced with the problem of reducing the costs of production.   One method adopted by many employers was to instal more
machinery and to employ more women and girls. . . .   We find that
it is really through a movement for reducing costs of production that
women have entered the industrial and commercial field in large numbers
since 1921.   After analysing the Ministry of Labour's return of the
number of persons employed in manufacturing industries, including the
building trade, I came to the startling conclusion : comparing 1927
with 1923, I found that there had been a decline of 50,000 in the number
of male insured persons employed in the manufacturing industries and
an increase of 70,000 women in the same industries " (*Journal of Royal
Statistical Society, Part III*, 1929, p. 360).

of depression apart from the general wage-level, as the figures seem to suggest, it will continue to exert its influence even though the general wage-level be lowered.

Even in a labour-market divided into segregated groups, the lack of demand for labour in one industry consequent on comparative depression of that trade, may be expected to lead to lower wage-rates, and so a levelling of wage-rates between different industries is to be expected. As between men's and women's trades, the more efficient organization of the men counteracts this levelling tendency, but nevertheless it is occurring to some extent at the present time. Wage-rates and earnings in many men's occupations have fallen very low, and in some women's industrial occupations the earnings obtained by women (especially on piece-work) equal or exceed the earnings of many men in the depressed trades.

As a proof of the futility of a policy of segregation of men's from women's work aimed at the securing of higher wage-rates and earnings for men, such a state of affairs might be welcomed ; but when one considers the misery in many a home where families of young children are spending their days on intermittent or starvation-wages, or the dole, or Public Assistance, because of the depression in " men's " industries, one can feel no pleasure that women's employment and earnings may be increasing in this time of general distress, as compared with men's.

There are circumstances conceivable in which the preferential employment of women to men might be accounted in the long run a blessing, bearing hopes of more productive organization of industry in the future. If many present restrictions on women's work were removed, while at the same time wage-rates were equalized for the sexes and standardized by occupation, and separate provision were made for all dependents, an increase in the employment of women might be nationally profitable and give no occasion for regret. But the preferential employment of women at the present time appears as an unmitigated curse. Two especially of its evil effects may be noted :—

(1) A considerable number of the women recruits to

industry under present conditions would find, and would prefer to find, domestic work wherewith to occupy themselves, if their homes were adequately financed either by sufficient wages or in any other way. Their employment in industry represents a loss to national home-making and health, and brings an unnecessarily heavy burden to bear on the National Health Insurance Fund. This aspect of the present state of affairs has already been discussed in Chapters IX and X.

(2) A high percentage of unemployed men as compared with unemployed women represents a heavier drain on the Exchequer than an equal or reversed proportion would do, because payments for dependents have commonly to be made in the case of men which are not liable to be made in the case of women. Here we have an instance of financial burden spread over the whole nation, directly caused by the present system of differential occupational wage-rates of men and women in industry. For the fundamental reason men are to be paid more than women for similar work, under the present wage-system, is that they have wives and children to maintain. And the fact that they are to be paid more than women leads (though generally not through purposeful substitution of the one sex for the other) to the higher unemployment rate of men than of women at periods of depression. But the unemployment of men who are responsible for the maintenance of wives and children is much more expensive to the State than the unemployment of women. Thus as industry, forced to strip itself, often unwillingly, of every possible burden in the competitive struggle, throws off as much as possible of the cost of maintaining the next generation of labour, the Exchequer is forced to take it up.

The present wage-system encourages the employment of women by permitting their employment at a lower rate than that of men for the same job, or jobs of equivalent skill ; and in so doing it in effect offers to certain industries a supply of labour at less than the cost of maintaining *and recruiting* that labour. The differential unemployment of men and women indicates that industry

P

is being subsidized from the National Exchequer in the form of a disproportionate expenditure on Dependents' (Family) Allowances paid out as a part of Unemployment Benefit. Those who oppose reorganization of the wage system through the introduction of Equal Pay for Equal Work, made possible by a general scheme of Family Allowances, do not always seem to recognize the unfortunate form in which the State, in default of such reorganization, is already forced to pay a proportion of such allowances. It may be a reasonable proposition that a special subsidy is necessary from the Exchequer to industry in times of depression ; but that it should take a form only consistent with the employment of women in preference to men, only consistent with the preferential privation and degradation of men, childbearing women and small children, only consistent with an unequal encouragement of different industries without reference to their national value or the genuine demand which, in a labour market more sanely organized, might arise for their services— this is a proposition very difficult to defend.

It may be said that it is impractical to criticize the present wage-system on the ground of non-equivalence of wage between male and female groups of equivalent skill, since it would be impossible to draw up a list indicating the comparative skill required in different occupations, to ensure that where men and women do not compete they might still receive equivalent wages, and the industries in which they are thus separately employed would not undercut one another for custom and capital through wages. Certainly no such general imposition of occupational wage-rates would be practicable. But the present lack of comparability is chiefly a result of artificial segregation of the sexes. With the establishment of Equal Pay and the removal of restrictions on women's work, there is little doubt that women's labour would find more varied openings. War experience clearly indicates the likelihood of this. It also seems likely that some men would be employed for work now delegated to women. Such changes would in time provide the opportunity for a truer comparison of the economic value of, or the demand for, each type of work, irrespective of the sex of the worker employed on it. " Artificial " stimulation of demand in favour of industries employing women would cease, as a national force, and the international application of the same principle would tend to the healthier development of industry throughout the world.

There are many arguments in favour of *Equal Pay for Equal Work*, and also in favour of the payment by the State of Family Allowances. I know of none more cogent than the present condition of affairs in Great Britain, which is so unfortunately equalizing the earnings of men and women through unemployment of men, and forcing the State to pay most meagre Family Allowances to the children of the unemployed ! One may dive into the sea for one's health, but to be pushed under is to drown.

CHAPTER XIII

THE DIRECTION OF CHANGE (*continued*)

Provision for families—disadvantages of present system—schemes for change—cash payments—provide a basis for equal pay—extension of communal services to family—less effective—Future of the Home—as a family unit—as a small-scale unit—popular distaste for co-operative home-service. New Economic Basis for Marriage —failure of present legal basis—Christian teaching—Swedish law— voluntary agreements—mutual obligations. Future of Women's Work—still largely domestic—domestic work less like slavery— freedom of movement between domestic and industrial—based on special organization therefor—advantages of this freedom—for domestic woman—for gainfully occupied woman—for children under their care—for industry. Women's work more diversified—and of higher average grade. Conclusion.

The introduction of Family Allowances has been suggested as a necessary accompaniment to the establishment of pay by job rather than by sex, and of all that is implied in the formula, *Equal Pay for Equal Work.* But that is far from being the sole argument in its favour. Still more impelling is the present unequal and racially-dangerous incidence of poverty, which falls most heavily on those families in which young children are being brought up.

It is our custom that children are reared at the expense of their parents ; usually through the income earned by the father, and the domestic work of the mother. For over a century it has not been the practice in our country for children to contribute anything material to their own support, as they almost invariably used to do (either through gainful or domestic occupation) from their most tender years. And the upward age of childhood, in this sense, has continuously risen. So the parents' income has to an ever-increasing extent ceased to have relation to their parental responsibilities.[1] The

[1] The fall in the birth-rate noted since 1870 in most industrial countries is without doubt largely due to an attempt on the part of individual

income of the majority of families in which there are
young children is now derived solely from the payment
made to the father for his work as an individual.
There exists a theory that all employed adult men
receive, or should receive, sufficient from their work to
enable them to support a wife and three dependent children (a "standard family") according to a human, if
not a civilized, standard of living.[1] Studies of the cost
of living and wages, however, make it clear that in past
times even of prosperity there have always been numbers
of male workers whose wages did not reach this standard.[2]
Statistical examination of the actual distribution of population in family and age groups, and of the national income, make it doubtful whether a Capitalist system
ever could, or a Socialist system ever would, fulfil this
ideal of the "standard family" wage. For the Socialist
creed is to render to each according to his need,
which cannot be achieved by providing equal incomes
for families of different sizes. And under a Capitalist
economy such as we now enjoy, wage-rates fixed by
collective bargaining are determined rather by actual
average than by mythical "standard" liabilities. Only
about 6 per cent. of male workers over 20 years of
age support a "standard" family at any one time.
About 10 per cent. have more young children ; about
50 per cent. have none at all. The number of dependent
children per 100 wage-earning men over 20 years of age
was reckoned in 1921 to be 119.[3] To pay every adult
male wage-earner on the assumption that he has three
young children to support would involve making provision for 16 million non-existent children ; it would still
leave over a million children (those in the larger families)

parents to relate their income to their family responsibilities at the
standard of living to which they are accustomed, after such adjustment
ceased to occur automatically.

[1] The standard of living detailed in *The Human Needs of Labour*,
by B. S. Rowntree, offers the concrete example of what may be termed
a "human standard".

[2] The studies directed by Professor A. L. Bowley, and of Mr. Rowntree,
and Booth's *Survey of London Life and Labour*.

[3] *The Disinherited Family*, by E. F. Rathbone, p. 16 and p. 19 (note
3, quoting Bowley, *Economica*, May 1921, pp. 109, 110).

unprovided. Under a system of wage-fixing based on collective bargaining, these things in conjunction are not likely to happen. If the wage is to be uniform for the job, and if the worker is to be expected to maintain his family from wages, the wage will tend to be fixed (in so far as the worker's family responsibilities affect the decision, which in some way and to some extent they always do) according to the actual average liabilities of the moment among the workers in question. Phantoms pull little weight, even when their delusory nature is not recognized.

But families of different sizes cannot be adequately maintained on averages, even if the average be truly reckoned. Equal incomes determined by averages on a generous, a parsimonious, or a strictly " scientific " basis, cannot put equal amounts of food into the bellies of quite different numbers of people. An equal sum for rent does not provide equal house-room for members of large and for members of small families. An average number of socks will not clothe an exceptional number of feet. It would be as reasonable to serve out size nine in boots to the whole Army, on the ground that that is probably the average size among the rank and file.

Lack of regard for the fact that varying numbers have to be maintained from uniform individual wages ensures that whoever else suffers, the wage-earner's children will suffer first and foremost. Among groups of working-class families studied by Professor Bowley, Mr. Rowntree and Mr. Hill, a large number of those suffering most severely from poverty were found to contain young children.[1] In the normal life-history of a worker's family it is at the time when the children are young that the members of it suffer privation. Since the very presence of young children in the family is a cause of stringency of income, it follows that extreme poverty is the lot of a greater proportion of the child than of the adult population, and the studies quoted above prove this statistically. Furthermore, of the adult population, poverty is the especial lot

[1] Bowley and Rowntree, *op. cit.*; Hill, A. B. (*Journal of Hygiene*), *op. cit.*

of the parents of young children, and most affects the mothers who are bearing and nursing the new generation.

Thus the present system of providing for families stands condemned, above all, because it places the workers' children first in the firing-line of poverty and privation. Lack of sufficient suitable diet, house-room, home-service, which are the normal results of extreme poverty, affect young children more injuriously than adults ; and young children are suffering from them in greater proportion.

It is doubtful whether the system can be defended on eugenic any more than on humane principles. It seems improbable that poverty suffered in childhood is selective of qualities the nation would wish to encourage, especially since such poverty is not nowadays readily permitted to kill the young, but only to stunt or maim.

Suggestions that provision should be made for children by some method other than, or additional to, the present way of providing for them through paternal income, have been frequently put forward, and have come to the forefront of political consciousness since the war, particularly through the work of Miss Eleanor Rathbone.

The principle of special financial support being given by the State to those responsible for the rearing of young children (which is one, though not the only proposal put forward) is not new ; in fact it is already practised in this country in various forms, as for instance in the form of

(a) Rebates on Income Tax ;
(b) Pensions paid in respect of widows' or totally-orphaned children ;
(c) Allowances paid to unemployed persons in respect of dependent children ;
(d) Allowances paid to men, or widows of men, in the Defence Forces in respect of dependent children.

Free services are also given to dependent children by the State, in the form of

(a) Meals to undernourished schoolchildren whose parents are found to be unable adequately to support them ;

(*b*) Food to nursing or pregnant mothers, under similar conditions ; [1]

(*c*) Medical service to schoolchildren and to infants.[2]

These measures, framed to alleviate the economic burden placed upon individual parents and to secure the adequate care of dependent children do not (as do the measures alleviating the burdens of old age) form an integral system. They are designed to meet difficulties and palliate evils as they individually arise from the working of the present economic organization of society, rather than in any regular way to prevent them from arising. But they provide a suggestion of the framework on which a more complete system of provision might be built ; they indicate a general acceptance of the principle (at any rate among the income-tax-paying classes in respect of their kind), and a means of observing in little its physical and psychological results.

Among those who propose remedies for the present unsatisfactory method of family-provision, however, there is one line of cleavage which is of particular interest in connection with the subject of this book. Some consider present evils best remedied by the payment of a weekly sum in cash to the mother in respect of each dependent child (to be paid either from public funds—possibly through a system of insurance similar to national insurance schemes already in force—or else through regional or occupational pools of wages).[3] Others would prefer to see, alternatively to these plans and as a variant of the former, an extension of communally-provided services to children. Proposals on these different lines were recently put forward in the Majority and Minority Reports, respectively, of a Joint Committee of the Trade Union Congress General Council and the National Labour Party Executive.

The former plan would make Equal Pay for Equal

---

[1] There is a good deal of local variation in the conditions under which this assistance is given. It is not actually a free service, but offers such provision at or under cost price.

[2] Including service to the infant's mother, as such.

[3] The Family Endowment Society, 18, Abingdon Street, S.W.1. has published numerous pamphlets, etc., outlining schemes in force in other countries or proposed for our own.

Work possible, or bring it very much nearer the possibility of realization. It represents the method which has been actually adopted, in conjunction with the establishment of Equal Pay, in the Civil Service of Ireland, and other European countries.

The payment of Family Allowances to Civil Servants, so long as such allowances are not a part of a general State scheme, is rather in the nature of an Occupational Pool system, than a direct payment from the Exchequer. On the Continent the Pool system is common, being organized sometimes on a regional and sometimes on an occupational basis. The system of Family Allowances followed by the Wesleyan Ministry and with regard to salary payments of the teaching staff of the London School of Economics, are examples of Occupational Pools in this country.

The method suggested by Mrs. Sidney Webb, when she advocated Children's Allowances in connection with Equal Pay in 1919, was that of a direct payment from the Exchequer, provided out of taxation, and this is the ideal of many of the foremost exponents of the reform.

The method of making more adequate social provision for families by an extension of communally-provided social services would not provide any solution for the problems which arise from unequal pay ; and quite apart from this, such a system would seem to have a number of other deficiencies and disadvantages compared with a method of more direct cash provision. The social-service-extension method of family provision may be concretely studied in the Minority Report of the Trade Union Congress and Labour Party Joint Committee (which was subsequently adopted by the Nottingham Trade Union Congress).

In this Report it is suggested that cash payments should be made in respect of children under two years old and during the last year of school life, but that rather than provide them for the intermediate years, it would be preferable to establish out of public funds :—(1) a complete medical service (preventive and treatment) for all children from birth to school-leaving age ; (2) adequate pre-natal and post-natal maternity service ; (3) raised school-leaving age ; (4) nursery schools for children up to the age of admission to elementary schools ; (5) adequate healthy houses ; (6) elimination of tuberculosis and provision of pure milk.

In so far as these proposals can be seriously considered as *alternative* to the provision of Family Allowances, they are either ambiguous, or they may best be described as putting a second horse behind the cart. The desirability of more adequate maternity services, of the elimination of tuberculosis (and all other diseases), and of raising the school-leaving age, are already recognized. Whether and when they may be achieved, the case for Family Allowances will still stand exactly where it stood before. The case for State Nursery Schools is strong, but it is doubtful whether they are practicable for rural areas, or whether attendance at them should be compulsory. Their provision is therefore no alternative to an allowance for each child. What exactly is meant by the demand for the " full establishment out of public funds of the provision of adequate healthy houses " it is difficult to determine, but taken at its face value this would seem to imply expenditure as great as the complete scheme of cash allowances proposed by the Majority Report. If, however, houses for wage-earners with young families only, are intended to be provided out of public funds, is it suggested that the tenants should be evicted as the children leave school ? The failure of existent housing schemes to accomplish slum clearance in the way they were intended to do, has been shown to be largely due to the fact that those with dependent families who most need the new houses, are least able to pay even the subsidized rents charged for them, and so the houses are frequently taken by those who need the subsidy less, and the removal of the former families from the slums becomes an almost insoluble proposition.[1] To provide free house-

[1] The problem is discussed from this point of view by Mr. E. D. Simon, *How to Abolish the Slums*.

room for all, or even houses so subsidized that those who most need them could afford to rent them, is found to be financially quite impracticable. A more economical way of reaching the desired result would be to increase the income per head, or (what in this particular case amounts to the same thing) reduce the rental, for those families where there are dependent children. The Housing (Greenwood) Act (1930) has now brought the latter procedure within the powers of Local Authorities.

The Report recommends an extension of preventive medical services. What is wanted is not so much preventive medical service as prevention of the need for medical service. Initial prevention is the function of the home, which it should be manned and equipped to perform. So far as medicine (and particularly orthopædic medicine) really is preventive, it works through advice to the home-maker, and is powerless for good if she is unable to carry out such advice, as she nowadays may well be through overwork, ill health or poverty caused by funds inadequate to meet the demands made upon them. Every medical man will agree that so far as prevention of illness and growth-deficiency is concerned, the child depends more on the activity of the mother than of the doctor, and the beneficial activities of the mother depend chiefly on the amount of time and income she can spare for the child.

Nor can the mother's own health be secured simply by medical care on the occasion of pregnancy and child-birth, necessary as such care may be. If immediately after her confinement she must return to days of unregulated overwork, nights without adequate rest, insufficient food, and continual worry to ward off the innumerable ills that arise from insufficient family income, there is little hope that she will preserve the personal health and strength which are the safeguard of her children's.

The provision of pure milk, to prevent the carriage of tuberculosis from cows, may be extremely important ; but so is the provision of a sufficient nourishing mixed diet for the family in general, to give immunity against tuberculosis and other ills, and to safeguard the infant before and after birth through care of the mother.

But in fine the case for cash allowances and against communally-provided services as an alternative to them is, that so long as children are to be reared in homes, those homes should not be condemned to inefficiency. If it is considered better that children should *not* be reared in individual homes, it follows that child-rearing services *should* be provided in communal fashion from infancy, probably in institutions such as all-the-year-round boarding-schools.

Apart from such fundamental opposition as this, the chief difficulties which confront the advocate of Family Allowances are (1) the necessary cost of any such scheme, and (2) the possibility of dysgenic effect. Of the former objection it may briefly be said (since this is not the place to enter into details, which are available in books especially devoted to the subject) that in the main the financial problem is one of redistribution of wealth rather than one of extraneous expenditure (such as occurs in war-time). Certainly redistribution is a business exceedingly difficult to accomplish without destruction of wealth ; but since this particular form of redistribution is directly aimed at improving the quality of the race, it should, even in terms purely of financial economy, ultimately repay a certain additional capital expenditure, by increasing later production per head and diminishing the expenditure on health and public assistance services. A redistribution of wealth which is of immediate need and ultimate value, offers a problem which is the opportunity of the economist and the statesman, rather than a final check.

The problems of eugenics which schemes of Family Allowances bring to the fore are calling out for solution in any case. The propagation of mental defectives and of criminal types ; the disproportionate fertility of the less successful members of the community ; these occur under the present system of family provision, and the experience of the working of Family Allowance schemes on the Continent gives little reason to suppose that they are further encouraged to any appreciable extent by the provision of Family Allowances. The fertility of mental defectives seems commonly to occur without reference to economic considerations at all; and it seems possible that the disproportionate fertility of the very poor is often due to the very fact of their poverty, and might be discouraged by those payments in respect of existent children which would make the parents' lives more tolerable, and more capable of the self-respect, forethought and practical provision which are necessary for the intentional limitation of families, whether abstinence from sexual intercourse or other methods of birth control be the means of such limitation.

It is with some temerity that one refers to the direction of change, and yet presumes the survival of the family home. The disintegration of the family is commonly prophesied.

For centuries the family structure we have inherited from Rome, Germany and the Hebrews has been showing signs of stress and change. The further advance of the process in America and Russia than in Western Europe makes it absurd for us to suppose that our own present condition is likely to become suddenly static. But the changes in other countries are not identical, and our own will probably display further variety.

The emancipation of women, and its expected results, have formed the basis of many prophecies as to future methods of providing home-services. As more and more women (it is suggested) become unwilling to devote themselves to domesticity, or to produce a sufficient number of children to form a healthy individual-home environment for the young, or to live permanently with their child's father, children above the age of suckling will be despatched to professional or municipal " homes ". Men and women, each independently engaged in paid occupations, will form liaisons whose establishment and continuance will be independent of the law and yet consistent with social approval unless children are produced.

Intercourse leading to the birth of children, though it will require legal sanction, will involve no liability to permanent attachment, or permanent maintenance of one partner by the other. Home services will be supplied either through communal organization, or by private domestic service highly paid and reduced to a minimum by modernized architecture and mechanization. Elimination of all discrimination against women (or men) in respect of employment in any kind of work, and payment for work done without regard for sex, are taken for granted.

Since the latter condition is so far from being realized, it is perhaps a hardly fair criticism of such prophecies to point out that the emancipation of women does not seem at present to be producing effects along these lines. The demand for increased equality of the sexes and more sexual freedom for women is not in most cases combined, so far as one may observe, with a demand for personal irresponsibility towards their children, either by the fathers or mothers. Many women of modern outlook take more interest and give more personal care to the rearing of their children than their Victorian or Edwardian mothers did. Rather than give up child-care for the sake of work and independence, they are often inclined to do the opposite, not through undervaluation of independence but through revaluation of child-care. Nor do the mothers who continue to undertake non-domestic work after marriage tend to despatch their young children, nor do they or their husbands even seem to wish to despatch them to homes where the parents will no longer be directly responsible for their welfare. It seems that they prefer to keep them in their own home, partly perhaps for the selfish reason that they enjoy their company, but also because they believe that a home based on the two-parent family relationship is in most cases a good environment for a child's upbringing, and that if the family is (as modern families commonly are) small in numbers, and more widely spaced than those of previous generations, earlier day-schooling and the companionship of frequent child-visitors may counteract the difficulty.

So far as young children are concerned, there is little sign that the future is leading us towards a disappearance of the two-parent family home *as the normal type*, though variations may become more common and cease to rouse disapproval. The "scattered homes" envisaged by Mr. Eden Paul,[1] populated by "families" not bound together by blood-relationship, may develop and increase side by side with the more conventional type of family home, to supply a suitable environment for children of a gregarious nature whose parents do not wish, are not able, or are temperamentally unfitted, to provide them with homes of the conventional kind.

Where there are no young children, the family home is in more danger of disappearance. In middle- and upper-class society, the departure of the grown-up, un-married daughter from its shelter has been a feature of women's emancipation. The pressure of economy had expelled the poorer young woman at an earlier date, ex-cept in districts where neighbouring factories brought paid work within reach.[2] Trade depression is now taking the choice away from many who had it before. Cases are recorded in recent issues of the *Ministry of Labour Gazette* of unemployed single women who claim benefit while declining to apply for work away from their home dis-trict. In the majority of cases their claims are disallowed, and thus pressure is put upon them to leave their homes. The home as a family-habitation is being destroyed by society's preference for mobile labour.

In some sense the home may survive, whether or no it continues to shelter families bound together by ties

[1] *Chronos, or the Future of the Family*, by Eden Paul.

[2] The institution, with centralized industry, of the individual wage, brought a sense of independence to the wage-earning young woman, which was very early recognized as a danger to the survival of the family. In 1833 a writer described the individual wage as "another evil of the factory system" which "has led to another . . . grievous misfortune, namely, that each child . . . loses the character and bear-ing of a child . . . pays over to its natural protector a stated sum for food and lodging ; thus detaching itself from parental subjection and control. . . ." Many factory girls, at about sixteen years of age, made a practice of leaving their parents and going into lodgings. Pinch-beck, *op. cit.*, p. 313 (notes), quoting Gaskell, *Manufacturing Population of England*, 1833, and *Factory Commission (Evidence)* of same date.

of blood or marriage. Whether a home is conceivable without some form of personal service, is more questionable. Will the emancipation of women in Western countries affect the method of providing home-services and so tend to eliminate the individual home, as it seems to be doing to a great extent in Russia ?

The alternative to the individual home is communal or co-operative home-service. A good many examples of such services grew up during the war-period, which faded away afterwards. Two that survive, towards the upper and lower ends of the social scale, are service-flats and industrial canteens. Neither of these in practice seem to be subserving the emancipation of women from the home. Service flats, in which much or all the necessary domestic service is provided by the landlord, are generally inhabited by wealthy families or couples whose womenfolk follow the older convention of genteel leisure. Industrial canteens, which aim at providing workers with meals better planned and cooked than they would be likely to obtain at home, at prices which secure for them the economy of large-scale marketing, generally benefit men or women who take their home-share in the conventional type of domestic service, but who would otherwise suffer, as most do, from its present inevitable inefficiency.

So far as one can see at present, the movement for women's emancipation is not leading to, or closely connected with, the development of co-operative home-services in this country. This may be because such services are in themselves unpopular except when planned on lines beyond the means of the majority. The Elder Prophets of the Movement supposed that the New Woman would be willing, if not glad, to give up the family home for the sake of economic freedom. It seems she is not ; she wants both. There is no reason they should be incompatible ; and there may be sound reason in the preference for the home organized on a small scale. If it is to provide rest for the worker in industry, reaction from the stimulus of large-scale production is necessary ; the home-environment therefore has a functional reason for being planned on a small scale. Communal kitchens economically run cannot easily cater for individual taste ; but it is true enough that one man's meat is another's poison. Individual infant-care has value ; babies in crèches are subjected to ills and infections from which the separate nursery is comparatively free. Temporary individual economies cannot be accommodated to co-operative, as they can to separate, housekeeping.

A distaste for communal or co-operative home-services, often subconscious but not necessarily unreasonable, may well be part of the reason why the women who have succeeded to the heritage of the earlier suffrage societies, and the women of the Co-operative Guilds, are directing so much of their interest to the position of the woman in the home, without seeming to wish to get her out of it. Their attitude indicates for our future not the disappearance of the individual home, but a change of the status of the woman who works in it. Without the surrender of what she so highly values, she is asking for the economic independence and the chance of co-operation in an organized group, which the earlier prophets of change expected her to seek outside the functional limits of the home. There is no reason she should not secure all these together. Changes in the economic basis of marriage might give the woman equal economic freedom with her husband, without forcing her to seek it by work outside her home, if and when there are occupations which command her interest and demand her service within it. To bring about such changes in her status should therefore be more especially the aim of those men and women who value the individual home.

What changes in the laws and conventions of marriage are required, to reconcile the claims of the home to the wife's personal service, and her own claim to economic independence ?

Our present marriage laws are such a peculiar patchwork of ragged antiquity, and so ineffective to achieve any reasonable purpose, that were not men's actions regulated by more reasonable custom, marriage as at present instituted could hardly survive a month.

The anomalies of these laws have been frequently described : the ineffectual method of securing the wife's maintenance by permitting her to pledge her husband's credit or to apply for a maintenance order ; the liability of the husband to maintain his wife and children despite the fact that she may have separate property, income or earning capacity greater than his own ; the cessation of the husband's liability at his death, so that he may will all his property away from his widow and children and leave them destitute, and so on.

Attempts or suggestions for the reform of our insensate code of marriage legislation commonly meet with opposition, obstruction, and a blank wall of inertia. Sufferers from the effects of the law are less vocal than the herd, because they are conscious of social disapproval. Reasoned opposition is based partly on the view that marriage laws are of less effect than customs ; that our marriage customs are in advance of our laws ; that cases which come to the law courts are usually past cure ; and that to tamper with law may have the effect of loosening the sanctions of custom.

Doubtless marriage legislation is of a peculiarly delicate nature, and the reactions of law and social custom upon one another have to be taken into special consideration when it is reviewed. To enact a Marriage Code reasonable from the point of view of the economic development of a nation but far in advance of its social psychology might well be a grave mistake. To permit the survival of a Code consistent only in being irrational and out of date, is a course almost equally unwise.

As a means of regulating the economic basis of marriage our law is demonstrably a failure, for it provides no reasonable suggestion of a system of normal justice for the common man, and cannot enforce what it lays down without breaking up the marriage altogether. If the recruitment of the population were in every detail financed by the State ; if women had the same opportunities as men to

engage in paid work, and no greater customary obligations than they to shoulder the burdens of unpaid domesticity, there might be no need for any legal enactment
regarding the economic arrangements made by men and
women in marriage. But our society does not work on
these lines. As things are at present, the lack of reasonable laws to guide and safeguard the people in connection with the economic aspect of the marriage-contract
leads to many hard cases and injustice for individual
men, women and children, and it confirms and seems to
vindicate selfish actions by husband or wife which may
not only cause individual suffering but also be contrary
to the interest of society.

Changes in the law would not need to be in advance
of widely accepted ethical standards. Christian teaching
with regard to the economic aspect of marriage has been
for ages familiar to the people through the Church of
England Marriage Service, and although its principles
have not been incorporated into national law, they have
already accustomed the common man to the idea of an
equality of " worldly goods " between husband and wife.
New law might therefore suitably aim at expressing in
legal form the economic basis for marriage to which the
husband pledges himself in the Church Marriage Service
(1928 version) :—" All my worldly goods with thee I share."

In the drafting of new Marriage Laws much might be
learnt from the framing and working of the Swedish
Marriage Act of 1920. The clauses of this Act which
are concerned with the question of maintenance of the
family not only define the husband's obligation more
exactly than is done in English Common Law, but are
also of particular interest in that they lay the obligation
equally on both spouses, by including household work as
one method of maintenance :—

" The spouses are under obligation, each according to his
capacity, whether by supplying money, by household work,
or by other means, to contribute to the maintenance of the
family on a scale of living in reasonable accordance with
their position. The term maintenance of the family shall
be understood to include what is necessary for the house-

Q*

hold, for the education of the children, and for meeting the special requirements of each of the spouses." [1]

Provision is made against a grievance which every social worker will realize is deeply felt by many English wives to-day :—

"In order to be able to make perfectly fair estimates of the respective duties of support, incumbent upon both husband and wife, they are by law required to inform each other in full of their financial condition and resources." [2]

As Sir Anthony Fitzherbert said, they should each "make a true rekening and accompt" to each other, "for if one of them should use to disceive the other, he disceyveth himselfe, and he is not lyke to thryve, and therfore they must be true ether to other." An economic basis of the marriage partnership as necessary now as then.

With regard to husband's and wife's estate, the Swedish law has worked on a new principle, based neither on the guardianship of the wife's property by her husband (the former principle of Swedish law, and of English law before the passing of the Married Women's Property Acts), nor on the common estate administered by the husband (the principle of Scotland and certain other European countries), nor on a complete separation of the two estates. The new system provides for a combination of the estates of both on marriage, of which both shall then own one half, but each shall administer the estate he brought into the marriage, and shall account to the other for his stewardship. Administration does not include the right to alienation of the portion of the estate administered, without consent of the other spouse. For household debts they are conjointly responsible. [3]

Examples of laws of intestacy more equitable than English law may be found even nearer home than Sweden,

[1] *Draft Report . . . on Economic Provision for Wives and Mothers . . ,* prepared for I.W.S. Alliance; *International Woman Suffrage News,* May–June, 1923, p. 135.

[2] *Marriage and Divorce Legislation in Sweden,* by J. Thorsten Sellin (U.S.A.), p. 69.

[3] *The New Swedish Marriage Law,* by Fru E. Nilsson.

since in Scotland as well as in British Overseas Dominions a husband (or wife) is not legally able entirely to set aside at his death, the obligations towards his spouse and children by which he has been bound during his lifetime. On this point our social ethic is certainly in advance of our law.

A valuable step tending towards a new economic position for the married woman would be an increase of the custom of making agreements before marriage, defining the sharing of income and property. This custom would form an excellent basis for, and extension of, new marriage law. Such agreements are often verbally made nowadays among young people, especially of the middle classes of society, but except in the case of the wealthy they are rarely set out in form.

A normal pattern for such contracts (capable of wide variation) might suggest that a variable amount, perhaps commencing at the proportion of four-fifths, of the couple's total income should be devoted to joint family maintenance, and that each should keep half the remainder for personal or private use. The expenses of either spouse necessitated by outside work should be counted as part of family maintenance, and not as private expenditure. An agreement to inform one another of the amount of income received might well be explicit, if a joint household is planned, as is normally the case. Each item in the agreement should apply mutually ; the bride as well as the bridegroom should pledge herself to the sharing of worldly goods and income on the agreed lines.

Among those who do not realize the value to the family of domestic work, as compared with " breadwinning ", it would seem that the bridegroom alone, in most cases, was pledging himself to share with his family the reward of his work, and that the obligations undertaken by the spouses were far from being really mutual. The true position, however, is clearly stated in the provisions of the Swedish Marriage Law already quoted, and similar provisions might be included in private agreements.

In unions wherein the wife contributes neither household work (even supervisory), nor income, and the husband earns the joint income, their obligations are not in practice mutual; but since in such cases the woman's position has usually been occasioned by a convention to which the husband subscribes, it is just that the non-contribution by the one spouse should not remit the obligation of the other. But marriages in which the wife does not contribute either household work, unearned income, earned income, or some form of assistance in the partnership (such as the fulfilling of social duties valuable to the man in his career, the supervision of care of their young children, etc.) are very rare.

There are peculiarities of the law affecting the status and economic position of the married woman on which I have not touched—details of method of taxation, non-liability for torts, " restraint on anticipation ", etc. There are anomalies which cause legal men to dub the married woman " the spoilt darling of the law ", and make women themselves realize the disadvantage of being a spoilt darling in a workaday world. In framing new legislation, consideration would need to be given to such anomalies. There is, however, a danger that these peculiarities may be noticed when major inequities are overlooked. Their reform alone would not be sufficient. Unless wider action is taken, marriage as we know it may predecease by many centuries its necessary demise, while we are still unprepared with any substitute to fill its place.

The suggested new economic basis for marriage does not necessarily imply that women will continue to occupy themselves with unpaid domestic work in the same proportion as they do now; but it attempts to make some provision for the economic dignity and independence of the woman who does so.

It does, however, seem likely that a large proportion of women will continue to be employed in domestic work. While in civilized countries the depression of trade results in unemployment for industrial workers, it is improbable that large numbers of domestic workers will be absorbed in other work. When or if prosperity returns, the individual home with its individual service is not likely to be given up, because it is generally preferred. So long as we retain the individual home, the function of machinery and even of architecture in diminishing the numbers employed on domestic work is strictly limited. Much of the gain they win will be devoted to decreasing the work-hours rather than the number of those employed.

As the family-home tends to become a smaller unit— the young birds flying from the nest, male and female, as they are fledged—a considerable part of the gain from future increases of production per head (if such a gain does occur, and in so far as it is distributed, without absorption in the cost of mal-organization of labour) may be employed in the extra expense of maintaining smaller home-units than was customary in the past. Some of the difference may be saved by a decrease in the number of women genuinely unoccupied.

But if in the future the proportion of unpaid women home-makers changes less than some of the forward-lookers foresee, their mental outlook and their position in the national economy may be changed to an incalculable degree, both by the developments which will primarily affect the industrial worker (that is, the establishment of Equal Pay, accompanied with the removal of the marriage bar and other restrictions on women's industrial oppor-tunities for work and training) and by the more honour-able recognition of the value of their domestic work which would be secured them under the new marriage laws. Home-work will come to bear less resemblance to slavery, because the wife will be freer to leave it and because she will receive for it a recognized personal economic reward.

Her freedom to exchange domestic for industrial (in-cluding professional) paid occupation will be an import-ant factor not only in her individual status, but also in the prosperity of industry. Special organization will be necessary to secure this healthy freedom of exchange. For the industrial life of *the average* woman will con-tinue to differ from that of the average man. She will continue to retire, if not on marriage, then on the occasion of child-bearing, from non-domestic work, and to be chiefly occupied in her home for some years. Her household work will later diminish, and may demand only part of her time and energy many years before that energy is much reduced by age. At this stage of her life she may prefer to engage part-time domestic help and herself return to full-time occupation in industry, or she may seek part-time paid work, domestic or otherwise. It is in the interest of national economy as well as women's happiness that some attention should be paid to the problem of providing work for women under these conditions.

Such special organization is already being developed in the United States, where bureaux have been established in New York and Philadelphia (through the inspiration and generosity of a private donor) to deal with the part-time employment of women. These bureaux between 1922 and 1929 had been the means of filling 13,000 jobs with part-time women workers.[1]

The satisfaction of those desiring part-time paid *domestic* work has a double importance. It may solve at the same time the would-be employee's problem, and also set free another woman for full-time professional or industrial work. In this case some difficulty arises from the low status of paid domestic work at present, which tends to prevent women skilled and happy in domestic occupation, and desirous of part-time paid work, from seeking such domestic work outside their homes. The new economic basis for marriage, by raising the whole status of domestic work and the home-maker, may well cause a revolution in the attitude to home-service, which will go some way towards correcting this ; and the transference of responsibility for domestic employment from private Registry Offices to the State Labour Exchanges might also prove a valuable step in the same direction. This change was demanded at the 1931 Annual Conference of the Women's Section of the Labour Party.

---

[1] *The Married Woman and the Part-Time Job*, by L. Pruette, in *The Annals of the American Academy, op. cit.*, pp. 309–14.

A return of married women, after a period of domesticity, to the world outside home walls, would be of immense advantage to society in many ways. The importance of this freedom for industry proper has already been stressed : the whole trend of our modern economy is in the direction of production through centralized and divided labour, while the absorption of work by the solitary individual in the separate home, when it serves no purpose of individual happiness or welfare, merely clogs the wheels of industrial development. Its other advantages would be equally far-reaching, through its direct effect on the outlook of women, and its indirect effect on children. For many domestic married women it would add a new zest and stimulus to life, not only at the time of their outside employment, but throughout the days of their domesticity. At present so cut off are many of·them from the type of vitalizing social contact which comes through the impersonalities of employment, that they may well envy those primitive mythical villagers who lived by taking in each other's washing, and so did at least get opportunities of exchanging views on the mutability of linen, the quality of soap, and the variety in value of services. Many a young girl who remains in the factory after marriage, and dreads the permanent confinement to home with which child-bearing seems to threaten her, is moved by a sentiment which under other circumstances men have found noble : *Fellowship is life, and the lack of fellowship is death.*

Her present peculiar economic position, and all the restrictions, regulations and conventions which cut her off from the world of the paid worker, and its fellowship, tend to develop in the home-maker a dissatisfied and depressed mentality with regard to her working life, which is unhappy for herself, and especially unfortunate for society in view of her responsibility for the care of young children.

The unmarried woman would benefit as much as the married. If society not only permitted but encouraged, and developed the organization for, the greater freedom of women's labour to move to and from domestic work, the enforced and yet voluntary celibacy of the professional woman which is such a feature of our present middle-class life, would loose its hold. The result would be of physical and mental value : through the fertility of many women who under present conditions are unproductive, the *quality* of the next generation should be improved ; and through the altered bias of mind among teachers, a healthier mental environment would surround school-children.

Thus industry, the home, and society should feel the benefits of the greater liberty of women's labour.

And when women's economic renaissance has been accomplished, through the establishment of equal pay, the recognition of social responsibility for children and for the welfare of maternity, and the organization and encouragement of mobility between home-making and paid occupations, what changes should we expect to see in those aspects of woman's employment, described in the early chapters of this book : the distribution of their work as compared with that of men ; their average remuneration ; their opportunities for skilled employment ?

Not so much change, perhaps, as in their mentality ; in social welfare, industrial prosperity, and individual happiness. Under the new conditions the occupations of women will probably be a great deal more diversified, and perhaps those of men too. The sexes will seep into each other's preserves, for these water-tight compartments of occupation according to sex rather than to reason have less to recommend them in a civilized than in a primitive community. The more voluntary character, and shorter average duration, of women's marriage-retirement, will diminish the disadvantages which at present attach to their preparation for skilled work, and will thus lower the barriers which now shut them out from many occupations of higher grade. As they gain in average skill, and remain or return to industry with longer experience of life and work, and more capacity for responsibility and the management of their fellows, their average remuneration, under the new conditions, will inevitably rise.

Nevertheless, if the small-scale home operated by the woman home-maker is to survive, as it has been suggested that it will, men will still tend to secure the preponderating measure of skilled industrial work and direct remuneration, despite all these changes in the conditions of women's employment. The diversion of many women's energies in the prime of their working life,[1] to occupations which flow from or centre locally around their function of motherhood, will make this inevitable. Yet it is a prospect we may quite happily face ; for the inequality of the sexes in economic reward and in scope for the exercise of skill will, under the new conditions, be more apparent than real. The home-maker's skill will receive its opportunity and social and economic recognition, and this will provide the balance to the higher average status and pay of the man in industry.

Is this prospect Utopian ? Surely there is no need to take the wings of the morning and fly to the uttermost parts of the sea, to far Atlantis, to find its model, or the means for its realization ? Field-glasses, rather than a telescope, may bring it within our vision, and means of transport to it need but be taken, they need not first be invented.

So tracing in foreseeing imagination the Direction of Change, we find we are planning a Prospectus for a Company—the Company of Human Society—of which we are all Directors.

[1] The prime of working life for the professional worker, however, occurs much later than for the industrial employee. A professional woman who could arrange for a motherhood-retirement period at an early age—say 18 23—might thus prevent any vital interference with her career, and secure definite physical advantage. On the other hand, the ideals of celibacy before marriage, monogamy after it, and intellectual companionship throughout married life, combine with the economic pressure of middle-class life to cause postponement of marriage, recently very marked among women of the professional classes. It is difficult to foresee where these opposing currents will lead.

INDEX

Abstract of Labour Statistics for
1930, 204 nn.

Agriculture : at Industrial Revolution, 92–6, 98 ; before Industrial Revolution, 58–61, 66, 67, 69 ; numbers occupied in, 14 ; wages in, 31–7 ; *see also* Rural Life

America : family and sex relationships in, 1, 2, 184, 221 ; home-making in, 7, 149, 151, 156, 191–2 ; maternal mortality in, 175 ; organization of women's work in, 232

Ancren Riwle quoted, 60

Annual Register of 1812 cited, 100 n.

Asser, *Life of King Alfred* quoted, 65

Balfour Committee, *see* Industry
Birth Control, 168, 179, 221
Birth-rate, 5, 6, 40 (figures), 57, 65, 80 n., 128, 153, 212 n.
Blainey, J., *The Woman Worker and Restrictive Legislation* cited, 131, 138
Boot and Shoe trade, 110, 120
Bowley, A., 213 (notes), 214 ; *Numbers Occupied in the Industries of England and Wales* cited, 11, 15, 40
Brontë, Charlotte, 68–9, 186 ; *Shirley* quoted, 68–9
Brown, Bland and Tawney, *English Economic History, Select Documents* quoted, 58

Brush and Broom industry, 120–1
Building industry, 38
Burnett-Hurst, A. R., reported in *Journal of R. Statistical Society*, 1929, 207 n.
Burnham Scale, *see* Teaching

Carr-Saunders, A. M., and Jones, D. C., *Social Structure of England and Wales* cited, 12, 17, 19, 40
Catering trade, 24, 158–9
Cathcart, E., and Murray, *A Study in Nutrition (Report of Medical Research Council)* quoted, 162
Cathcart, E., and others, *The Relation between Home Conditions and the Intelligence of School Children (Report of Medical Research Council)* quoted, 163
Census, General Report on (1921), quoted, 12
Chain-makers, 117–8
Charwomen, *see* Domestic Service
Chaucer, Geoffrey, *The Canterbury Tales* quoted, 60, 62
Chemical industry, 77, 143, 195
Children : care of : maternal, 41, 150–3, 160–5, 188, 191, 219, 221–3 ; in early times, 57, 61 ; effect of industrial employment on, 67–9, 80
— professional, wages for, 28 and n.

237

Children: employment of, in domestic work, 64 n.; in textiles, 93 n.
— maintenance of, as cause of sex-differential pay, 49–50, 209
— pensions proposed for, when dependent on women, 83; *see also* Family Allowances; Widows' Pensions
Church, economic position of women in early, 58
— of England, Marriage Service of, 227
— of Rome, agreements preceding mixed marriages in, 185–6
Civil Service: employment of women in, 43, 157; expense of qualification for upper divisions of, 44
Civil Service, Report of Royal Commission on (1912–15), 195, 198; (1931), 1, 195 n.; quoted, 43
— sex-differential remuneration in, 36, 198, 217
Clark, Alice, *The Working Life of Women in the Seventeenth Century* cited, 61, 92, 99; quoted, 63, 64, 66, 69
Clerical work: classification of, 15 n.; healthfulness of, 143; status of women occupied in, 17, 33; wages for, 32–3
Clothing industry: numbers occupied in, 14, 15; remuneration in, 23, 159, 195; Trade Boards in, 23, 26, 158; *see also* Tailors
Coffin Furniture industry, 121
Commerce, Banking, Finance, 14, 16, 17, 37
Consumers' Councils, 190–1
Cotton, *see* Textile
Coulton, G. G., *Social Life in Britain from the Conquest to the Reformation*, document quoted, 64 n.

Crawley, E., and Besterman, T., *The Mystic Rose* cited, 54
Cunningham, E., *Growth of British Industry and Commerce*, 66

Davies, Rhys, *Are Women taking Men's Jobs?* (*The Political Quarterly*, March 1931) cited, 206
Defoe, Daniel, *A Tour through . . . Great Britain* quoted, 93 n.; *The Behaviour of Servants* quoted, 63
Distributive trades, 16, 24, 26, 32
Domestic Service (paid private): numbers occupied in, 11; shortage of supply of, 72, 139, 150 and n., 173; unemployed women drafted to, 202; wages and conditions in, 27–9, 143, (juvenile), 34; *see also* Personal Service
— Work, 6, 47, 82, 85–6, 95, 149–60, before twentieth century, 58–70; heaviness of, 18, 143–5; numbers occupied in unpaid, 12–14; value of, to community, 153 and n.; to family, 124, 229; undertaken by women industrially occupied, 95, 117, 137, 173–4
Drake, Barbara, *Women in the Engineering Trades* cited, 81; quoted, 88, 89, 106; *Women in Trade Unions* cited, 81, 106; quoted, 107, 108, 115, 172
Drapery trade, 24, 33
— *and Allied Trades, Report of Ministry of Labour on . . . Rates of Wages . . . in the* (1926) cited, 34
Dunlop, O. Jocelyn, *English Apprenticeship and Child Labour* cited, 92; quoted, 44

Electric lamp industry, 39 and n.
Engineering industry : numbers occupied in, 15 ; Trade Union's views on women's work in, 110, 116 ; war work of women in, 72, 76, 77, 89
Equal Pay, see Wages
Equal Pay for Equal Work, Report of Labour Party on, 5
Examiner, The, of 1832, 108–9 ; quoted, 103–4

Factory Acts, see Legislation, Industrial
Family, see Children, Inheritance, Marriage ; future of the, 193, 221–3
— allowances, case for, 212–21 ; payable under Unemployment Insurance, 209–11 ; proposed by Mrs. Webb (War Cabinet Committee Report), 84–5, 188 ; Reports of T.U. Congress and Labour Party on, 216–19
Fitzherbert, Sir Anthony, The Boke of Husbandrye, quoted, 61, 228
Florence, P. Sargent, A Statistical Contribution to the Theory of Women's Wages (The Economic Journal, March, 1931) cited, 52 n., 203 ; and quoted, 122–5
Food, Drink and Tobacco trades, 153 n., 159 ; numbers occupied in, 14, 15 ; Trade Boards in, 24, 120
Frazer, Sir J. G., The Golden Bough cited, 55
Fur-dressing industry, 120
Furnishing industry, 16, 159

George, M. Dorothy, English Social Life in the Eighteenth Century, documents quoted, 93 n., 99–100

Germany, action of, in respect of industrial legislation, 129–30 ; home-making in, 148, 150, 191
Gladstone, W. E., 102, 187
Guilds, women's economic position under, 43, 63–4, 91–2

Hammond, J. L., and B., The Skilled Labourer cited, 93 ; quoted, 99, 100, 101 and n.
Health Insurance, National, claims of married women workers under, 172–4 ; maternity benefits, 175, 179, 180; exclusion of home-makers from, 163, 179
— Ministry of : Annual Report of (1927–28) quoted, 165 n. ; Annual Report of Chief Medical Officer of, for 1930, quoted, 161 ; Interim Report of Committee of, on Maternal Mortality and Morbidity, cited, 176 et seq. ; Report of, on Training and Supply of Midwives, cited, 176 et seq. ; quoted, 32 ; Report of, on Protection of Motherhood, and on Maternal Mortality, by Dame Janet Campbell, 176 ff.
Hill, A. B., A Study of the . . . Diets of Workers in Rural Areas (Journal of Hygiene, Oct., 1925) cited, 213 ; quoted, 164 and n. ; Sickness among Operatives in Lancashire Cotton Mills (Report of Medical Research Council) cited, 196 n.
Home Work, Report of Select Committee on, quoted, 155
Home-making : definition of, 146–7 ; health of those occupied in, 19, 68, 127–8, 144, 151, 163–6, 172–82 ; num-

Home-making (*continued*) :—
bers occupied in, 12–15 and
15 n. ; *see also* Children ;
Domestic Work
Hosiery trade, 76
Hours Convention (Washington),
130, 132
Hutchins, B. L., *Women in
Modern Industry* quoted, 48,
52 ; cited, 40
Hutchins, B. L., and Harrison,
A., *History of Factory Legislation* quoted, 137 ; Preface
by Sidney Webb quoted,
129, 201

*Industry and Trade, Report of
Balfour Committee on the
State of,* cited, 12, 24 ;
quoted, 10–11
Inheritance, laws and customs
of, 8, 44–5, 62, 228–9
International Labour Organization : and Equal Pay,
119, 120, 129 ; work of,
especially affecting women
workers, 113, 130–1, 140–1,
189
*International Labour Organ-
ization, The First Decade,*
cited, 130
— *Report of, on the International
Protection of WomenWorkers,*
quoted, 140 n., 189
*International Woman Suffrage
News* of May, 1923, quoted,
227

Jenks, E., *Husband and Wife
under the Law* quoted, 57 n. ;
*Short History of English
Law* quoted, 57 n.
Jute industry, 24 n.

Kneeland, Hildegarde, *Woman's
Economic Contribution in
the Home* (*Annals of the*

Kneeland, Hildegarde (*cont'd*) :—
*American Academy of Poli-
tical Science,* May, 1929)
cited, 151
Knowles, L. C. A., *The Industrial
and Commercial Revolutions
in Great Britain* quoted, 135

Labour Party, *see* Equal Pay ;
Family Allowances
— *What's Wrong with Domestic
Service ?* quoted, 29
*Lancet Commission on Nursing,
Second Interim Report of,*
cited, 31
Laundry industry, 25, 158–9
Lecky, W. E. H., *History of Eng-
land in the Eighteenth Cen-
tury* quoted, 94 n.
Legislation, industrial : differ-
entiating between sexes,
102–9, 112–4, 127 ff., during
the war (1914–18), 74, 81, 84;
early (1197), 66, (1773), 100 ;
see also Trade Boards
Locke, John, *Report to the Board
of Trade,* 93 n., 94 n.
*London Labour and the London
Poor,* edited Mayhew, cited,
30
*London Life and Labour, Survey
of,* edited Booth, cited, 213
*London Life and Labour, New
Survey of,* edited Sir H.
Llewellyn Smith, cited, 28
Luddite riots, 100–1 and n.
Lynd, R. S. and H. M., *Middle-
town* cited, 156

MacDonald, J. Ramsay, *Women
in the Printing Trades* cited, 39
Marriage : age of women at, 4,
5, 57 ; laws regarding, English, 57 n., 184–6, 225–30,
Swedish, 227–9
Married Women's Property Act,
12 n., 228

Matchmakers, strike of, 116
Maternity, Convention (I.L.O.),
    130
— national provision for, 83,
    179–82, 188, 190, 219, 234
May Committee, see National
    Expenditure
Medical profession, numbers oc-
    cupied in, 16–7 ; training
    and practice of, in care of
    maternity, 176–8
Metal industry : numbers occu-
    pied in, 14–16 ; remuner-
    ation in, 24, 195 ; Trade
    Unionism and women's work
    in, 106, 115–17
Midwifery profession : remuner-
    ation in, 31–2 ; status of,
    177–8 ; see also Health,
    Ministry of ; and Medical
    Profession
Mining industry : women's work
    in, 98, 101–2, 105, pro-
    hibition of, 108–9, 131, 133,
    135
Mortality rates : infant, decline
    in, 80 n., 153, 174 ; mater-
    nal, causes of, 144, 176–82,
    figures of, 175–6 ; see also
    Stillbirth

National Expenditure, Report of
    May Committee on (1931)
    cited, 30
National Federation of Women
    Workers, 88, 116, 172, 198
National Union of Societies for
    Equal Citizenship, Women
    and the Lead Paint Bill
    (1926) cited, 138
Newman, Sir George, Citizenship
    and the Survival of Civil-
    ization quoted, 175
Night-work Convention, 130, 137
Nilsson, Fru E., The New Swedish
    Marriage Law cited, 228
Nursery schools, 6, 191, 218

Nursing profession : remuner-
    ation in, 31 ; see also Medi-
    cal Profession

Paul, Eden, Chronos, or the
    Future of the Family cited,
    223
Personal Service, numbers gain-
    fully employed in, 11–14 ;
    see also Domestic Service
Pinchbeck, Ivy, Women Workers
    and the Industrial Revo-
    lution cited, 93, 99, 100,
    106, 114 ; quoted, 67, 95 n.,
    96, 97, 98, 101 n., 102–4,
    109, 223
Pollock and Maitland, History of
    English Law before Edward
    I quoted, 57 n.
Porter, Alan, article in The
    Spectator, Jan. 31, 1931,
    quoted, 1–2
Pottery trade, 16, 106
Printing and Paper industry :
    division of labour between
    sexes in, 39 and n., 43 ;
    numbers occupied in, 14,
    15 ; Trade Boards in, 24 ;
    value of women's work in, 76
Professional work : distribution
    of sexes in, with reference to
    skill, 16–17 ; celibacy of
    women occupied in, 234 ;
    numbers occupied in, 14,
    16–17 ; remuneration for,
    30–2, 37
Prostitution, 29–30 and n., 101 n.
Pruette, Lorine, The Married
    Woman and the Part-time
    Job (Annals of the American
    Academy of Political Science,
    May, 1929) cited, 232 ;
    quoted, 149

Rathbone, Eleanor F., The Dis-
    inherited Family cited, 49,
    213 ; quoted, 150, 164

Rowntree, B. Seebohm, *Poverty, A Study of Town Life* quoted, 164, cited, 213 ; *The Human Needs of Labour* cited, 213

Rowntree, B. Seebohm, and Kendall, May, *How the Labourer Lives* quoted, 164

Rubber industry, 16

Rural Life, Report of Ministry of Agriculture and Board of Education on Practical Training of Women for, cited, 13 n., quoted, 150 and n., 191, 192

Russia : economic relationship of sexes in, 2–3, 187 ; the family in, 221 ; home-making in, 7, 224

Sellin, J. Thorsten, *Marriage and Divorce Legislation in Sweden* quoted, 228

Sells, Dorothy, *The British Trade Boards System* cited, 35, quoted, 119–21

Shaftesbury, Lord, 97, 108, 112, 127

Shaw, Bernard, 184, 200

Shop Assistants : status of women, 18 ; Trade Boards affecting, 24 ; wage-rates of, 33–4, 35, 119
— — National Union of, 33 and n., 119

Short-Time Movement, 102, 104, 109, 112–13, 136

Silk industry, conditions in London, during eighteenth century, 99–100, 114 and n. ; wages in, 41

Simon, E. D., *How to abolish the Slums* cited, 218

Smith, Adam, *The Wealth of Nations*, 100

Standing Joint Committee of Industrial Women's Organizations, *Protective Legislation and Women Workers* cited, 132–3 ; quoted, 135

Stillbirth, 138, 144–5

Tailors, Lodge of Female, object to male restrictions, 108 ; Society of Journeymen, oppose employment of women, 107

Teaching profession : numbers occupied in, 16–17 ; remuneration in, 30, 36 ; restrictions on married women's employment in, 157, 199

Textile industry : in early times, 61–2, 66–7, 93 nn., 96 n., 97–101 ; numbers occupied in, 14, 15 ; prosperity of, in relation to wages, 154–5, 200, 201 ; Trade Union activity in, 23, 112–5, 118 ; wage-relation of sexes in, 23, 97–101, 103, 121–2 ; wages in, 24, 41

Tin-box manufacture, 15

Todmorden, Female Operatives of, 103–4

Trade Boards : effect of, on recruitment to Trade Unions, 54, 117–8 ; grounds for establishment of, 22 ; proportion of men to women in trades under, 23 ; trades under, 24, 32, 158 ; wage-fixing methods of, 25–6, 35, 41, 119–21, 131, 136 ; wage-rates fixed by, 27, 32, 35

Trade Unions : attitude of men's, to women's employment : during the war, 71–4, 80–1, 89 ; in early times, 92, 99 *et seq.* ; in general, 51–4, 127 ; effect of, on women's wages, 122–6 ; organization

Trade Unions (*continued*) :—
  of women in, 53–4, 89, 108,
  114–8, 134
*Unemployment Insurance, Report
  of Royal Commission on*
  (1931), 206–7
Unemployment rates, Table VI
  and accompanying Chart,
  204–5

Vaughan, Dr. Kathleen, *Maternal Mortality . . . (Proceedings of Royal Society of
  Medicine,* Dec., 1929) and
  *The Shape of the Pelvic Brim
  as the Determining Factor in
  Childbirth (Brit. Med. Journal,* Nov. 21, 1931) cited,
  144
Veblen, Thorstein, *The Theory of
  the Leisure Class* cited, 153 n.
Vernon, H. M., *Industrial
  Fatigue and Efficiency*
  quoted, 162

Wage Convention, Minimum,
  130–1
— National Minimum, proposed
  as equal for men and
  women, 84, 188 ; proposed
  for women only, 82–3
Wages change from family-
  earned to individual, 5, 93–
  5 ; of juveniles, 21, 34–6,
  37, 41 ; of women, Chap.
  III *passim* ; sex-differential, inimical to men's
  employment, 50–4, 71, 96
  ff., 202 ff. ; " standard
  family " ideal of, 213 ff. ;
  see also Trade Boards, and
  under separate trades

Webb, Beatrice (Mrs. Sidney),
  *The Wages of Men and
  Women ; Should they be
  Equal ? (Minority Report of
  War Cabinet Committee on
  Women in Industry, q.v.*)
Webb, Sidney (Lord Passfield),
  see Hutchins, B. L., and
  Harrison
Webb, Sidney and Beatrice,
  History of Trade Unionism
  cited, 81, 100 ; quoted, 101,
  108, 111, 113, 116 ; *Industrial Democracy* quoted, 71
  n., 72 n.
Westermarck, E., *The History of
  Human Marriage,* and *The
  Position of Women in Early
  Civilization,* cited, 55 n.
Widows' Pensions, 83, 188, 215
Women : economic position of,
  among primitive peoples,
  55 ; in early England, 57 ff.,
  in the future, 234–5
— gainfully occupied : age of,
  117, 128 ; geographical distribution of, 20 ; health of,
  142–3, 172–4 ; industrial
  distribution of, 14, 15, 18–
  20, 75–6, 98, 133, 234–5 ;
  numbers of, 10–11, 14 ;
  proportion of married, 12
— married, proportion of, 12
*Women in Industry, Report of
  War Cabinet Committee on,*
  cited, 8, Chap. VI *passim,*
  104, 121, 192, 195 ; quoted,
  72 n., 110, 197–8
Women's Trade Union League,
  108
Woolf, Mrs. Virginia, *A Room of
  One's Own,* 45

For Product Safety Concerns and Information please contact our EU
representative GPSR@taylorandfrancis.com
Taylor & Francis Verlag GmbH, Kaufingerstraße 24, 80331 München, Germany

www.ingramcontent.com/pod-product-compliance
Lightning Source LLC
Chambersburg PA
CBHW050418280326
41932CB00013BA/1906

* 9 7 8 1 0 3 2 2 7 3 1 0 5 *